CHURCHILL'S
NAVIGATOR

CHURCHILL'S NAVIGATOR

AIR COMMODORE
JOHN MITCHELL
LVO, DFC, AFC

with Sean Feast

GRUB STREET • LONDON

Published by
Grub Street
4 Rainham Close
London
SW11 6SS

British Library Cataloguing in Publication Data

Mitchell, John.
    Churchill's navigator.
    1. Mitchell, John. 2. Flight navigators, Military--Great
    Britain--Biography. 3. World War, 1939-1945--Aerial
    operations, British. 4. World War, 1939-1945--Personal
    narratives, British. 5. Churchill, Winston, 1874-1965--
    Travel.
    I. Title II. Feast, Sean.
    940.5'44'941'092-dc22

ISBN-13: 9781906502744

Cover design and formatting by Sarah Driver
Edited by Sophie Campbell

Printed and bound by MPG Ltd, Bodmin, Cornwall

Grub Street Publishing only uses
FSC (Forest Stewardship Council) paper for its books.

CONTENTS

ACKNOWLEDGMENTS

My first thanks go to the Rankin (and extended) family, and especially Hugo and his mother, Anna. Without this connection, and Anna's habit of buying my books, I would never have met John, and had the very great privilege of helping to write his story. Both at Micklefield Hall, and in Lymington, I was always met with great kindness, which made the task of getting John's thoughts and memories down on paper such a tremendous pleasure.

Correspondence with Wing Commander 'Jeff' Jefford of the RAF Historical Society gave me a steer on style and tone, and I am grateful for his comments. The notes of David Walters, who has conducted much research into his father's own experiences with 58 Squadron in 1940/41, were also useful in conveying the atmosphere of Linton in those early days of the bomber war.

My work colleagues Iona, Alison and Alex have now mastered the art of feigning interest in my extra curricula activities, but I am grateful for their support, nonetheless. I thank also Charlie, Paul and Mike for their inspiration, and their (occasionally) sensible input. Perhaps next time, Paul!

To Grub Street I owe an enormous debt of gratitude once again. This is now our fourth collaboration, and the fun and excitement of working with John and his team is as great today as it has always been. One day I will run out of ideas, but hopefully not quite yet.

A word of thanks of course goes to the genius and financial controller that is my wife, Elaine, and my two boys Matt and James – James in particular for choosing his friends so wisely. And Matt - Facebook will never catch on you know!

And finally I would just like to record the passing of my father, Don Feast, during the preparation of this book. A familiar figure at previous book launches, and a great supporter of my work, he served underground at Kelvedon Hatch during the Cold War, watching the skies for Russian invaders. More recently he was a key figure along with my mother in organising a series of extremely successful RAF reunions for all those who served down 'the hole'. They miss him, and I do too. Per Ardua Ad Astra.

Sean Feast, Sarratt, June 2010

PROLOGUE

My pilot was shouting at me. Indeed he was swearing. Squadron Leader John Bartlett, B Flight commander, 58 Squadron was a dour man of few words, but this evening he was making an exception. He had quite a bit to say, largely profanities and most of them directed at me.

The night of June 30, 1940 was dark, very dark in fact, and we had already gone around twice looking for the target. Our Whitley V (coded P4951) – one of the RAF's laughingly named 'secret weapons' in the war against Germany – had seen us safely from our base in Linton-on-Ouse to Düsseldorf. Now I was peering down into the gloom, trying to identify the Reisholz oil refinery, our primary target. We were one of eight 58 Squadron aircraft operating that night, but had seen nothing of our colleagues since taking off at 21.15 on that summer's evening.

I wondered if I would ever find the target. And I wondered how, as a twenty-one-year-old pilot officer in the RAF Volunteer Reserve (RAFVR) I had come to be in this bomber, on this night, with less than ten hours night-time navigational experience to my name – my first operational sortie.

CHAPTER ONE
FINDING MY WAY

As a young man I had lived a very conventional, even ordinary, existence. Born in Sanderstead in South Croydon on November 12, 1918, the day after the Armistice, with a father who had not been subjected to the horrors of trench warfare on account of being too old, having flat feet and working in what was a relatively 'reserved' occupation. He was a civil servant, and by all accounts quite a senior one, working in the Inland Revenue.

I was one of four, with two sisters and a younger brother. At the age of twelve I passed the school entrance exam for Whitgift Grammar, and was excited about going. My father, in his wisdom, decided instead to pack me off to his old boarding school, Bancroft's in Woodford Wells, where I was to spend a thoroughly miserable first few years. In fairness I don't think it was Bancroft's fault as such, but rather that I hated the whole idea of boarding schools at that time. It was ironic that my father, who I actually got on quite well with, decided to send me away, and that my brother, with whom my father struggled, was allowed to stay at Whitgift.

Bancroft's was typical of the period: masters ruled with an iron discipline, and we had our fair share of fagging (junior boys serving their seniors) and bullying. The buildings were of an imposing redbrick, designed by Arthur Blomfield, and the grounds of more than four acres were similarly impressive. The school was founded in 1737 following the death of its founder, Francis Bancroft, who left a large sum of money to the Worshipful Company of Drapers (which continues to act as a trustee for the school). Alumni included such exalted old boys as the famous geographer and geologist Sir Dudley Stamp; Sir

Kenneth Peppiatt, the chief cashier of the Bank of England; Tommy Hampson who won a gold at the 1932 summer Olympics; and Lieutenant Colonel Augustus Newman who led the military forces as part of the famous St Nazaire raid and won the Victoria Cross as a result.

Later, perhaps, I would learn to understand the benefits of my school days, particularly having chosen a career in the services. The ability, for example, to get on with people in trying circumstances never left me.

My time at Bancroft's was relatively unremarkable. I played 1st XV rugby, and enjoyed 2nd XI cricket, but couldn't pretend to be very good at either. In terms of schoolwork, I did have a natural aptitude towards maths and the sciences, and even managed a distinction in physics. This was to be of significant help to me in later life.

My lack of serious academic promise, however, was of concern to my father. Perhaps because of this, and no doubt the practical consideration of saving on school fees, I was told that university was not an option and that I would leave without completing my second year in the sixth form. This meant I never had the opportunity of taking my Highers, or the chance of a scholarship that may – or may not – have been in my reach. And so, a little earlier than I had planned, I found myself considering my future.

One opportunity that appealed to me was the Post Office research laboratory at Dollis Hill (where they later got the first programmable electronic computer working); industrial chemistry was also attractive. Both stemmed from my inclination towards the sciences. Investigating further, however, a four-year stint at the Beckton gas works and concurrent evening classes to achieve a Bachelor of Science (BSc) degree was not appealing, and so – with an air of inevitability – I followed my father into the civil service.

My father, I should stress, did nothing to advance my career, but neither did he do anything to hamper it. The civil service at that time was highly regulated, and hierarchical, and having passed the requisite exam I found myself a part of the department of scientific and industrial research (DSIR). The DSIR administered premises such as the National Physical Laboratory in Teddington and various other major research establishments. I joined as a clerk, effectively to serve my apprenticeship.

Customs and Excise appealed to my sense of humour and involved a considerable amount of travel. As a young officer, my task was 'the protection of His Majesty's revenue' and to this end we had enormous powers, even to the extent of breaking down doors if we thought the revenue in danger. I remember clearly listening to the abdication speech of Edward VIII, and managed to watch the coronation procession of George VI first hand. As the new boy I had won two tickets to the event in the DSIR's 'draw'. I spent a most pleasant afternoon on the Embankment, watching the procession go by. I then took yet another exam on my own initiative to join HM Customs and Excise, the start of a most agreeable time.

One of my first 'postings' was to Birmingham Collection, where we unattached officers, as we were ranked, were in the charge of the eponymous Mr Smith who in keeping with all collectors – and all of my later AOCs – was god. I shared excellent digs in Moseley, owned by Mrs Prudence, a professional landlady who seemed, unofficially at least, to be part of the overall chain of command.

One of the main scams in my orbit at the time concerned Sportman's gin, a cheap alcohol from a local distillery in Langley Green near Wolverhampton. The gin was being transported in barrels to Blackpool, where it was then bottled, and sold, as Gordons. This was a common occurrence and kept us busy. There were plenty of unscrupulous landlords who were prepared to refill their optics with cheap product but still charge their customers full price.

The hours were not always sociable and when working at a bonded warehouse we took our lunch when we could. I recall one occasion taking some packed sandwiches along with me. The head porter asked if I would like something to go with them as he'd just opened a rather fine 'pipe' of port. He poured me a tumbler and I soon after fell asleep.

From Birmingham I was sent to Manchester, specifically to work on the import of tobacco at the Salford Docks. The accommodation this time was as awful as my first digs had been superb, and overlooked the local cemetery.

Working at the docks we were kept very busy, 'rummaging' (as it was called) on board ships for illegal goods. We would talk to the captains of the boats and look at the cargo manifests. Drugs were not popular in those days, but other potentially less lethal products still had real value. Imported sugar, for example, had a high duty on it to protect our own sugar beet industry in Lincolnshire. As a result, smuggled liquid saccharine – which was used by brewers and confectioners – became a desirable commodity. We once managed to find an entire stash – completely by chance – that had been hidden inside a shipment of teddy bears. The bears had been packed in crates, and the smugglers had the misfortune of dropping one of the crates on the dockside. The box smashed open and we were confronted by this sickly smell. It was immediately apparent what we had found.

In Ireland there were customs offices at the border crossing posts in a vain attempt to stop what was a tremendous smuggling racket, especially in horses. It was an impossible task, as there was no way we could keep watch on all of the roads that littered the countryside. It seems strange to think of the IRA as being at any stage 'friendly' but in those days it all seemed a bit of a game. They would regularly burn down our huts to destroy what records we had, but always made a point of letting us know when they were going to do it.

Given the events on the world stage, the subject of war was never far from our minds. Neville Chamberlain's promise of 'peace in our time' was looking decidedly unlikely and so our thoughts turned towards which branch of the services we should join.

The civil service had strong links with the Royal Naval Volunteer Reserve (RNVR) but this held little attraction for me. The army, too, was similarly unappealing; it seemed such an 'uncomfortable' existence. My preference, especially since I had always been interested in aircraft, was towards the Royal Air Force.

My family had friends in Birmingham with a son, Keith Jeffries, at Cranwell, who had won the coveted Sword of Honour. Keith's cousin had been accepted for a short service commission and although Cranwellians tended to look down on their short service colleagues as being second best, this myth was exploded when the cousin in question – Denis Smallwood – went on to become a highly decorated air chief marshal and C-in-C Strike Command. Keith never got beyond group captain OBE. Denis (or 'Splinters' as he was usually known) flew a Gloster Gladiator single-seat fighter from Castle Bromwich on an Empire Air Day demonstration, and seeing him emerge from the open cockpit resplendent in his white overalls and spotted blue cravat had me decided that the RAF was the right choice.

It might be worth here just explaining a little bit about the pre-war RAF Volunteer Reserve (RAFVR). From the mid-1930s the Conservative government belatedly began re-armament in earnest and a number of schemes were launched to create a reserve of pilots and observers who would be selected and embark on the initial stages of aircrew training whilst still in their civilian occupations. Inevitably the bias in recruitment was towards pilot training, and the Air Ministry drew upon civilian assets – especially the private flying clubs and a small but growing number of the commercial operators – to provide what support it could.

Fortunately, a number of far-sighted ministry staff in the policy branches of the air training world recognised that the new generation of larger aircraft then coming into service required expert crew with specialist skills. The manning of what was hitherto considered a 'part time' job in the rear cockpit actually now needed all-purpose aircrew who could navigate (beyond simple 'pilotage'), aim the bombs and fire the guns to defend the aircraft, whilst also executing the visual reconnaissance and photography then demanded by co-operation with the army. This led to the requirement to recruit 'observers' – men with similar educational qualifications to pilots, but whose eyesight would prevent them from flying.

So it was that I found myself reporting to my local VR town centre (as the administrative headquarters were called) applying to join the reserve. My academic record was not a problem, but the medical proved somewhat more tiresome, with my eyesight not sufficient to train as a pilot. Therefore instead I was recruited as an observer (under-training) and given the only rank open to me at the time: leading aircraftman (LAC).

The usual pattern of training was to join an initial training wing (ITW), a structure established by the former Royal Flying Corps

Brigadier Alfred Critchley (famed as the founder of the Greyhound Racing Association), and many of them were housed in former Butlin's holiday camps. ITWs were important starting points, as they schooled new boys into the ways of service life, its structure and routine, as well as getting them physically fit for the challenges that lay ahead. Here I was unlucky, because shortly after my attestation at our Birmingham town centre and well before I had any time to settle into any regular attendance at lectures of any sort at Colmore Row, I was moved to Salford. I was therefore obliged to ask for a transfer to the Manchester town centre, where ground school training was not as well developed as my previous posting.

Summer passed and war seemed inevitable. The Germans made their move with the invasion of Poland on September 1, 1939, and we were formally mobilised. (This was an important distinction for any reservist at the time and today – that is to say we were 'mobilised' and not 'called up'.) I at once reported to our headquarters and we were immediately organised into a pay parade at which I received (for the very first time in my life) some crisp, white five pound notes. I was sent home and told to await further orders.

Rather than going back to South Croydon, I opted instead to use the address of my friends in Birmingham. Manchester was easier to reach from the Midlands and I sat out a pleasant few weeks helping in a catering business in Solihull, in great comfort.

I was posted on a course on November 12, and so found myself celebrating my twenty-first birthday not quite as intended, on a night train to Prestwick in the company of a number of Mancunians, none of whom I knew, but all of them the same as me – LAC observers under training.

Our destination was 1 Air Observers' Navigation School (AONS), run by Scottish Aviation, and under the command of Wing Commander Duncan McIntyre. McIntyre was in the reserve of air force officers (RAFO) and held the Air Force Cross (AFC). He was somewhat of a celebrity, famous pre-war for his flight over Mount Everest in 1933 with the Marquess of Douglas and Clydesdale (later Group Captain the Duke of Hamilton) in a specially built Westland aircraft. McIntyre was commanding officer and chief flying instructor of 12 Elementary Flying Training School (EFTS).

Scottish Aviation already owned Grangemouth aerodrome and had begun to establish a civil air navigation school there (as well as 12 EFTS at Prestwick). The company had benefited considerably by having the Duke of Hamilton on its board. The duke was both an active member of the auxiliaries and one time CO of 602 (City of Glasgow) Squadron, and had boundless energy and enthusiasm that was employed to great effect.

The establishment of the AONS had been cleverly planned. They recruited a number of ex master mariners from the world of the Merchant Navy, well schooled in the art of dead-reckoning, maps and charts, magnetism and compasses etc, albeit at a different speed. These men could, it was reasoned, provide the bulk of navigation experience at a cheap price. Just what value it might be to us, however, was more doubtful.

For the purpose of air exercises, the school had acquired three second-hand Fokker FXXII and F36 airliners that had originally been built for KLM. They were great lumbering beasts powered by four Pratt & Whitney engines and could accommodate some twenty pupils and their instructors at any one time. The Fokkers were in turn supplemented by a handful of Avro Ansons.

We arrived at Prestwick station in the early hours of the morning and were soon marshalled outside the nearby Red Lion pub which became our town headquarters, or assembly point, for we were all billeted in the surrounding village and still wore our variety of civilian outfits. Our immediate mentors were two ex-army senior non-commissioned officers (SNCOs) dressed in snazzy warrant officer-style uniforms with the Scottish Aviation company's crest on their caps and buttons. They soon smartened us up and we were marched off to classes/duties in two platoons under the command of the two tallest students who had been 'promoted' corporal.

Classroom accommodation was good; textbooks, however, were few and far between, and indeed some among our number had even bought their own copies of *Martin's Air Navigation*, an accepted 'text' of the period written by an RAFO flight lieutenant of the same name. He turned out to be our instructor for met. Although the airfield was cold and under snow our billets were warm and my hostess gave us a big breakfast and high tea, as well as comfy beds – quite unlike my boarding school. It all seemed like great fun. There was no organised sport or PT, and with the exception of morse code I found the syllabus relatively easy.

I took my first flight in the Fokker (coded G-AFZR) on November 17, an air experience flight of an hour-and-a-half with Flight Sergeant Palethorpe. I flew again with Palethorpe and with two different flight lieutenants, Vetch and Cane (Peter Cane was later a captain with BOAC and with his experience on Comets became special duties pilot assigned to the VC10), throughout the course of the next six weeks on a series of map-reading and other navigational exercises. I also flew with another, Flight Lieutenant Thomas who post-war went to work for Airwork at Blackbushe. A brief record of each flight had to be recorded in ink in my observer's flying logbook that was to become my constant companion in the months and years ahead.

My trips in the three Fokkers (along with G-AFZR were G-AFZP and G-AFXR) were interspersed with cross-countries in the station's Avro Ansons. We were allowed home for Christmas and by February 16 and the completion of the first stage of my training I had recorded just short of fifty flying hours in total, and had been rated 'above average' by the chief instructor.

The group was then split into two, one half heading north to Evanton, and the rest of us being sent to a 'proper' RAF base, RAF Aldergrove in Ulster. Aldergrove was home to 3 Bombing and Gunnery School (B&GS) and had on its inventory a mixed bag of aircraft including an old Westland Wallace, an open-cockpit biplane with a phenomenal rate of climb. We also had our very own Fairey Swordfish – the venerable 'stringbag' of Fleet Air Arm fame. The Swordfish could take two pupil air gunners who had to change places in flight! Most of our training, however, would be flown in a Fairey Battle – a comparatively fast single-engined monoplane on which much hope of success had been pinned but that would soon fail to live up to expectations with disastrous results.

Aldergrove was very different from what we had been used to. By now we were properly kitted out in our uniforms with the 'propeller' of our rank sewn on our sleeves. We slept in barrack blocks on hard mattresses – colloquially known as 'biscuits' – and were obliged to leave our barrack room in the approved service way, with all of our gear appropriately stowed. We patronised the NAAFI and off base consumed unrationed suppers of steak, eggs and chips at the Abercorn Hotel in Belfast – although we were steered clear of the Falls Road, in uniform at least.

It was also different because, as well as our training school, the airfield was the operational base for 502 (County of Ulster) Squadron engaged on anti U-boat patrols. Seeing them there kitted out in Mae West life jackets and a parachute harness was the real deal. Watching them take off with their few small depth charges to battle the might of the German Kriegsmarine was our first sight of the RAF at war.

At B&GS we received armament training. What this amounted to in essence was an introduction into the mysteries of aiming bombs at targets floating in Lough Neagh, barely ten minutes flying away. The theory of bomb aiming and the handling of the pre-war Mk IX bombsight were taught by an armaments officer, but 'bombs and comps' (as 'bombs and components' was known) was the responsibility of elderly flight sergeants who had learned their trade in the Middle East and fighting on the Northwest Frontier.

I remember two characters in particular: the station commander, Group Captain Richardson, a tall, imposing man known locally as 'King Dick'. He was to be chairman of a local commissioning board to which I found myself summoned at the very end of the course. The second personality, and equally tall, was the station warrant officer by the name of Armstrong. The SWO was responsible for the conduct and discipline of all airmen and NCOs on the station and a man not to be crossed.

Of our pilots, most were again elderly flight sergeants with the occasional younger commissioned pilot thrown in. Organisation, however, was as chaotic as it had been at Prestwick. There was virtually no pre-flight liaison with the pilot when better co-ordination might have ensured a more profitable use of (flying) time. We might have benefited, for example, in better understanding how the pilot aligned the aircraft with the target or the drogue. As mere sprogs, however, we didn't speak to the pilot unless spoken to.

One of my gunnery details in the Westland Wallace – a two-seater general purpose biplane – was flown by a sergeant pilot who seemed to be quite experienced; the opposite was the case in the Swordfish where I was in the hands of a junior midshipman (I believe his name was Tattersall). I often wondered what sort of 'black' he had put up in the wardroom to have earned a posting to Aldergrove, stooging up and down the ranges on Lough Neagh with the likes of us!

As part of our familiarisation with our weapons, in this case the .303 gas operated (GO) Vickers machine gun, we learned how to strip the gun and how to load the drum magazines, which were then stowed in the rear cockpit on brackets within easy reach of the gunner, standing with the fairing open to the slipstream. On one particular sortie it was bitterly cold; we were not able to wear gloves, as we needed our fingers free to manipulate the weapon. I had to change the first drum, having discharged its contents, and struggled to latch the second one onto its fitting when, instead of bringing the gun completely inboard, I allowed it to catch the slipstream and the gun slipped out of my grasp, the drum fell overboard, and down into the water below! I was lectured afterwards, it could have fallen into the hands of the enemy, in this case the IRA if they had dredged the lough.

I was lucky to escape court martial. I can only think that they could ill-afford to lose any of us partially trained observers at such an early stage in the war. I got away with a severe dressing down from our chief instructor, Wing Commander P.J. Barnett MC.

I wasn't exactly a star pupil, but at the end of the course we all seemed to have passed. For my own part I had completed around thirteen hours of gunnery exercises and eighteen hours of bombing. For this endeavour I passed my ab initio gunnery course with a score of 81% and 79% for my bombing.

The course ended in the last week of April 1940, but just before it did, Basil Sayers and I – the two of us had rather paired off during the course – were told to smarten ourselves up and report to the commissioning board in station headquarters. It was a bit of a mystery. I had done reasonably well but my shooting could have been better and as for my bomb aiming, perhaps that was best left to the Germans and the Italians to judge in the months to come.

I sat in front of the interview board, chaired by Station Commander Richardson, the chief instructor, Barnett and a squadron leader (general duties) armament specialist. They asked me about my education and career to date, and seemed interested in why I had opted for the RAF. Luckily they did not seem interested in my mishap with the machine gun! Basil and I discussed our relative performances and decided not to worry about the outcome. Then came the news that we had both been recommended for commissions, after which we were given railway warrants and told to go on leave and acquire the appropriate uniforms from Gieves.

There was no instruction given to us on becoming an officer in the RAFVR and even less in becoming an RAFVR observer, having missed out on the ITW course. At Gieves, beside the correct uniform and advice on the matter of uniform allowances, we were given gratis a 'guide to commissioned service' and a little about mess routine. Nothing else. This was to be our officer training manual, and we were expected to pick everything else up as we went along. I duly bought my observer's brevet, the flying arsehole as we called it, but had no instructions as to when we could 'put it up' (wear it). Unlike pilots obtaining their wings, there seemed to be no commissioning parade but then life was too short. I had become an observer with only fifty hours of practical navigation and thirty hours or so on armaments. I remember also having to learn the army co-operation code in which to describe and report enemy troop movements exactly as if we were on the Western Front in 1918.

We were told to report to RAF Benson in south Oxfordshire – an operational training unit (OTU) – the final stage in our journey to a front-line squadron. It was early afternoon when Basil and I were picked up from Wallingford railway station by RAF truck and deposited outside the mess in the late afternoon.

Our first action was to 'warn in', we learned, in effect signing the visitors book. This enabled the mess secretary to count his numbers for catering purposes and accommodation. Next we reported to the mess secretary's office to be allocated a room, or to be more precise, a bed in a room, since all junior officers were required to 'double up'. Our kit had already been deposited – we weren't in the same room – and we set off to find the batman who was to look after us. This mission successfully accomplished, we sauntered off to the dining room where we supposed – correctly as it transpired – tea would be served. We were learning how to fend for ourselves.

The following morning we checked in with the OTU adjutant and reported to the chief instructor, complete with his dog. Neither seemed particularly interested in where we had come from or what we were doing, and simply allocated us to our respective flights, in my case A Flight of 1 Squadron. I never did discover what the other 'squadrons' were for at an OTU, but I later surmised they must have been the 'engineering' and 'equipment' squadrons.

We had to be kitted out with our flying clothing, navigation necessities (logbooks, pencils, plotting instruments and other paraphernalia) as well as our parachutes. Parachute types varied, and ours were the observer-type, stowed separately in the aircraft, usually in easy reach, and then clipped on to a harness that was worn all of the time. Pilots had 'chutes that they sat on. We were then allocated 'flying lockers' in which all our kit could be stowed.

Benson was a permanent RAF base, and very modern. It had been built in 1937, part of a major expansion programme to meet the threat emerging from Nazi Germany. Two squadrons had arrived in April 1939 – 150 and 103 – equipped with the Fairey Battle. Both squadrons left for France in September to become part of the Advanced Air Striking Force (AASF) and both were badly mauled. By the time of our arrival, RAF Benson had become 12 OTU, still equipped with Battles with which we were already well acquainted. The 'station master' was Group Captain Wilfred Dunn, a former seaplane pilot who stood out for his rather splendid mutton-chop whiskers.

Before I had a chance to begin flying or 'crew up' with a similar u/t pilot, I found myself performing several days of navigation exercises, including one with the CI, Wing Commander Anderson in an Anson, to the armaments practice camp at Penrhos on the coast of

Cardigan Bay. This was a hutted camp for temporary detachments to practice on the sea ranges, but had become notorious as the target of Welsh Nationalist arsonists. They preferred in those days to attack military targets rather than holiday cottages! I was to encounter one of the perpetrators (who had gone to prison) later in my career, as SASO of 25 Group. By that point the man had risen to become principal of the University College of Wales at Aberystwyth, and I was obliged to ask him whether we could use 'his' campus for recruiting cadets into the university air squadron of Wales. Despite his past, and the fact he was now a pacifist, he did not object.

I soon found myself flying with a splendid bunch of pilots from New Zealand who had completed their wings course back home and arrived in the UK by ship via the Cape. They had been trained on elderly biplanes and flew the Battle with considerable zest, as though it were a fighter. We completed a number of cross-country exercises with a wireless operator and employed radio navigation bearings for the first time. The full crew was three, but it made for a very crowded aircraft. As observer, I sat amidships with no direct view outside except downwards through the bombing hatch. We slowly climbed to 22,000ft with a (dummy) bomb load to experience flying with oxygen masks on and began using 'homing bearings' to help with navigation – an easy exercise assuming the w/op could raise the required station.

Low flying was fun, especially with our kiwi pilots, and we were introduced to the use of poison gas to be sprayed on enemy troop concentrations – if they were foolish enough to provide such targets. Spray canisters were mounted under the wings on bomb racks. For training purposes these were filled with soapsuds, and at least one poor Oxfordshire tractor driver – though no doubt well accustomed to our low-flying antics – must have been surprised to find himself enveloped in (rapidly dispersing) soapsuds. The defensive use of poison gas must have been considered in higher echelons, if the invasion of the UK had been launched.

Bombing training was included, usually at the Otmore range nearby (now a nature reserve) but this was at low level with the aiming and weapon release being under the control of the pilot using a mark etched onto his windscreen. So much for our high-level practice bombing over Lough Neagh! We learned later that high-level formation bombing had been employed in France against vital pinch points such as bridges and road intersections but at an appalling price.

May and June were glorious months for flying, but not so in France. The inadequacy of the Fairey Battle in modern day warfare was by now badly exposed. On May 10, while I was enjoying a brief spell of leave, Battles of 12 Squadron made their ill-fated attack on the bridges at Maastricht, an attack in which two aircrew won posthumous Victoria Crosses – the first to be awarded to members of the RAF in the Second World War. Four days later, an all out effort against German pontoon bridges at Sedan by Battles of five separate squadrons resulted in the loss of forty out of an attacking force of seventy-one aircraft.

In my time at Benson I flew with various pilots of equally varied ranks and seniority: Wing Commander Anderson, Squadron Leaders Grey, Lewis and Lane (the latter being the commanding officer of 1 Squadron), Flight Lieutenant Johnston, Flying Officers Simpson, Collins (who signed my logbook as A Flight commander) and Wilson, Pupil Pilot Officers Auliff, Andrews and Alexander. By the end of June I had accumulated some 130 hours of flying to my credit – but still only three of those hours (including the one at Prestwick) had been at night. Nevertheless I felt ready for my next challenge, and was excited when the posting notice came through and I was told to collect my camp kit from the stores. This comprised a heavy canvass bedroll containing my camp bed and washbasin. I already had a gas mask, of course, which had to be carried tediously at all times except when flying. I also collected my webbing, a harness worn like a soldier (for my revolver, water bottle and other accoutrements of a military nature). From the armoury I was given my .38 revolver and a small box of ammunition that was carried in a further pouch added to the webbing.

My posting was to 98 Squadron in France, a squadron with a proud tradition dating back to the First World War. The squadron had been in Nantes since April 1940, in essence a reserve squadron that acted as a replacement 'pool' for those other Battle squadrons in the front line. Events, however, had already superseded my orders. And fortuitously so as it later transpired. Just as I was given my railway warrant to transport me to Hendon (from where I would be flown to France), I was stood down, my posting cancelled. France was being evacuated; no further aircrew were required.

It was a bitter disappointment to me, although I was soon to discover that I would have arrived to find no aircraft and no squadron. They were, in fact, at that very moment making for St Nazaire from where they would be evacuated. Many were loaded onto the former Cunard liner *Lancastria*, which was then sunk by Junkers Ju87 'Stuka' dive-bombers with the loss of more than 4,000 military personnel including many with whom I had recently trained. Among them was Pilot Officer Auliff, a strong swimmer who – I believe – saved several lives. (He also did well after the war at the Aircraft and Armaments Experimental Establishment – A&AEE – at Boscombe Down.)

It was an enormous anti-climax, but the fact was that we had little real knowledge of the progress of the war, especially on land. We were aware, of course, of the unequal struggle of our few fighter squadrons against the might of the German Luftwaffe. As Churchill said: "The Battle of France is over; the Battle of Britain is about to begin." For my part I was told to return to my flight and await further instructions – an order I was by now rather familiar with. Drinking in local bars had become unpleasant, particularly if we should meet any 'pongos' (soldiers) who were all too quick to ask where the hell the boys in light blue had been whilst they were getting strafed on the beaches of Dunkirk.

Fortunately I didn't have long to wait before I once again received orders, this time to report to 10 OTU in Abingdon only a few miles up the road. Abingdon, like Benson, was a permanent base, but a little older, and reputed to have the finest rose garden in the RAF (though not for much longer as the non-essential civilian staff drifted away). Group Captain Herbert Massey, later to become well known as the senior British officer in Stalag Luft III, the scene of the 'Great Escape', was the station commander.

My confidence had returned, but as the only one to be transferred, I felt quite alone. Not only was the base unknown to me, and the personnel unfamiliar, but also I had never before seen the aircraft in which I was to fly: the Armstrong Whitworth Whitley. I was also acutely aware that whilst I had been trained for daylight bombing operations, this was a night bombing aircraft.

The Whitley could trace its roots back to an Air Ministry Specification B 3/34 issued in July 1934, and the first prototype (K4586) flew on March 17, 1936. It appeared in public for the first time at the RAF display at Hendon that same year. The Whitley, a twin-engined mid-wing monoplane, was much admired by the Air Ministry and chosen with the Wellington to re-equip the front line heavy bomber squadrons. Early variants used Tiger IX radial engines, each of 795 hp. By the Mk III, the engines had been upgraded to 920 hp, but it was the arrival of Rolls-Royce Merlin X engines giving (ultimately) 1,145 hp for the Whitley IV and the major production variant, the Mk V, that the real improvements in performance were realised. I was looking forward to finding out for myself.

Once again I 'warned in' and found myself doubled up with a very odd character, a senior flight lieutenant by the name of Folkard, who was said to have completed the 'short nav. course'. I never did discover whether he was the station navigation officer and he took no interest in me, but I soon found out that he was most distressed with the mess secretary for making him share. Having reported to the unit adjutant, I found myself allocated to E Flight commanded by Squadron Leader Bickford, who like all senior officers I had come across had a dog, in this case a white bull terrier. He (Bickford, not the dog) was not especially friendly, and with no particular interest wanted to know what I was doing there. Having given him what explanation I could, he told me that there wasn't any course of any kind for me to join. I was just an odd 'bod'. Not to be defeated, I then set about scrounging half an hour local 'air experience on type' in an Mk IV Whitley (N1374) with a Pilot Officer Robson, and was left to my own devices. I had a good look over the aircraft, to discover she was fitted with an automatic Mk 1 bombsight – the first I'd seen. Indeed I had never heard of it, which was a little disconcerting. No-one seemed in a rush to tell me about it either. Again I managed to scrounge a couple of trips in an Anson to the Otmore range, but watched as the pilot aimed and released the practice bombs, just as he had done in the Battle.

By the end of the first week, I had still only flown in a Whitley once, and had amassed less than two hours flying time. Having been so close to joining a squadron from Benson, I now seemed to be further away from the war than ever. Soon I would be further away still, when from Abingdon I was sent to join the unit's detached armament flight (C Flight) at RAF Jurby on the Isle of Man. The flight operated very elderly Whitley Mk IIs and IIIs, fitted with the Tiger engines that evidently gave endless servicing troubles.

Happily, I began flying almost at once, starting with the C Flight commander, Squadron Leader J. H. Barrett. The first few sorties were spent familiarising myself with the front-powered turret fitted with a solitary Vickers K gun. Unlike the bombsights, I was most familiar with the Vickers from my time at Aldergrove, and contentedly fired 200 rounds at a drogue towed over the sea off the coast of Ramsey, taking care to miss the local fishing fleet!

The glorious summer of 1940 continued, and we flew several practice bombing sorties early in the mornings, dropping our bombs near targets floating at sea from about 8,000ft. Climbing any higher wasted time, and often caused the engines to overheat. I continued to scatter my bombs all over the range, on one occasion allegedly dropping one 20lb missile (smoke filled) outside of the range. Nothing was ever said, so I assume no harm was done. The simple truth was that I could not get to grips with the bombsight and received no intelligent instruction as to its use. It was a gyro-stabilised device, with the aiming graticule driven at the correct groundspeed, assuming that the correct wind speed had been set and the pilot flew at the airspeed briefed. The sight itself was restricted in its vision, and in reality I was forced simply to guess the forecast wind and hope for the best. There was no time for measuring the drift, which might have made our bombing more accurate, but it would have lengthened the sortie too much. My results were indifferent, and my colleagues' reactions were the same.

I left Jurby after precisely two weeks, having dropped the required number of bombs and fired off the requisite number of rounds in the front turret. Apart from a pilot (Pilot Officer Fletcher) going sick, forcing an early return, and my wayward bomb, there was not much to report. I returned to E Flight at Abingdon, again to be received with supreme indifference. It was difficult being the odd man out, without a crew or any structured training. It was, I think you would call it today, rather shambolic. In the course of a further week I flew one night cross-country flight of less than six hours. But even that wasn't all that it sounds. In the event, all that I did was keep a log; the pilot actually did the navigating, with the second pilot calling out and noting pinpoints along the way. It was such a fine night, and the blackout so poor, that roads, rivers and buildings were easy to see. My night flying experience had now trebled to nine hours in total.

As with the Battle, I recall one sortie in particular where the objective was to climb to 18,000ft for oxygen experience. We tried to go higher, but the Whitley – an Mk V in this case and the very latest model (N1503) – refused to oblige. A further low-level sortie on the Marham bombing range with a Flight Lieutenant Tomlinson brought my OTU experience to an end, and my logbook was dutifully stamped and signed by the chief instructor, Wing Commander 'Streaky' Cattell. I had flown the grand total of 158 hours and thirty-five minutes, but had received no proper crew training whatsoever, so that even the basics of dinghy drill or escape procedures were still alien to me. It was ironic, because in just a few short weeks I would need both skills in abundance.

My posting came through: 58 Squadron. At last I was going to war.

CHAPTER TWO
TO WAR
IN A WHITLEY

Squadron transport arrived to meet me off the train at York station. I had travelled first class! It was July 28, 1940.

The squadron to which I had been posted, 58 Squadron, gloried under the motto *Alis nocturnis* − on the wings of the night. It had been formed at Cramlington on June 8, 1916, initially employed on advanced training duties. It went to France in January 1918 and its aircraft (the redoubtable FE 2bs) flew their first night-time bombing operations the following month. The squadron was flying the mighty Handley Page O/400s by the time of the Armistice. After Vickers Vimy and Virginia bi-plane bombers, the squadron took delivery of its first Whitley monoplanes in October 1937, although it had teething troubles with its original Whitley IIs and was obliged to take several Heyfords (another bi-plane) on loan from Leconfield to fill in the gaps.

It was finally with the Whitley III that 58 Squadron went to war, when seven of its aircraft dropped leaflets over the Ruhr. After a brief sojourn with Coastal Command and escort patrols, the squadron returned to Bomber Command and 4 Group in February 1940 and converted to the Whitley Mk V. With the German invasion of Norway, bombing attacks began on April 17, by which time it was firmly established in its permanent home, Linton-on-Ouse, where it would remain for the next two years.

The mess at Linton was similar in layout to RAF Benson. At

Linton, however, I was given a room to myself in one of the married quarters (now evacuated) not many yards from the main building, and immediately came across a most curious character – a civilian batman – who took all of my clothes and had them pressed! I had been lucky, depending on one's point of view, to have short-circuited the initial training wing where I would have learned the very structure of the RAF and, above all, the hierarchy and how my life was to be conducted. Having offloaded my kit, therefore, I was left alone to take stock.

The station commander was Group Captain Ivelaw Chapman DFC, AFC. 'Chaps', as he was known, was a highly distinguished airman who had served with 10 Squadron in the First World War, mainly in artillery observation, before flying with distinction on the North West Frontier. (Later he would achieve fame as the man from the planning directorate who Churchill ordered killed lest he should reveal secrets of the invasion of Normandy after he went 'missing' over enemy territory, flying operations without permission.) He was a very kindly man, greatly concerned with the welfare and morale of his men and much admired.

Wing Commander John Sutton whom everybody called 'The Maestro' and who already held the Distinguished Flying Cross (DFC) commanded the squadron. Although not a thinking man, he was a CO who everybody held in the highest regard, and had contempt for anyone outside of Linton. He was especially dismissive of those at 4 Group headquarters, and it was heavily ironic that he later left us to join those same officers (as wing commander operations I believe) who had done so much to torment him. Sutton was a real leader, although I would recognise later he was not actually a good squadron commander. Too often we were allowed off base to York and the Half Moon, one of our favourite watering holes. There was none of the professionalism and discipline that would come later in the war, but his briefings were always memorable, with plenty of fiery language encouraging us to "smite the hun".

The squadron was divided into two flights – A and B. The A Flight commander was Squadron Leader Michael Hallam who was soon after succeeded by Squadron Leader John 'Hustler' Tuck. Hallam was an officer in the reserve, awarded the DFC in 1940. Hustler I remember especially for his dog, Parker. Parker was a white bull terrier who his owner tried to teach to pull the 'chocks' away from the undercarriage when he needed to take off. I don't think Parker ever succeeded, but he was particularly successful at biting any airmen who came into range.

I learned that I had been posted to B Flight, whose commander was also a memorable character but for different reasons. Whereas Hustler was very cheerful and kindly, Squadron Leader John Bartlett was rather a gloomy man of few words. A Londoner, from South Kensington, Bartlett was a regular and very close to being tour expired.

There were other notables among the more senior officers. Flight Lieutenant Peter Cribb, for example, had been operating almost from day one of the war, and was just coming to the end of his first tour. He was extremely professional, an expert pilot and navigator and highly intelligent. He tried once to explain to me the workings of the astrograph – a disastrous piece of equipment that was supposed to help navigation by projecting pre-calculated astro position lines on to the chart. We loaded an appropriate 'film', dependent on our latitude, and the relevant lines would be displayed. Trouble was, my nav's table was quite often disturbed – usually when the co-pilot got up from his seat or put his coffee flask on it – and if the table wasn't level and stable, the projections were utterly useless. I believe they were of slightly more use in a Wellington, but I'm not convinced.

Overseeing the day-to-day administration was the squadron adjutant, Flight Lieutenant Evershed, who wore the 'Mutt and Jeff' medals of the First World War as well as his pilot's wings. He seemed positively ancient but was pleasant enough to us sprogs.

The other memorable senior officer was another ancient, the station intelligence officer, Squadron Leader Ivor Jones. He was known affectionately as 'The Colonel' and was a great one for the 'blood and guts' language of the time. He was actually a retired officer from the Indian Army who had found happy employment in the ground defence role (before the days of the RAF regiment) but commissioned into the administrative branch. The administrative branch covered a multitude of duties, especially the operations officers. His team, all of them 'wingless wonders', were mainly elderly flight lieutenants who had been solicitors or accountants in civilian life. One, John Lloyd, was the High Sheriff of Montgomeryshire!

The danger of operations in these early stages of the war cannot be understated. Whilst all of the attention in the summer of 1940 has been focused on the efforts of Fighter Command, and the legendary 'Few', there were a great many in Bomber Command fighting and dying whose sacrifices were largely overlooked. Shortly before my arrival our squadron lost some fourteen men killed in three weeks, at a time when we could ill-afford to lose any crews with experience.

My own chance to get to grips with the hun (as 'The Colonel' would have said) came scarcely forty-eight hours after my arrival. I had reported to the B Flight commander and Bartlett had told me to get myself organised with flying kit, parachute harness, Mae West life jacket etc and the necessary accoutrements of a navigator such as pencils, plotting instruments, log sheets and so on. He was taking me on my first night operation.

We were to be part of an attacking force of some seventy-six Hampdens, Wellingtons and our own Whitleys – the three mainstay bombers of the period – against various targets including Homberg, Cologne and Hamm. Our own target was identified as one of the oil refineries (the Reisholz refinery) on the outskirts of Düsseldorf, and our squadron was to contribute eight aircraft to the overall plan. The crew for my first sortie comprised the captain, Squadron Leader Bartlett, Pilot Officer Eric Ford – the second pilot, Sergeant Allan – the wireless op, and Pilot Officer Dickie Fennell as rear gunner.

In those days, once the instructions had been received from group, the stations and squadrons were largely left to their own devices in terms of planning their route to the target. Rather than the huge bomber 'streams' that would come later in the war, and that would see hundreds of aircraft passing through a target in just a handful of minutes, we could stooge around the darkened skies of France and Germany in one's and two's all night. We had a 'time on target' (ToT), but how we got there and the route we took was decided at station level. The intelligence officer might suggest certain routes, and known 'hot spots' to avoid (such as the Friesland Islands, for example, where there were known flak concentrations), but other than that we were on our own.

The briefing itself was also nothing like the size and sophistication of bomber operations from 1942 onwards. Pilots and navigators would gather in the briefing room around a large table where we would be issued with our target folders. There was no big unveiling of a map behind a curtain, or gasps from the assembled aircrew of "God, not Berlin again". Mostly we didn't know where the target was, and it took some finding on the charts we were given. The detail of the information within these folders, however, was considerable. They came from the Air Ministry, and we would be given precise aiming points and told that if we hit this particular generator, at this particular point, for example, we would render the whole plant u/s. Of course it was nonsense for night operations, and lacked all sense of proportion. Even a near miss was unlikely to damage a target to the point that it would be destroyed, and we were scattering our bombs all over the place. Not that we knew it necessarily at the time.

After the main briefing, the wireless ops would then receive a separate briefing by the station signals officer. They would be told the frequencies of the night-fighter beacons that would be working to help with navigation. No-one bothered to tell the navigators, however, the relevant co-ordinates, so they were rather useless to us. We didn't, at that stage, have a station navigation officer either.

On this particular summer's evening we took off late, at 21.15, in our Whitley V (P4951) and slowly, laboriously climbed to our operational ceiling. To say I was ill prepared would be an understatement: I hardly knew how to connect my oxygen mask or where the R/T socket for the nav table was situated (it was behind me of course). As for R/T procedure and use of the crew intercom, I would have to learn as I went along.

We had a maximum speed of 230mph at 16,400ft, according to the manufacturer's own figures, and could climb – in theory at least – to 26,000ft, but at that height, remembering that we had no electronic navigational aids in 1940, it was virtually impossible to make out any ground details with any certainty. Not that we ever did get to

26,000ft. Mostly we were lucky to make half that height, out of range of the light flak.

Navigation at night was by dead reckoning, and we relied on seeing the ground to attack our targets, letting down through cloud when we thought we were due at the destination, and hoping to recognise any prominent landmarks from our maps. In the dark, only rivers, lakes or shorelines offered any positive identification, and even this depended on the moon or the half-light of dusk or dawn.

That night I learned many lessons: I learned, for example, that you can see best 'up moon' and next to nothing 'down moon', whereas the reverse is true of sunlight. As it was, I couldn't find the target. The darkness was intense. I thought we were close, but I had had to leave my navigator's charts and squirm my way forward under the co-pilot's legs and down into the bomb aimer's position in order to drop the bombs, since this was also my responsibility. (The RAF would take some time before they realised the nonsense of abandoning navigation just at the point it was needed most.) Try as I might, peering into the gloom below, I could not, with any certainty, indentify the refinery we were looking for, let alone line it up in the bombsight.

It was at this point that our usually mild-mannered pilot and flight commander became rather exasperated, and demanded to know why I couldn't see the target, at which point I told him to go around again! Needless to say he wasn't impressed, but then I could hardly explain to him that I had actually only ever flown in a Whitley at night once, and that was on a navigation exercise around England in rather more gentle circumstances. Nor did it seem relevant to tell him that my total night flying experience amounted to less than ten hours. As it was, I was less concerned about the captain shouting at me, and more worried about the searchlights. They were dazzling, and I felt utterly naked when several of the beams came together into a large 'cone'. I was also worried about the flak, and had received my first experience of being shot at just a few minutes earlier from the defences of Münchengladbach. To use a sporting analogy, I had had no second XI experience before being shoved into the real thing.

I never did find that target and we decided to bring our bombs home. I managed to crawl back to my nav's table, reconnect my oxygen and R/T leads, and tried to work out where we were. Somehow I managed to make sense of our position and we arrived back at Linton after a flight of six hours and forty minutes.

Notwithstanding my flight commander's displeasure, he picked me again to fly with him for the squadron's next operation, against the same target. I did not have a regular crew in those days, and was chosen to fly with a variety of different pilots as the need dictated. For August 1, the 'crew' comprised Bartlett as pilot with Sergeant Colin Hughes (second pilot), Sergeant Gibson as w/op and the improbably named Hunter Muskett in the rear turret. I navigated our aircraft to the target area but owing to ground mist was again not able to identify the aiming point with any certainty. As it was we attacked a secondary target about three miles to the north west of Reisholz in what they called 'a gliding approach', reducing height from 10,000ft to 8,000ft, then levelling off to drop our bombs. We had the satisfaction of starting a number of fires.

(Officially we carried a maximum of 9,000lbs of ordnance – usually six 1,000lbs and six 500lbs bombs – but many of the crews also had the habit of carrying a few incendiaries, in a box, in the bomb aimer's position, which we would throw out of the escape hatch over the target. It never crossed our minds just how dangerous carrying such bombs inside the aircraft could be, and the sergeant armourer was always keen to let us have them off the inventory. It was all very childish, but somehow, again, indicative of the time.)

The following week I was detached to the school of air navigation (ex Manston) at St Athan, near Cardiff where I spent a fortnight learning the art of astro-navigation. We had no time or transport to explore the delights of the city, and despite the title of the school we couldn't fly at night because the Luftwaffe regularly targeted the city's docks. We therefore learned our skills with the bubble sextant on two and a half hour sorties out in the Bristol Channel in broad daylight, taking shots of the sun through the open roof hatch of the Anson. I passed the air observers advanced navigation course with a rather satisfying comment from the chief instructor inscribed in my logbook that said: "His interest in the subject should make him a confident astro-navigator with experience." Time would indeed tell.

In the wider world, the RAF was desperately anxious to learn to navigate at night without sight of the ground. Multi-engined aircraft were being fitted with astrodomes, with all-round vision of the heavens from which sextant shots could be taken. The operational planners, however, had never asked how the unfortunate observers, trussed up in heavy flying gear, Mae West and parachute harness, were to achieve such a feat. Nor did they consider that the last thing a pilot wanted to do on a bombing mission was fly straight and level for the two-minute run required by the RAF's standard bubble sextant, or that he would have to do this three times for the navigator to obtain a fix, of doubtful accuracy.

While I was away, our squadron bombed Berlin in retaliation for the German Luftwaffe's raids on our own capital. It had been a far from one-sided affair. One of our aircraft, captained by Pilot Officer Neville Clements, ran out of fuel on their return and abandoned the bomber short of base. Tragically, though all five aircrew baled out safely, Sergeant Matthew Hill's canopy was caught in a strong shore breeze and carried out to sea where he drowned. He was a local man, and only twenty-one years old.

Running out of fuel was always a danger, especially with the long-distance targets such as Pilsen or Stettin. A run-in with flak or a night-fighter – however unusual – could consume precious gallons at an alarming rate. On September 2 we were briefed to attack one such long-range target – indeed one at the very extreme of our range – Genoa in Italy. As a target, it was reckoned to be a doddle, especially as the Italian anti-aircraft gunners were reputed to take to their shelters as soon as the air raid sirens sounded. It did, however, involve a ten-hour flight across the Alps, and planners at group therefore arranged for us to stage at RAF Honington in Suffolk in order to top up our tanks and shorten our flight time.

We took off therefore in the late afternoon in a Whitley V (N1427) for the hour-long trip from Linton to Honington, with Squadron Leader Bartlett once again at the controls. The rest of the crew this time comprised Sergeant Frederick Kerr (second pilot), and Sergeants Coubrough, and Caryll de Tilkin, w/op and gunner respectively. After a brief stopover, we were on our way by 20.00, one of eight 58

Squadron aircraft operating that night. Six of us would attack Genoa, and the remaining two would target Frankfurt.

It was a long and arduous journey – and a mystery to me why they routed us over the Alps at an unnecessarily high safety height when we could just as easily have avoided the highest ranges. Switzerland may have been neutral but nobody seemed to mind that much later in the war. As it was we used considerable amounts of fuel gaining the necessary height that would see us safely over Mont Blanc and back again – fuel that might be vital later. And so it proved.

Conditions were against us all of the way, and once we reached the target we were met by a considerable barrage of anti-aircraft fire. It seemed to be particularly intense above the town, and bursting at various heights between 4,000ft and 15,000ft. More than one of our aircraft was hit, though mercifully we encountered no searchlight activity to add to our troubles. As it was, I managed to find and then bomb the target and gave our captain the course for home. By now there were head winds and it was soon clear that we would be lucky to make it home. I was keeping an anxious eye on the fuel gauges and calculating at what point we would finally run out. Manston was just too far.

Land was in sight, North Foreland. We had been in the air for ten hours and twenty minutes. Our luck and our fuel were fast running out. Bartlett had to make a decision and gave the orders to take up crash positions for ditching. In my case, that meant finding a safe place behind the main spar at the back of the bomb bay.

We had heard that the sea was harder than the land and we were about to find out. Bartlett sensibly feathered one of the engines in order to conserve what little fuel we had left. Ditching was a delicate operation, and required power. He could not risk losing that power in the final crucial moments for we would drop like a brick. As it was he did rather well, keeping the aircraft's nose up until we stalled just above the water.

The aircraft skimmed the waves for a short distance before finally coming to a halt and rocking in the swell. I had not until this time practiced any dinghy drill but it didn't seem to matter. The dinghy was released from the top part of the wing and automatically inflated, remaining tied to the aircraft by a short cord. One by one we clambered out of the escape hatch and onto the wing. Although the weather was fine and the sea benign, it did not stop us all getting soaked. A mixture of seawater and aviation fuel had flooded the fuselage, some of it finding its way into my underpants and onto my balls, and I don't mind admitting that it hurt like hell.

Bartlett was calm throughout and took charge, and we started to paddle towards shore. As I plunged the paddle into the water I looked over my shoulder at the sad sight of our once proud aircraft as she sank lower in the water, her tail still visible above the water line, like a giant fin. I'm not sure how long it would have taken us to paddle to shore, because fortunately a passing fishing boat threw us a line and took us in tow back to Margate. The lifeboat was elsewhere, overworked with Battle of Britain casualties. After the noise and excitement of the ditching, the world now seemed strangely silent and calm.

In my logbook I wrote the words: "Forced-landed in sea off North Foreland. Aircraft sank." In Bill Chorley's *1939-1940 volume of Bomber Command War Losses*, a most comprehensive study, I am not listed in the crew, but I can assure you I was there!

The local superintendent of police soon took us in hand, and he was most helpful. First we were taken to a nearby gas works to dry out and then on to a local girls school (the girls had long ago been evacuated I hasten to add) for a hot and most welcome shower. It was a tremendous relief to wash the petrol from my body. My jacket and most of my clothes, with the exception of my trousers, were no longer fit for purpose, so our policeman had the idea of allowing us to help ourselves from a selection of attire kept at the local mortuary! The humour of the moment affected us all. It was like being in a fancy dress shop, and some of the clothes were fancy indeed. For myself I selected an ancient frock coat, accompanied by a silk scarf and a pair of white plimsolls. When the superintendent saw my rig, he found me a hat to match from the mayor's parlour, and so the outfit was complete.

We spent the rest of the morning in the town, stopping at a street corner to help a group of locals collecting for the Spitfire Fund. Word

John in garb from the local morgue having been rescued at sea.
Sergeant Kerr is rather more traditionally attired.

had got around about these strange airmen walking about town, and inevitably the press were soon on the scene taking photographs of Sergeant Kerr and me. (I still have a copy. The headline the next morning in the *Daily Sketch* described the picture somewhat embarrassingly as typifying 'the amazing spirit of the RAF'.)

Our brief moment of celebrity did not last long. The superintendent had been busy, and had 'phoned Linton to let them know that we were safe, and that we would require transport back to base. It was arranged that a De Havilland Dominie would pick us up from Manston. By a strange quirk of fate the aircraft was from 24 Squadron, a squadron with which I was later to spend two years of my life. As it was, there was a problem and we were obliged to overnight at RAF Hendon, it being too late to return to Linton.

This was where the fun ended. The station commander, a group captain, looked me up and down and steadfastly refused me permission to enter the public rooms of the mess on the grounds that I was 'improperly dressed'. It was a hard lesson learned. I was shown into a room where I munched a sandwich and drank a mug of coffee whilst contemplating the last few hours. The fact that I had been in the air for more than ten hours, shot at by the Italians and then survived a forced-landing in the sea was irrelevant against the fact that I was not wearing the right uniform.

We returned to Linton the next day.

It was a great relief to be back at base. Although we were at war, life was carefree. We were almost blasé. The French were out of it and we now only had ourselves to worry about. We were standing on our own with our backs to the wall. And it felt good. With 'The Maestro' in charge, we felt we couldn't lose.

On my return I penned a letter to the chief constable in Margate, William Palmer, to thank him and his officers for the assistance they had rendered us during our short stay in his town. I also wrote out a cheque that the chief constable put towards the police widows and orphans fund.

As a result of our misfortune I was obliged to attend group headquarters with the captain and be interviewed by the AOC, Air Vice-Marshal 'Maori' Coningham (who was later to achieve fame in the desert). No conclusions were drawn, but it was clear that better routing might have saved the aircraft. The weather hadn't helped, and although I had seen the lights on the shores of Lake Geneva on the way out, I cannot recall getting a single fix by map reading at any point during our return journey. The AOC was not best pleased, for we were not the only ones to come down in water that night. Flight Sergeant Dennis 'Dinty' Moore found himself in a similar predicament and also ditched, fifteen miles north east of Harwich. His crew too were able to clamber into the dinghy and were later rescued whilst drifting off the Suffolk coast by HMS *Pintail*, a Kingfisher Class patrol vessel. (*Pintail* was lost the following year after she struck a mine off the Humber estuary.)

Dinty was in A Flight and highly experienced. Indeed it is worth here saying something about our NCO pilots who tended to be among the very best. Most were apprentices who had been selected for pilot training, and because so few places were available, the RAF could afford to be choosy. Those that made it, like Dinty, were invariably very calm, well disciplined and proficient. It did not surprise me that many went on to be commissioned later in the war, and attain relatively senior rank.

Dinty was fortunate that night to be flying with another A Flight officer, and another accomplished pilot, Peter Elliott. Peter and Dinty were later to 'star' in a famous photograph, taken for propaganda purposes, extolling the virtues of 'The Few'. The fact that the photograph shows pilots and airmen from a bomber squadron was an irony that was not lost on us at the time or now.

Propaganda played a big part in those early days of the war. As well as our 'poster' publicity, an official press photographer also spent some time with us at Linton taking a variety of shots for use in the media. They include various 'staged' photographs of an operational briefing, with a group of twenty or so of us gathered around a senior officer, listening intently to his every word, with target maps and papers scattered across the table. It is a world away from comparable briefings later in the war, with up to a hundred or so pilots, navigators, bomb aimers etc seated at rows of trestle tables and chairs ten or fifteen deep in front of a dais and blackboards detailing weather conditions, take-off times, and pathfinder techniques. The photographer has also managed to capture a number of evocative shots of our aircraft at dispersal, and ground crews labouring hard to see those aircraft refuelled and re-armed. They are all now part of the Imperial War Museum collection.

The men at the ministry had also taken to sending young fighter and bomber crew out to the factories and manufacturing plants to thank the workers for their vital contribution to the war effort. I took my turn with a talk on the industrial shop floor of one such plant, the Armstrong Whitworth factory building Whitleys at Baginton (now Coventry airport). They were very kind to me, and although I remember little, I did my best, standing on a box, to say all of the right things. Whether it had any impact in terms of boosting production, however, I very much doubt. The Luftwaffe had blitzed Coventry in the first of the raids employing their beam bombing system. This was a navigation system developed from the Lorenz beam landing system employing a very narrow radio beam aligned with the runway. It was built under license in the UK by the Standard Telephone Company and installed at Croydon aerodrome before the war. It was used by the RAF under the name of standard beam approach (SBA).

Throughout this time also we would receive various 'signals' and 'messages' from the air officer commanding-in-chief, Bomber Command – Air Chief Marshal Sir Charles Portal – acknowledging our successes in taking the war to the enemy. Several are glued into my logbook and vary in length and tone. One dated August 14, 1940 simply states:

"Please pass to all squadrons who took part my heartiest congratulations on the success of their operations against Italy last night." Another, from September 1, is much longer and is an interesting propaganda piece in that it refers to the fact that "the great majority of pilots brought their bombs home rather than loose them under weather conditions which made it difficult to hit the precise military objectives prescribed in their orders". This, the message goes on to say, is evidence of "the high standard of poise and self-restraint preserved by the Royal Air Force in the performance of their dangerous duties", which, it says, "is in marked contrast with the wanton cruelty exhibited by the German flyers."

Portal's most damning lines are reserved for the end:

> "All this is another sign and proof that the command of the air is being gradually and painfully, but nonetheless remorselessly, wrested from the Nazi criminals who hoped by this means to terrorise and dominate European civilisation."

I returned to the war on September 8, but this time with Sergeant Cyril Boothby, and a commissioned second pilot, Pilot Officer

Thomas Robison, a New Zealander who never stopped cursing the Germans. We attempted to raid the docks and shipping around Ostend, but once again we were unable to locate the target owing to very bad weather conditions and returned to Linton with our bombs. On September 10 I navigated to Bremen, to attack shipping and warehouses, this time with Flight Lieutenant Ned Harding (later B Flight commander) and Sergeant Hughes in the co-pilot's seat. Indeed this was to be the manner of attacks in the weeks that followed, with our main efforts being focused on destroying harbour installations and shipping that might be used to support an invasion – when we could find them of course. The cloud was so thick over Bremen that I couldn't be sure of our aiming point and so bombed an area between the target and the railway marshalling yards without observing any results.

The threat of invasion was never far from our minds. On September 12, that threat looked like becoming reality when church bells began to ring out their warning.

We were drinking in our favourite pub, the Half Moon, run by Harry and Ida Moore, the landlord and landlady, who were most hospitable. They were like Jack and Jill, he was as thin as a rake, and matched the building which was tall and narrow; she was large, rotund and seemed to fill the small premises. Evidently, Linton had been ordered by group headquarters (situated at Heslington Hall, now a part of York University) to bring all squadrons to readiness for probable operations at first light on the following day, against an expected German landing on the east coast. The squadron duty officer knew where to find us. So it was Ida who called out, above the usual din, for someone from Linton to take the call. Her stentorian voice silenced the crowded bar and one of our number had to announce the dismal news that our evening was spoiled. We crowded into a small car, with The Colonel packed into the back, loudly announcing that he'd act as tail gunner, and drove through the blackout back to the camp.

When nearly home we were stopped by a red lamp being waved at us in the middle of the road. The local home guard were already in action and had felled a tree across our path, but being locals, they showed us how to get to the main gate and we tumbled into the mess ante-room, for a drink. The station master duly addressed us: every aircraft that was serviceable to fly was being bombed up and we should disperse to our squadron crew rooms to await orders, captains and crews being duly assigned.

In the event, nothing happened. It was a false alarm – though rumours were widespread that bodies had been washed up on the south coast. The sea had been set on fire with burning fuel, but such was the blackout on news that we never did discover the cause of the alarm. It has, however always stuck in my memory.

We had better luck for our attack on Dunkirk on the 13th with Boothby again at the controls. This time I could make out the target quite clearly, and Boothby executed an attack from 9,500ft and saw our bombs explode on the southern side of the commercial docks. There were nine of our squadron involved in the raid, and for once everybody dropped their bombs in the right place. As we left, and I gave Boothby the course to steer for home, there were several large fires underway, orange and yellow blobs in an otherwise darkened canvas.

It was a pattern of operations at that time that we would regularly lose crews, and our losses continued to mount. Pilot Officer James Thompson and his crew, for example, were lost over Bremen. All were later reported safe as prisoners of war including the second pilot, Pilot Officer Trevor Hadley, one of two New Zealand brothers, one in each flight (they had consecutive service numbers).

It was also a pattern of operations that we constantly changed pilots and crews. I was never convinced it was a good idea but had little choice in the matter. The operational training units in the first two years of the war were little short of shambolic. We were not yet at the stage where aircrew would leave OTUs in ready-made crews, and be posted accordingly. We would receive replacements in ones and twos. I arrived on my own, and flew with whoever I was detailed to fly with by my flight commander. Perhaps Bartlett, and 'The Maestro', should have been more rigorous in their crew selection and especially in their training. Training was virtually non-existent once you were on a squadron, and continuation training for pilots – which today would be considered essential – seldom took place, beyond being sent (usually on rainy days) for a few hours on the Link trainer, a primitive flight simulator for instrument flying. One could find the wireless operators on occasion in a huddle with the signals staff, but only the gunnery leader – Dickie Fennell – organised any formal training that I remember, and that was a clay pigeon shoot. It was a miracle that any of us made it through those months alive.

On September 18 I was paired with Pilot Officer 'Brownie' Brown, another of the squadron stalwarts. He was my skipper for the next five trips: Zeebrugge (in bright moonlight) that night, followed by Berlin (September 24), Le Havre (September 26), Magdeburg (September 29) and Stettin (October 2).

These operations were not without incident. We had to abandon our trip to Berlin only an hour or so into the journey because of our air gunner yelling on the intercom that he couldn't go on. Officially he went 'sick', but in my logbook I have written the word 'mad' in brackets. I read somewhere that our Whitley was met when we landed, and the rest of us were told not to leave the aircraft until the RAF police had arrived and taken the unfortunate man away. I do not recall the incident in that way, but it was probably one of the early examples of what the RAF would later call LMF, where aircrew were said to be 'Lacking in Moral Fibre'. It was a cruel soubriquet for what is now widely understood as being combat stress.

We similarly had to abandon our raid on Stettin because of 10/10ths cloud over the target, and on the way back bombed the Hindenburg Dam on Sylt instead. Le Havre was more successful, and I had the satisfaction of seeing one stick of our bombs burst across the docks south of the power station, causing a large explosion.

Again we suffered the loss of several good men and their crews: Bert Crossland was lost with his entire crew on September 18, his aircraft having been seen to be on fire by other members of the squadron. A week later Sergeant Herbert Cornish crashed on take-off just beyond the airfield boundary. The aircraft immediately caught fire and soon after there was a terrific crump as the bomb load exploded.

Cornish and two of his crew were killed; two more were injured. Such were the dangers we faced at the time. Crews were as likely to be lost to accidents as they were to enemy action, and night-fighters were still a relatively unusual sight.

In between these operations, there is a note in my logbook dated September 25 that lists a flight with Brownie to search for a missing aircraft, downed in the North Sea the previous evening. This is confirmed in the squadron operations record book that says we were searching for a missing aircraft from 77 Squadron. The aircraft, a Whitley V, was skippered by Pilot Officer Dunne DFC. Although we had no luck finding him or his aircraft, two survivors were picked up four days later, one of whom later died.

There was no let up, either in operations or in casualties. Whilst we were on our way to Stettin, Bill Espley, one of our Canadians, took off to attack Frankfurt an der Oder. His aircraft, (Whitley N1434) failed to return. Five nights later and the squadron lost another of its commissioned pilots, the second of the New Zealand brothers, Flying Officer Ronald Hadley. Having successfully completed his attack (the target was Gelsenkirchen), the twenty-year-old Aucklander was last heard of having trouble with his port engine. Subsequently the squadron was informed that his aircraft had crashed while trying to land at an airfield in Norfolk, killing the entire crew. One of my fellow commissioned observers and friends, Richard Phillips, was among those who lost their lives.

Friendships, in those days, were fragile things. As I had arrived on my own, there was no-one in particular to whom I had any especially strong bond. I knew those who were married – men like Hustler Tuck with his charming wife who lived out and one of our intelligence officers, Bo Seymour, who lived in York. Life was almost 'pre-war' in so many ways. I was lucky that an elderly (and very academic) aunt of mine had a friend who was headmaster of Archbishop Holgate's Grammar School in York, so I used to go there for supper with him and his wife whenever I could get a lift. I also went out on one occasion when some well-established local family had rung up the station adjutant and asked that the CO nominate a junior officer to be 'sent over' for dinner. It was a most enjoyable evening at a fine table, and they felt that they were doing their bit for the war effort.

There were other diversions: there was all manner of sport for those that were so inclined, but station teams required regular support, which operational aircrew could not guarantee. Solo sports such as squash tended to be more practical and could more easily be fitted around our flying schedules.

Meantime I had been paired with yet another different pilot, Squadron Leader Kenneth Smith, for the raid on the Fokker aircraft works in Amsterdam. Our crew comprised Sergeant Stiles as second pilot and Sergeants Falkingham and Keatley as wireless op/air gunner and gunner respectively. Falkingham I particularly remember as an unflappable Yorkshireman. We called him 'Smokey Joe' on account of the fact that he was always smoking a filthy little pipe. He would wait until we had dropped our bombs and he had transmitted the 'time-on-target' signal to base and then he would light up as we were heading for home. His position was always shrouded in smoke.

There were only three squadron aircraft up that night and we all attacked the primary target. One, flown by 'Brookie' Brooke, had more of an adventure than most. They suffered a 'hang up' when one of their 500lb bombs refused to release. This was a nerve-racking experience for any crew, as there was always the danger of the bomb working itself loose and exploding, especially with the vibration caused from landing. As it was, they got down safely at Stradishall, to discover their port wing peppered with flak. The aircraft returned to Linton later that afternoon.

One of our sergeant pilots, Bill Christie, became – perhaps more than any other – my 'regular' skipper until the New Year. He had joined the squadron with me in July, and like Dinty Moore was a quiet and efficient airman. I was once asked whether it bothered me, as an officer, flying with a sergeant pilot. I can honestly say that it never did. Officers and NCOs messed separately. That was the way it was, but it was a pity. After operations it would have been good to discuss the detail of the raid with those who had been on it. When we were in the air, the captain – of whatever rank – was in command. It might have been interesting had we come down in the sea (again) and found ourselves in a dinghy, for then I assume I would have been in charge, and my leadership qualities as an officer (such as they were) would have been expected to come to the fore!

Our op to Holland, at just over five hours, was one of our shortest trips. The next two raids to the oil refineries at Leuna and Pollitz (Stettin) took more than nine. Both were successful, especially the Stettin raid. When we arrived, the handiwork of previous raids was much in evidence, and there were several buildings alight. Our second stick demolished two chimneys out of the four standing at the start of the attack, and we could still see the glow of the fires when sixty miles from the target.

My longest trip to date, however, took place on October 21 when we left at 19.00 to attack the Skoda works at Pilsen and returned more than eleven hours later – at the very end of our endurance – having been unable to identify the target because of cloud, and attacking the goods yards at Bonn instead. I remember the raid well, because the whole of Germany was covered in a sheet of white, and I not so much 'aimed' my bombs as rather jettisoned them 'live' wherever I could. Forget what you may have read about every crew 'pressing on' to ensure his bombs hit only legitimate military targets; as far as I was concerned, if they fell on Germany and killed Germans, then that was good enough for me.

I should perhaps add a note of explanation about bombs being jettisoned either 'live' or 'safe'. If the bombs were 'live', they would explode, and the arming pins would be retained in the aircraft; if they were dropped 'safe' – perhaps in an emergency or over friendly territory – they would not explode, and the arming pins went with the bombs. There were two incidents I recall in particular: the first involved a squadron commander, 'Crack'em Staton, who led a spectacular raid on the *Tirpitz* early in the war and managed to drop his bombs right down the battleship's funnel. Unfortunately when he got home his 'Chiefy' noted that the arming pins were not in the aircraft and the bombs had been dropped 'safe'. On another occasion, our squadron was on its way to Brest when one of our aircraft accidentally released its bombs 'safe' over York but was oblivious to the fact until all aircraft were contacted by group signals and told to check their bomb load!

Such long hauls took their toll. On the operation to Pollitz (Stettin) on the night of October 14/15, another 58 Squadron crew came to grief but fortunately without injury. 'Brookie' Brooke was once again in the wars, running low on fuel and coming down five miles east-north-east of Driffield. In the crash that resulted, the aircraft lost most of its starboard wing but miraculously no-one was hurt. Less than a week later and Brookie came to grief again, this time injuring himself whilst ditching in the River Humber on his way back from Pilsen. Despite crashing in fog within 50 yards of the shore, Brookie and his crew spent three hours in their dinghy before being rescued. In the conditions, they had not realised how close to safety they had been.

Indeed this was a bad and busy night for 58. Another Whitley (P5089) piloted by Pilot Officer Arthur Wilding had engine trouble, resulting in the bombs being jettisoned 'live', and lack of fuel forcing them to ditch off the Norfolk coast. A local lifeboat rescued the crew. Wilding and his crew were fortunately none the worse for their ordeal. Tragedy befell the pilot and crew of Whitley T4171 however. Close to base on their approach, the crew failed to notice an approaching intruder and in the ensuing combat the Whitley burst into flames and crashed, killing all but two of the crew, one of whom subsequently died of his injuries. Among the dead was Sergeant Marcel Caryll de Tilkin who had been in the same aircraft as me when we'd ditched in September. It was only luck that I was not with them that night.

Such intruder sorties by the Germans would become a feature of later life, and perhaps we never took the threat of such an attack seriously enough. Our instructions should an intruder be identified in the circuit was to fly to a particular beacon and circle until told to return. The runway lights would be extinguished and we would all hope for the best. The Luftwaffe would also regularly send fighter-bombers to attack targets of opportunity and particularly to disrupt bomber operations, and on more than one occasion we would hear the sirens go and take to the shelters as an enemy aircraft appeared overhead.

Sightings of night-fighters over enemy territory were also still relatively rare. The German Nachtjagd was still in its infancy, although 'Tommy' Gunn, one of our more excitable characters, would regularly report being stalked by an enemy Messerschmitt or two. We never took Tommy too seriously however, as he was nearly always at the source of any shenanigans that were going on in the squadron, and would tease 'sprog' pilots mercilessly that if they showed any signs of weakness they would instantly be 'sent to Matlock' – Matlock being one of the recognised mental asylums of the period.

John Sutton, our 'Maestro' found himself tour expired by the end of October and he was posted from the squadron at the start of November. My erstwhile flight commander, John Bartlett was also posted, and on November 22 notification of his well-earned DFC appeared in the *London Gazette*. Sutton's job as commanding officer passed to Kenneth Smith, who was duly promoted acting wing commander.

Smith was ex-Cranwell, and a good pilot. He had flown one of the first operations of the war, and would later receive full reward for his leadership qualities. As observers we could sum up our pilots' abilities pretty quickly, and Smith inspired great confidence. It would take a little time, but he also began to organise the squadron more efficiently. 'The Maestro' had been great for morale, but Smith began to bring a sense of professionalism that had until then been woefully lacking.

B Flight, meanwhile, was given to Flight Lieutenant Harding, who was promoted acting squadron leader. It was a busy period of change, both on the squadron and in the higher echelons of the service. We had, for example, a new C-in-C. Sir Charles Portal had left to become chief of air staff and Air Marshal Sir Richard Peirse took his place. Oil was to be our continuing priority target, but a long list of other preferred targets was also now being discussed, especially in the major German cities such as Berlin and Hamburg.

It was whilst attacking Hamburg that we lost yet another of our NCO crews on November 7 when Sergeant Francis Elton was believed to have come down over the North Sea on his way back from the target. Though his wireless transmissions were received, his aircraft was never found, despite an extensive search. Elton was only nineteen years old.

I myself flew only two operations in November. The first, on November 14, was a disaster, both for the squadron and for the command.

We were briefed as one of fifty aircraft to attack Berlin, flying with Bill Christie in Whitley P5028. Of course we didn't know we would be one of that many; we only ever had a worm's eye view of the war. It was a long slog, and weather conditions were against us and in the end only twenty-five aircraft (of which we were one) actually managed to find and bomb the target. We landed back at Linton in the small hours of the morning after a noisy, cold and very tiring trip of a little over ten hours.

After every operation we were debriefed by The Colonel and his team (including at least one WAAF intelligence officer), so that their intelligence reports could be sent to group, and they could build a clear picture of the success or otherwise of the raid. (I am not convinced of the accuracy or reliability of these reports; the second pilot probably had the best overall impression of a raid and the rear gunner never saw much until he was leaving the target!) What became clear quite quickly in the ops room was that a number of our pilots were overdue. Then it became clear that three of them would not be coming back at all.

This was our worst night of the war so far. We lost Flying Officer John Champness and his crew (in Whitley T4170), shot down by flak. Champness, at thirty-two, was quite old to be a pilot and had survived a ditching the previous month whilst flying as second pilot to Pilot Officer Wilding. We also lost Sergeant Kerr and his crew (Whitley T4239) though all were later reported as prisoners of war. Kerr had been with me in our own ditching off North Foreland. The biggest personal loss to me was the news that 'Sinbad' Webb was missing. Ival Webb was a twenty-two-year-old sub-lieutenant in the Royal Navy – hence his nickname – and a particular friend. He had been 'on loan' to 58 Squadron from HMS *Daedalus* at a time when the Fleet Air Arm (FAA) had insufficient aircraft to absorb the flow of trained pilots.

My second raid in November was significant as it was one of the largest undertaken by Bomber Command up to that point, and I was flying with the squadron CO. I think he had wanted to check me out, although he didn't put it that way at the time. Some 130 aircraft were briefed to attack four targets in Hamburg, our own being the Blohm & Voss shipyards. Although reports of the raid subsequently pointed to limited success, we were satisfied with our own performance and landed back at Linton just after three in the morning.

The death toll in those weeks, through enemy action and accidents, had been high, and we very nearly added our own names to the list of casualties with two accidents in quick succession. The first was on November 26. It was to be another raid on Turin, and once again we were detailed to fly south, refuel, and then take the arduous route over the Alps. It took about an hour to get to RAF Wyton, and after we landed, the local ground crews marshalled us. The airfield, however, was unfamiliar to us, and in the confusion we managed to bump into another aircraft. The collision was not especially bad, but sufficient damage was done to the pitot head to render our aircraft u/s, and our operation was abandoned. We returned to Linton in a relief aircraft flown by Sergeant Herbert Walters.

Five days later I was with Sergeant 'Johnnie' Johnston, flying to Hendon, when we were unfortunate enough to be involved in another accident. Whitleys were coming to us from the maintenance units without modified radios, and we were obliged to fly them down to Hendon to have new equipment fitted. Johnston and I thought it would be a splendid idea to take one such Whitley and stop over in London for the night. Hendon, however, is in a 'saucer', which means that it is prone to winter fog. We left a little late in the day and arrived over the airfield in thick fog. The obvious thing to do would have been to divert to Abingdon, or even to have gone back to Linton, but the draw of spending an evening in the city was too much, and so Johnnie attempted to land. The runway in use was the shorter one of the two as we would soon discover. The runway lights were on, but every time we caught sight of them and turned in for a final approach, we kept losing them in the turn. The controller, in his caravan on the ground, kept firing white Very cartridges, but these simply made matters worse with the smoke.

Eventually, Johnnie managed to turn the Whitley on a sixpence, and keep the lights in view as we approached. He straightened up, closed the throttles and crossed the airfield threshold too high. Try as he might, he couldn't get the aircraft to 'sit' until he was at least half-way down the runway, by which time we realised we did not have enough runway left in which to stop. Johnnie wasn't unduly concerned, as he figured he could slew the aircraft to one side and still stop without damage or overshooting. What he hadn't bargained on was the station commander's pet aircraft, an old Hawker Hind that was kept for searchlight co-operation exercises, in his way. The collision was inevitable, and although we were unharmed, both aircraft were damaged. The station commander, not surprisingly, was unimpressed, not least because he had only just had his aircraft painted. Despite damaging two of His Majesty's aircraft, thankfully neither of us were court martialled or even disciplined.

A bizarre accident befell the crew of Sergeant Gosling (with Pilot Officer Jack Kerry in the co-pilot seat) that same day when on the way home from Lorient. Their Whitley (T4207) hit a dummy aircraft at one of our 'K' sites at Cold Harbour and was badly damaged. 'K' sites were decoy airfields to fool German raiders, complete with lights but no runways.

The next few weeks were fairly uneventful. I flew three raids on December 11 (Mannheim), December 16 (Mannheim again) and December 20 (Berlin), all with Bill Christie. Our second visit to Mannheim was particularly noteworthy since it signalled a change in strategy by our higher command, and the first of what the German civilians would later call 'terror attacks' and the perpetrators (that is to say, us!) 'terror flyers'. Bomber Command had been authorised by the War Cabinet to carry out a 'general' attack on the centre of a German city in direct retaliation for the heavy attacks our own cities had suffered, notably in Coventry and Southampton. Some 200 aircraft were assembled for the attack, including thirty-five Whitleys, although the results were far from impressive. Only a few fires were started, and most of these were outside of the city centre. The attack still warranted the word 'Blitz' in my logbook, rather than a specific target.

In terms of casualties, only on the night of December 23/24 was there further dismay when the Whitley of Sergeant Stronach Smith, another of our Kiwi pilots, was lost with all hands and the aircraft of Flying Officer Cresswell Clementi[1] very nearly came to grief having returned early from Boulogne. Coming in to land, some idiot had parked an unmarked Lysander of 4 Squadron, unlit, in-line with the runway and a collision was unavoidable.

Both aircraft burst into flames, and Clementi was badly burned helping his wireless operator to escape. Sadly the rear gunner was killed in the subsequent fire. It was a stupid and useless waste.

So 1940 drew to a close and the New Year began. I was now no longer the novice, having logged more than 167 hours of night-time flying, the vast majority of which had been on operations.

I flew just the once in January, a brief thirty-minute air test and some local flying with a Pilot Officer Owen before going on leave. A formal 'tour' system had not yet come into being, although it was generally accepted that we had 'done our bit' at around twenty to thirty ops. It was noticeable, even then, how some of the pilots would become 'twitchy' as the end was in sight. I certainly noticed that with Bartlett, and wondered if I would feel much the same way when my own turn came.

While I was away, the squadron suffered further casualties, William Peers, one of our married officers, being shot down on the night of January 15/16, and Sergeant Barlow going missing the following night. Peers was killed; Barlow luckily survived.

I returned to operations on the night of February 6, a comparatively short trip of less than five hours, bombing the docks and shipping in Calais. Our intended target was Dunkirk, but when we arrived we found it obscured by 10/10ths cloud and bombed what we thought was Calais. Indeed of the eight squadron aircraft operating that night, only three located and bombed the primary target. As well as our own attack on Calais, one bombed the aerodrome at St Omer, one the searchlights at Fort Risbon, and the last aircraft brought its bombs

---

[1.] Clementi was the son of the late Sir Cecil Clementi, the governor of Hong Kong. He had an illustrious career in the RAF, attaining the rank of air vice-marshal CB, CBE, and was part of the British nuclear test party in 1958.

back as they would not release owing to an electrical fault.

It was not immediately obvious to us at the time, but this period has subsequently been coined as 'the arrival of the heavyweights', when Bomber Command's four-engined 'heavies' came to the fore, and squadrons began taking delivery of the first Short Stirlings and Handley Page Halifaxes. Technically these were far superior to our faithful Whitleys, with an operational performance we could only dream about, and the latest technological aids to make life easier for pilot and crew. With the advent of these aircraft, the crew was augmented by the addition of a further air gunner to man the mid upper turret and a bomb aimer who would specialise in the art of map-reading, thus relieving the observer of his need to change position on approach to the target at the crucial prelude to the attack. A flight engineer was also substituted for the second pilot – with obvious training savings – to assist the pilot in fuel and engine handling.

For the time being, however, we had to put up with what we had, and the danger of getting lost and running out of fuel.

Two of our sergeant pilots – Fullerton and Walters – found themselves in just such a predicament on their way back from Bremen on the night of February 11/12. Fullerton abandoned his aircraft in the area of Bagthorpe, near Nottingham; Walters abandoned his Whitley fifteen miles south east of Glasgow. To put their efforts into context, however, there were eighteen aircraft lost that night on their return from Bremen and a second target, Hannover. Not a single bomber was lost to enemy action; all were either abandoned or crashed attempting to land.

Ivelaw Chapman mentions this incident in his biography, *High Endeavour*. He described the evening as "a traumatic night in our ops room". He wrote at the time that:

> "Of the twenty-one aircraft (*sic*) that had taken off from Linton, six crews baled out, ten landed at Drem, one at Kinloss, one at North Coates Fittes, one at Leuchars, one crash-landed and one only landed back at Linton after two unsuccessful attempts at 05.30hrs after having been in the air for some ten-and-a-half hours."

It was with Fullerton that I was to fly my next – and what turned out to be my final – bombing operation with the squadron on February 22. Sitting alongside Fullerton in the co-pilot's seat was Pilot Officer Ronald Carrapiett, with Sergeants Keatley and 'Smokey Joe' Falkingham making up the rest of the crew. Seven of our aircraft were detailed to attack Düsseldorf, but only four of us managed to identify the primary target. Because of thick cloud, however, we were unable to observe any results, and landed home at Linton at 08.05hrs.

Later that day I was spoken to in the mess by the station commander and told that my time with the squadron was done. I was a little confused as I hadn't yet completed my tour, but 'Chaps' was adamant and told me that the adjutant would fill in the details.

My logbook shows that by the end of February, my night-time flying amounted to just over 178 hours, most of which was spent on operations dodging searchlights and flak. It was certified by Leslie Crooks on behalf of the OC B Flight, Squadron Leader Ned Harding.

I learned that I was to be posted to 31 Air Navigation School in Port Albert, Ontario where I was to attend 12 Specialist Navigation (abbreviated to 'Spec.N') Course. I learned also that along with Squadron Leader Tuck and Flight Lieutenant Crooks, I had been awarded the Distinguished Flying Cross, and was delighted to receive various letters of congratulations, including one from The Collector of Customs and Excise, my previous employer in more peaceful times. There were Distinguished Flying Medals (DFMs) for seven of our non-commissioned pilots and airmen – two of whom had sadly been killed in the weeks preceding the awards' formal approval.

I had had a good innings, and survived when many of my friends and compatriots around me had been killed. Subsequently, aviation historians have highlighted how the Whitley squadrons of 1940/41 were the proving grounds for airmen who went on to greater glory, especially in the Pathfinder Force. However, not all of them got the chance.

Ron Carrapiett, for example, would be dead within a handful of weeks, the victim of an attack by Oberleutnant Paul Gildner, a contemporary of Prinz zur Lippe Weissenfeld of 4/NJG1. Carrapiett and all of his crew were killed with the exception of Sergeant Mason who became a prisoner of war. He was only twenty-one.

Sergeant Cyril Boothby, my pilot for two operations, was later commissioned and added the DFC to his already well-earned DFM. He was killed in 1943 as a flight lieutenant with 624 Squadron, operating from North Africa. I believe he had been dropping agents and supplies to resistance forces in Italy and southern France. His second pilot for at least one of our sorties, Pilot Officer Robison, was killed in action in June 1941, as a flight lieutenant whilst operating with 35 Squadron.

Sergeant Bill Christie, with whom I flew almost half of my tour, later rose to flight lieutenant with 7 Squadron, Pathfinder Force (PFF). He won the DSO before being shot down and killed in December 1942. He had been on his way back from Torino having been hit by flak, and managed to keep the aircraft in the air long enough for the rest of the crew to bale out. The wireless operator was none other than Flight Sergeant 'Smokey Joe' Falkingham DFM, who owed his life to the selfless bravery of his skipper.

Sergeant Walters, who often flew as second pilot with Christie, survived the war – but only just. After completing his tour he was posted to 10 OTU at Abingdon, when on a training flight in September 1942 his aircraft – a Whitley V – caught fire. He was seriously injured in the resulting crash and badly burned, but continued to serve as a staff officer, achieving the rank of squadron leader.

My first commanding officer, John Sutton, survived, and indeed our paths would cross later in the war. His successor, Kenneth Smith, was later awarded the DSO for displaying "exceptional powers of leadership, courage and determination" and was twice Mentioned in Despatches. He was killed with 9 Squadron in April 1943 on his fourth sortie having taken command of the squadron the previous month.

John Bartlett went on, I believe, to take command of 255 Squadron as a wing commander before being killed in action on August 22, 1941. The squadron had just converted to Beaufighters, flying night-fighter sorties.

Others survived and some did rather well: Sergeant Colin Hughes would later be awarded the DFM and be commissioned. He was shot down in June 1943 whilst flying Stirlings with 7 Squadron, PFF as Squadron Leader Colin Hughes DSO, DFM. He survived as a prisoner of war; Ned Harding finished the war as Wing Commander Ned Harding DFC; 'Hustler' Tuck also survived the war, only to be discharged as medically unfit in 1948. He had survived a serious collision whilst serving on four-engined 'heavies'.

Leslie Crooks, who had certified my logbook, went on to win the DSO as the commanding officer of 426 (Canadian) Squadron before being killed on the famous Peenemünde raid, the eighth operation of his second tour. (He was a former apprentice who had been a sergeant pilot in Iraq in 1935.) Flying Officer Mervyn Fleming also went on to command a Canadian squadron, 419, and win the DSO and DFC.

Peter Cribb, who was just coming to the end of his first tour as I started mine, finished the war as one of the most highly decorated pathfinder pilots, retiring as Air Commodore Peter Cribb CBE, DSO & Bar, DFC & Bar. Another contemporary, Pilot Officer 'Pat' Daniels, a live-wire who joined the squadron in September 1940 also went on to become a leading pathfinder winning the DSO & Bar and DFC & Bar, and Pilot Officer Jack Kerry became a flight commander with the famous 35 Squadron before being killed in action. His best friend Pilot Officer Peter Elliott was another early pathfinder killed with 35 Squadron in March 1943 as a squadron leader, DFC.

We had a saying at the time that I remember to this day: "*58. Never late. Flying straight. Through the gate. Germans hate.*" I don't know if they did actually hate us, but we did everything we could to help them.

CHAPTER THREE
THE WAY
TO THE STARS

Having been told by the adjutant that I was being sent on a special-ist navigation course, I did not immediately know where the course was being held. It therefore came as somewhat of a surprise that I would be heading for Port Albert and had to reach for an atlas to be sure of where we were going. First I took the train to Gourock on the Clyde where I would board my ship, the M/S *Batory*.

M/S *Batory* was an ocean liner that was part of the Polish merchant fleet and which had sailed the Gdynia/New York route in happier times. We were to sail in convoy with one other vessel, but no other escort ships as far as I can remember. We would be relying on our speed to avoid any lurking U-boats.

We were a mixed company comprising pilots and observers who had completed ops on Whitleys, Wellingtons, Blenheims and Hampdens, as well as some who were ex-Coastal. We were far from lonely, for we were part of a group that included an entire flying training school that had crated up its equipment (including its air-craft) to relocate to Canada. The officer in charge on the trip was Group Captain A'p Ellis, the CO of the FTS we were carrying.

The voyage across the Atlantic was mercifully short and unevent-ful, and we disembarked at Halifax with the help of a highly efficient movement unit and entrained that evening for Montreal. We were billeted overnight in the city, just long enough to have a drink or two in the Mount Royal, a regular watering hole for RAF aircrew in tran-sit. By pure chance I bumped into Danny Falconer, ex-58 Squadron, on his way home, having completed the Spec.N course, and he told me what to expect when we got to Port Albert. Sadly it was the last time I saw Danny alive.

It was another day/night journey to Toronto and finally to the rail-head on the shores of Lake Huron at Goderich. We all peered out into the wilderness, half expecting to see a 'Red Indian' or two galloping over the plain. We were wide-eyed innocents abroad, and took full advantage of the endless amounts of food that was supplied, which after the shortages back home was most appreciated.

At last we arrived at Port Albert, Western Ontario, our home for the foreseeable future. The camp had only recently been completed, and as the snow had only just receded, it was a sea of mud. Whilst the infrastructure may have been primitive, there was no criticising the camp spirit, which was positively engendered by the station commander, Group Captain Paul Robertson. The groupie was a fascinating character, ex-Royal Naval Air Service (RNAS), and memorable because he only had one eye and a badly burned face. He wore over his breast pocket the ribbon of the Albert Medal in gold, and I learned later that this was for trying to rescue his pilot after their seaplane had crashed into marshy land and burst into flames.[2]

Robertson was one of the old school, an excellent administrator who ran a tight ship very well. A young yet quite senior Canadian AOC told him once that he was going to be sent a number of Canadian WAAFs to help with the camp's administration. Robertson told the officer in question that he had no desire to have any women on his base, since they only caused trouble.

The AOC insisted, tapping his head and saying: "Don't worry about Canadian WAAFs, they've got it up here." Robertson replied: "I don't care sir, wherever it is, my men will find it!"

Port Albert was the top school for ex-operational pilots and navigators with the very best senior instructors. It was to all intents and purposes a complete RAF 'base' that had been transported from the UK and 're-located' in Canada, away from the dangers of wartime

---

[2.] Robertson's award of the Albert Medal appeared in the *London Gazette* on June 18, 1918. The pilot, Flight Lieutenant Hubert Lemon, died of his injuries.

Britain. Among the staff pilots was John Searby, later one of the RAF's great bomber leaders and the first 'Master Bomber'.[3]

This was an early example of the Empire Air Training Scheme in action, a scheme that had been well constructed and well planned before the outbreak of war, and from which we were now reaping the benefit.

The course, which lasted four months, focused primarily on the complicated theory and understanding of astro (what the US preferred to call 'celestial') navigation. The British, of course, had long ago understood the importance of being able to navigate using a compass and the stars. This understanding had led to the first astrodomes being fitted into our aircraft. The Americans, however, were not so trained. They relied on radio navigation aids, flying from beacon to beacon, and as such were expert instrument flyers. It is not too much of an exaggeration to say that some very important products of the Spec.N course, such as those who found themselves part of the British Air Commission in Washington, had an important influence on how US aircraft were subsequently equipped with hydraulic gun turrets, astrodomes and even where the compasses were sited so that they did not deviate excessively.

I qualified as a Spec.N with an average of 78.4%, with my logbook certified by Squadron Leader Mervyn Stanley, OC 31 ANS. Now, looking back, I realise that the Spec.N syllabus was already out of synch with the Bomber Command thinking of 1941/42 that was beginning to move away from astro-navigation in favour of electronic aids such as Gee (and much later H2S). Keeping a bomber aircraft straight and level long enough for the navigator to get an accurate fix was increasingly impractical in the hostile skies of northern Europe, and sure enough by 1943 the Spec.N course was brought back to the UK and appropriately adapted, as the 'new series' Spec.N course.

On completing my studies, some of my contemporaries were posted to the newly opened 32 ANS at Mount Hope, Hamilton, as instructors. Others reported to Dorval for repatriation as working aircrew on Ferry Command aircraft, as required. I fully expected to be re-absorbed within the Bomber Command family, almost certainly within an OTU

[3.] Air Commodore John Searby DSO DFC died in 1986.

where I thought my operational and navigational experience would be most in demand. The authorities, however, had different ideas.

I found myself appointed project officer on the development of a new astro-navigation training device then under construction. The celestial navigation trainer (CNT), as it was called, had been dreamed up by a few senior RAF Spec.Ns and given to the famous Link Aviation business to build for the RAF, the RCAF and the USAF. As its name implies, the CNT was primarily a navigation trainer with the ability to obtain astro fixes (with a sextant from certain collimated stars, radio D/F fixes and map reading) from a projected ground image beneath the cockpit.

The pilot (twin-engined controls and instruments) could 'fly' it as a conventional instrument trainer and perform blind approach training, either on the radio range or standard beam approach (SBA). From the floor of the nav. position, where an Mk IX bombsight was installed in a bombing window, the navigator/bomb aimer could direct the pilot on a simulated bombing run to attack a pre-selected target projected rather crudely on a screen beneath the cockpit body.

The instructor, at the standard Link desk, could set the 'sky' for the exercise by rotating the dome and setting its starting latitude. He could pre-position radio beacons for use with the radio compass and could – if he were multi-dextrous – set the terrain 'plate' in the projector for the target to appear in co-ordination with the progress of the 'flight' of the trainer. A standard Link 'crab' enabled him to do this; the same crab could be used to monitor the pilot's blind landing if required. For navigation exercises, the table was covered with a constant scale chart, appropriately marked with turning points, radio beacons, targets etc, with the scale set relevant to the distances needed.

A team of RAF tradesmen had already helped with the assembly of the device and were to be the technical instructors for future maintenance crews. By reason of their undoubted abilities, they were an enormous help to Link on the design and manufacture of the CNT's workings.

At first I was concerned with the development trials of the prototype and the development of suitable training exercises at Port Albert, alongside US personnel from the Link factory. Later, however, I worked at the factory itself on the first production model for shipment to the UK, under the 'lease-lend' agreement.

I also wrote a training manual for the device, and created 'ready-made' exercises for embryonic navigator/bomb aimers to perform, whilst at the same time showing how its many facilities could be fully utilised. At all times I liaised closely with the Link factory over the latest modifications that were being suggested.

Throughout this time I had a most able and effective 'number two' in Flying Officer George Watson. 'Doc' Watson had come up the hard way. He had been an armament fitter or some such and was most proud of the brass bullet he had worn on his sleeve that denoted he was a gunner of the old school. Above his breast pocket he wore the distinctive ribbon of the DFM & Bar, the first of which he had won for operations in Waziristan in 1938 as an LAC. He took part in one of the first daylight bomber sorties of the war, and told me that when his squadron had re-equipped with Blenheims, he was effectively ordered to attend a short navigation course at North Coates Fittes, and being RAF, he did as he was told. I shared a room with 'Doc' and his dog called Aries, which kept making a mess of the floor. We were friends, though very different and with especially different tastes. With his big moustache and thick black hair, he was always one for the ladies and women positively swooned in his company. He was no intellectual, but incredibly shrewd, and could sum up senior officers straight away.

It was an interesting period for all who were involved, and as our guinea pigs we managed to rope in some of the most experienced and senior officers then in Canada. These included the new station commander of Port Albert, Group Captain Richard Crofton (known as 'Auntie' because he was a bit of an old woman, especially compared to his one-eyed predecessor) and as many Spec.N students as we could lay our hands on.

Our work came to be well-known and attracted a good many visitors, including Ed Link himself who used to fly in to see us in his own little Amphibian, a Grumman Widgeon, accompanied by a number of his factory specialists. Among the senior air force visitors were Air Commodore Brookes, the AOC No 1 Training Command, Toronto; his SASO Group Captain Mackeson and his Air 1, Wing

Commander Wilf Oulton. I managed to sneak a flight with Wilf – a much decorated and highly experienced coastal pilot who by co-incidence commanded 58 Squadron after it transferred from Bomber to Coastal Command later in the war. He was a most brilliant staff officer who I much admired. I also managed to fix a few private fly-ing lessons with a Miss Hamilton in a Piper Cub at the London Flying Club (in Ontario). At the back of my mind I think I still har-boured some dreams of becoming a pilot, and whilst I enjoyed flying, it was not something that came naturally to me.

Trials of the trainer were conducted all through the summer of 1941 until the spring of 1942, by which time I had been detached to the British Air Commission in Washington DC. I had also been elect-ed as a fellow of the Royal Meteorological Society (dated December 3, 1941) and been awarded my air navigators' certificate 2nd class (February 9, 1942).

During this time, I was frequently required to sing for my supper and do my bit of PR for the local community. In my case this meant giving talks at local Rotary and Lions Clubs, with my every word reported in detail in the local press.

Some of the coverage was especially excitable. On one occasion I was photographed with the local sheriff having given an address to the Binghamton Lions Club. The picture appeared beneath a caption that states simply: "Sheriff shakes with one who drops bombs." I saw no reason at the time not to tell the Canadians the truth, and the truth was that I had killed women and children during raids over enemy territory and this too was reported in graphic language: "I admit I have killed women and children, and I must say I am not ashamed of it," I was reported as saying. "That might sound blood-thirsty to you but after all they have made rather a nasty mess of England!" I also suggested that the Germans "will feel the full fury of war until the myth of their much vaunted impregnability sinks into their thick Teutonic skulls". Stirring stuff.

I made a good many friends in Canada. The social life was out-standing, and the locals incredibly friendly. They were intensely pro-British and looked upon our antics with studied amusement. I think they thought us all mad, and found some of our customs and tradi-

Sheriff Shakes With One Who Drops Bombs

Hands across the sea became a reality at the weekly luncheon meeting of Binghamton Lions Club yesterday when Sheriff Earl J. Daniels and Flight Lieut. John L. Mitchell of the RAF put on a demonstration of the policy. Also shown in the picture are left to right, Thomas A. Sutphen, club program

The author's celebrity as 'one who drops bombs' was of considerable interest to the US media.

tions difficult to understand. One of our more 'informal' clubs was the 'Dead End Kids' – in effect an officers drinking and social club. Members could be distinguished by the way in which they held their beer pots, with the thumb on the rim and little finger on the base. It had been started by Sammy Mather, a former Halton apprentice. Sammy was another tremendous character who had been head 'plumber' (wing commander engineer) at Manston before being shipped out to Port Albert.

Trials of our CNT were proving very successful and by July 1942 my job was ostensibly done. Now they wanted me to spread the 'gospel' further afield and establish the equipment within the OTU network at home. Leaving 'Doc' Watson in charge, I made my way via B24D Liberator back to the UK. Flight Lieutenant Bill Longhurst (attached to RAF Ferry Command, Montreal) flew the aircraft and I navigated her from Dorval to Goose Bay, and then overnight to Reykjavik in Iceland. The final leg took us from Reykjavik to Prestwick.

Fortunately, my time spent flying a desk would not last too long.

CHAPTER FOUR

MEETING THE OWNER

On my return to the UK I reported to the Air Ministry Directorate of Navigation Training. From a personal point of view, the posting was a fortunate one for it enabled me to get married to Brenda, my girlfriend. We were married at All Saints in Sanderstead on Saturday, September 19, and had our reception at the nearby Selsdon Park Hotel. Captain Allen Thompson, an old friend from my younger days, was best man, and our honeymoon was briefly interrupted when I was obliged to attend Buckingham Palace to receive the DFC from the king. It was not the only time I was to meet His Majesty.

Although a 'desk job', I was able in the November to wangle a week's flying with 24 Squadron at Hendon, navigating both Hudsons and Electras (both similar twin-engined monoplanes from Lockheed) on a series of UK trips. My return to Hendon was somewhat friend-lier than my last visit to the base, as a sprog navigator who had just been fished out of the Channel, and my reception in the mess was decidedly more welcoming.

While I was there I caught sight of a strange new aircraft in the famous 'Grahame White' hangar. It was similar in size to the Avro Lancaster, with familiar wing-shape and four engines, but its fuselage was entirely different. I didn't know what it was, neither what it was doing at Hendon. I certainly didn't know just how closely I was to become associated with this aircraft – an Avro York – over the next two years.

My work at the Air Ministry kept me busy over the winter, and my chances to fly were few and far between. I did, however, in the March of 1943 manage to sneak in an operation – my first in almost exactly two years. It came through Kenny Lawson, one of my very best friends, and a fellow Spec.N student who I had got to know well in Washington. Kenny was ex-3 Group Wellingtons, who always said that he had no use for any living German. He was also an expert navigator who had spent his time in the US going around aircraft factories such as Consolidated and Douglas advising them where to site the compass in new aircraft. Now he was a squadron leader DFC on pathfinders, and I asked him whether he could wangle me a trip to keep my hand in, as it were. I went up to Warboys, where he was based, and they found me a berth on a 156 Squadron Lancaster piloted by a Squadron Leader Donaldson. It was only a short trip over to St Nazaire where I could come to little harm, and I believe we were a 'backer-up', ensuring the target was marked as required by the master bomber.

The following week I wangled another few days with 510 Squadron, local flying with my boss, Group Captain Kenneth Niblett, in the unit's lumbering Ansons.

Events began to unfold quickly after that. Although comfortable in my role, I had been actively looking for a new challenge. I had kept in touch with John 'Jackie' Sproule, a Canadian Spec.N pilot (he was later a group captain DFC), who had been an instructor at Port Albert and was now the navigation officer with 44 Group (the UK Ferry Group). He knew of my anxiety to get out of Air Ministry, and my name was evidently put forward to a selection board being assembled to interview for the position of navigator to fly the VVIP 'York' that I had seen at Hendon. The idea of using my navigation skills in long-range flying very much appealed to me, and in time I was interviewed at Adastral House (a straightforward affair) and afterwards was accepted and reported to A&AEE at Boscombe Down for training with the rest of the 'specially selected' crew on our equally 'specially selected' aircraft.

It quickly became clear just exactly what we had been let in for. Until that time, the organisation for transporting the prime minister had been a somewhat haphazard affair. Apart from the royal flight that had been established in 1936, there was no RAF aircraft provided between the wars for VIP flying. What little VIP flying which was required had been provided by 24 Squadron from Hendon in a variety of operational aircraft slightly modified to give the passenger some modicum of comfort. Although Ramsay MacDonald made some use of 24 Squadron Fairey IIIF aircraft to fly to and from his Scottish constituency, very few politicians travelled by air, and when they did it tended to be by Imperial Airways scheduled services. For Neville Chamberlain's historic flight to meet with the German chancellor in 1938, a Lockheed 12A had been specially chartered from a small firm operating from Heston called British Airways.

It was Winston Churchill, beyond all others, who was fully to exploit the inherent flexibility that air travel provided to conduct official business. He first used 24 Squadron when he was The First Lord of the Admiralty to visit his opposite number in Paris in March 1940. He flew to France no fewer than five times in May and June of that year to try and keep pace with a rapidly developing military situation and to stiffen the French resolve to fight.

After the fall of France and victory in the Battle of Britain, Churchill continued to use air travel for himself and his closest staff, returning from the first Washington conference in January 1942 in the BOAC's 'Berwick' flying boat having journeyed out on the battleship HMS *Duke of York*. For the second conference he took another BOAC aircraft (Bristol) both ways.

With unusual foresight, three of these Boeing 314 'Clipper' flying boats had been bought by Harold Balfour on his own initiative for the British government (with the inevitable row with the treasury) from Pan American Airways at the beginning of the war when it had been realised that a transatlantic service could not be operated by the corporation's 'C' and 'G' class boats built by Shorts. With civil registration markings and flown by BOAC crews in civilian uniforms, the Clippers could use neutral Foynes and Lisbon. We had entered the war with the RAF and the civil airlines ridiculously short of any long-range passenger/troop carrying aircraft. The last large civil land plane to enter service before September 1938 had been the Armstrong Whitworth Ensign class for the Empire Air routes of short stage lengths. Neither this type, nor the Short Empire flying boats had the range of the transatlantic operations. Rapid access to North

America had suddenly become a crying need. The gap was temporarily filled, albeit uncomfortably, by employing the early versions of the B24 Liberator in both directions for priority traffic, passengers and light freight.

By now the prime minister had discovered for himself the means to satisfy his desire to take decisions on the spot with other world leaders. He was anxious to be in on the action, or at least reasonably near, in suitable comfort and quickly. However, it was not easy or indeed practical for the PM to expect to be able to take over one of these three vital flying boats, or have one on stand-by, whenever he had the urge to travel. It didn't stop him from trying, however!

One such occasion occurred in the summer of 1942. Our military fortunes in the Western Desert were at low ebb, and Churchill had determined that decisive action was required and he needed to be on the ground to take it. A Clipper was an option, although it would have to make the journey via Gibraltar and Takoradi, and thence by the Central African reinforcement route to Khartoum and so north, down the Nile to Cairo. The chief of air staff (CAS) suggested the use of a Liberator instead, then part of what came to be called the return ferry service (RFS) based in Dorval. One of the Liberators, named 'Commando', had been adapted for VIP purposes, and was diverted for the PM for Operation Bracelet, his flight to Cairo and on to Moscow in August 1942. The captain of the aircraft was an American civilian, Bill Van der Kloot, and the navigator, specially added to the crew by the RAF, was Squadron Leader Charles Kimber DFC.

On their return, the CAS personally debriefed Kimber, and it was apparent that the RAF had some criticism of the planning and briefing at various stages of the PM's journey, some of it stemming from the employment of a rather 'independent' American civilian captain. Kimber had not always been properly warned of the requirements in sufficient time to prepare his plans. This was partly down to security, though of all people, the navigator has to be privy to the flight plan. Weather briefings had been rudimentary and there had been a haphazard approach to flight safety in terms of the timing over the routes to be flown, and the likelihood of encountering enemy opposition.

Churchill was still determined to use the aircraft again five months later for Operation Symbol, the codename given to the conference in Casablanca in January 1943. He flew from Lyneham direct to Casablanca, meeting the US president and the American joint chiefs of staff who had themselves flown directly from the US, mostly in Douglas C54s. Less than two weeks later, with his 'air taxi' effectively 'on call', Churchill could not resist another trip to the Middle East to see how his decisions had impacted the success or otherwise of the Eighth Army.

Meanwhile there had been developments on the home front. At much the same time that the prime minister had been venturing out on Operation Bracelet, aircraft manufacturers A.V. Roe had unveiled the first prototype of its York military transport. The Air Council decided that the third prototype, LV633, was to become a VVIP aircraft, and be furnished accordingly. It was also to be put at the disposal of the PM for his future visits to the Middle East, Russia and India.

LV633 was instantly recognisable as the only York with square windows. It was also given a name: Ascalon. The lance (or in some versions, the sword) with which George had slain the dragon.

The comfort provided within the aircraft was everything the 'Commando' wasn't: there was a state-of-the-art state room and en suite toilet aft. There was to be a dining room with a central table seating eight, which could double as an onboard conference room. The accommodation in the rear of the aircraft was separated by a galley – albeit a rather primitive one – and forward comprised two Pullman-style bays of four bunks in each, two up and two down like an American sleeper car. Two more Elsan chemical toilets, with folding washbasins, were situated between the bays.

Following the CAS's debriefing of Kimber, the air staff felt that responsibility for flying the prime minister by air should be given over entirely to the RAF, with its crew taken only from within the service. There were practical as well as proprietary reasons behind the decision, not least of which was the issue of command and control, and the intimate liaison that would be required in London for planning future flights at Cabinet level. There had been apparently an exchange between the CAS and the PM's office over the matter, with the PM minuting that he liked to travel with people he knew. His wishes to stick with the American crew were overruled, however, and it was agreed that an RAF crew was to be selected, with instructions that it was to be 'one crew to be solely responsible and screened from posting'.

The 'one crew' to which I would belong was made up of some exceptionally talented and experienced aviators, all experts in the respective fields. The captain, Wing Commander Henry Collins DFC, had been the first to be chosen, and as commanding officer of 24 Squadron, was perhaps the most obvious choice as pilot. 'John' Collins was a regular of the old school and so 'old' that we referred to him as 'Dad'. After a five-year short service commission between 1926 and 1931, John spent eight years as a pilot with Imperial Airways. As a captain he had flown the Argosy, Atlanta and Hannibal Class aircraft on the Empire Air routes. Recalled in 1939 to serve with the commandeered aircraft of the civil airlines, in 1940 he had flown an unarmed Ensign pre-war luxury airliner to the beleaguered units of the British Expeditionary Force (BEF) in and around the Calais enclave with quantities of urgently needed anti-tank ammunition. Coming under attack both on the way in and on the way out, he had won a well-deserved DFC for his extreme coolness under fire.

Joining Collins on the flight deck was Squadron Leader Ernest 'Bill' Fraser. The job had been initially offered to an ex-Bomber Command officer called Crackston, but he had wanted to return to his squadron. Bill, however, was far from second best. He was an experienced transport pilot who had come up the hard way pre-war, being selected for sergeant pilot training in 1934 after RAF entry via an apprentice school in 1928. This was a tough elimination process, for the number of NCOs accepted for pilot training was then far too few. He learned to fly at 4 Flying Training School at Abu Sueir in Egypt and then served his early flying years with 70 Squadron in Heliopolis, operating throughout the Middle East.

Our flight engineer was Flight Lieutenant Sydney 'Jack' Payne AFM, a particularly interesting character. Jack was the eldest of us all at forty-one, an ex-Halton 'brat', as the Halton apprentices were known, who had seen airman service in India and later became one of the first commissioned flight engineers. In civil life he had worked for the American Texas Oil Company and later for Bristol Aeroplane Co. He came to us from A&AEE Boscombe Down where he had been working on the acceptance trials of all of the new four-engined aircraft. Like most of the early-stage flight engineers, Jack was an experienced fitter on both engines and airframes (before the two disciplines were separated to accelerate learning). More than this, Jack also held various civil ground engineer licenses and was thus qualified to 'sign out' the serviceability of the York at any time without the say-so of an RAF ground branch engineer officer. Arguably one of his finest qualities, however, was his ability to make friends wherever he went, always at the level that would benefit us most.

Completing the crew was our wireless operator, Flight Lieutenant Willie 'Jock' Gallagher, ex-Coastal Command. Jock, a fierce Glaswegian, had considerable experience of transatlantic ferry operations, and I believe had flown several times with the coastal ace, Squadron Leader Terry Bulloch.

Our instructions were simple. We were to fly the York when required to do so by the prime minister, and that meant being on virtual permanent stand-by. The aircraft would be operated to the requirements of 10 Downing Street through a direct channel. This channel was to be via the CAS to the air officer commander-in-chief (AOC-in-C) at Transport Command, direct to the captain of the aircraft. Fortunately for all of us, the senior air staff officer (SASO) of this newly-formed Command situated at Harrow (which was also taking over the transatlantic ferry operations of Ferry Command in Dorval) was one Air Vice-Marshal 'Brackles' Brackley, a former operations manager for Imperial Airways who had been instrumental in getting Collins command of the York, and a strong advocate for our needs.

Whilst based at Hendon I was 'living out' at Richmond which, apart from being rather too close to a noisy anti-aircraft battery, suited my purposes well. We spent the next three weeks shaking down as a crew, whilst conducting handling trials of the aircraft at Boscombe Down.

My first flight in LV633 took place on May 2, 1943 at Boscombe Down, a forty-minute trip with a test pilot, Group Captain Purvis. My first impressions were encouraging. The flight deck was relatively commodious, with a fine navigator's position from which astro-

The author's crew position in Ascalon.

observations could be made without leaving the table. My only comment, and complaint after the maiden flight, was that the navigator's seat was too plush and took up too much space when standing in action with the sextant. Perhaps I should have stayed quiet. No-one had ever heard of a crew position being too comfortable! A folding stool was substituted and proved more than adequate.

The majority of our handling trials then took place under the watchful eye of the test pilot in charge of B Flight (the 'heavy' flight to which we were attached), Wing Commander Charles Slee AFC. We had consumption trials, and tested the automatic pilot and the calibration of our IFF (identification friend or foe) system. Endurance tests and API tests were complemented by our first fully loaded (63,000lbs) take-off trials – happily successful. Our first flight with Collins in command took place on May 17, and the following week we were ready to meet The Owner. (For this, or prime minister was how Churchill was always referred to by the crew.)

We were required to position in Gibraltar by May 27 and await the arrival of the prime minister and personal staff from the third Washington conference, Operation Trident. They were flying in on the BOAC flying boat Bristol.

Issues with runway lengths (the runway simply wasn't long enough for a large aircraft like ours) meant that we had had to leave Hendon and move to RAF Northolt, where the York would now be permanently stationed. It was conveniently situated on the A40, half way between Chequers and Number 10. It was from Northolt, therefore, that we departed on May 25 for the short trip to Portreath, intending to cross the Bay of Biscay that night. The weather, however, was against us; we would be flying into an Atlantic low, with all of the problems that would give us, and decided to think again. We were carrying our first passengers: John Peck of the Foreign Office, one of the PM's private secretaries; and Group Captain George 'Jimmy' Jeffs, the Command air traffic officer who was going to accompany the whole trip to organise ATC services at the various landing grounds we might expect to visit. Also, flying as first pilot but not in command was Wing Commander Slee, whom the AOC-in-C Transport Command had ordained should accompany the crew in view of the relatively few hours of development flying that the aircraft had undergone, and us with it.

It became clear that a crossing that night was not on, and our only alternative, if we were to make our rendezvous, would be a daylight sortie the next day. We eventually made Gibraltar without incident after eight hours, only to be told that the prime minister and his party were delayed, and would not be arriving until May 28. We could also see that an American C54 (Skymaster) aircraft had arrived via Gander to provide a VIP aircraft for General Marshall and senior American officers of various ranks who were to accompany the prime minister's North African tour, no doubt to prevent him from trying to bully General Eisenhower into doing something the president would not have approved of! Trident, by all accounts, had resolved little.

Collins positioned Ascalon at the end of the runway nearest the flying boat base. We assumed that the party might want a quick transfer from one aircraft to the next, and an immediate departure with the minimum of exposure to the public gaze. As it was, they were to stop over at 'the Convent', the governor's residence, and Churchill seemed to be in no mood to heed the advice of his security staff and conceal his presence. As it was he was seen by a great number of locals and service personnel, and no doubt his presence was soon communicated far and wide.

The use of Gibraltar for VIP transits to Algiers and all points further east was always open to security criticism. The duty spy, as he was known, was said to be situated on the high ground above La Linea at a site known as Queen Catherine's Chair, with binoculars focused on the comings and goings of all aircraft. Within minutes, the information he gathered on all aircraft types and numbers could be with the German Embassy in Madrid and transmitted onward to Berlin. It was also known that the Reina Christiana Hotel in Algeciras – even though British owned – had a whole wing given over to Italian and German intelligence staff.

The Owner finally joined us, a big man in every sense, and we set off for Algiers (Maison Blanche), a trip of around two-and-a-half hours that we would take with a fighter escort – a group of P38 Lightings from their base at Oran. I remember it very clearly as the excitement for the fighter boys of escorting one of the most important men in the western world meant they came a little too close for comfort. The RAF Spitfires from Gibraltar always kept a discreet and useful distance and height from us, from where they could in fact defend us from enemy attack. Not so the Americans. They seemed more interested in getting close enough to see the great man himself, who didn't help matters by waving at them and giving his ubiquitous 'V' sign from his state room window!

It was understood that our VVIP aircraft was to be run as a luxury yacht, albeit an airborne one. As we had taken off after lunch, we did little more than provide a running, or rather flying, tea buffet for the passengers. Besides the PM, our passengers included General Marshall (USA), Anthony Eden, the chief of the imperial general staff (CIGS), Air Marshal Arthur Tedder, General Ismay, Commander 'Tommy' Thompson (the PM's aide de camp) and Inspector Thompson from Scotland Yard. The PM was also travelling with his loyal valet, Sawyers. Whilst the ADC, Thompson, was our principal go-between, Sawyers was an invaluable interpreter and temperature gauge as to Churchill's mood. We found later that he was a bit of an old fuss-pot, and that his reading of a situation could occasionally be confused – especially if he had been serving drinks and helping himself as he returned to the galley!

We landed in the late afternoon and, having offloaded our passengers, headed into the centre of Algiers. Jimmy Jeffs had the good sense to use the PM's metaphorical 'weight' to secure us rooms at the Aletti hotel – rooms more usually reserved for officers of brigadier rank or above – and we spent three delightful days and nights in luxury.

We returned to the airfield early on the morning of June 1, to prepare the aircraft for a short hop to a United States Air Force (USAF) base at Châteaudun du Rhumel, near Bône. The journey was uneventful and the prime minister and his party disembarked to attend a briefing of B17 crews for an attack on Pantelleria. They were escorted by some very high-ranking US airmen, including Generals Cannon, Eaker and Spaatz, who stood by in the heat of the North African sun as the aircraft took off. Corporal Shepherd, who had been brought along with us as a steward, rustled up a cold lunch; we were yet to discover the secret of victualling the aircraft from local resources, so on this occasion had to ensure that at least the beverages were adequate!

The following day and we were ordered to position the aircraft at an airstrip at Grombalia, south east of Tunis, which was more convenient for our passengers, who had by now been joined by General Sir Harold Alexander. We had expected to fly as far south as Enfidaville and onwards to inspect the Mareth Line, perhaps proceeding on to Tripoli. But we had yet to learn the vagaries of The Owner's travel requirements, and how quickly he could change his mind. No sooner had we circled the Kasserine Pass, where the Americans had been bloodied in spectacular style against a German Panzer division, than he decided he wanted to return directly to Algiers. The whole flight took less than two-and-half hours.

We knew that Churchill had, at an earlier time, flown with 24 Squadron as a pilot under training at the same time as Lord Londonderry. His lordship had passed; the prime minister had not. That did not, however, put him off from the joys of wanting to fly, and on our return leg we were joined in the cockpit by the PM, who took the co-pilot's seat. He asked Collins whether he could try out the controls and our captain, with a barely perceptible hesitation, agreed. Collins, of course, was no risk taker, and attempted to smooth out some of the resulting attitudes of the aircraft with discreet use of the tail trimmer, at which point The Owner admonished him. He soon conceded that perhaps they would share the controls: Collins to work the rudder and he would try climbing and diving. He was clearly enjoying himself, much to the consternation of his passengers who were being thrown about in the back, and to the astonishment of the USAF fighter escort who were trying to keep station, and decided to back off. On landing at Maison Blanche, Collins was quick to explain to our escort commander who was doing the driving.

We spent two more comfortable nights in Algiers before starting out for our return flight to the UK. We left our US fighter escort behind over Oran where we picked up a Spitfire wing, much to the PM's pleasure. Again The Owner wanted to come to the flight deck, and as the flight engineer was able to take the necessary landing actions from his position between the two pilots' seats, the captain was comfortable with the PM occupying the co-pilot's seat.

All went well until the captain was holding off for a three point landing and realised that he couldn't pull the control column back sufficiently to get the tail down. Gibraltar did not have the longest runway and I remember thinking that the aircraft was taking quite a distance to settle. We did, however, make it down safely, and it was only afterwards, when the PM was safely out of earshot, that Collins explained that he couldn't get the control column back far enough because the PM's belly was getting in the way! The captain resolved that if the PM wanted to stay up front in future for the landing, then he had better sit at the navigator's table where he was more comfortable and we were at less risk.

At Gibraltar we saw that the flying boat Bristol was on stand-by to take the PM home; we guessed it was there in case he had not taken to the York. As it was, the PM was more than happy with 'his' new aircraft and was ready on board in good time for our departure to Northolt. I plotted a route out into the Atlantic (to the longitude of 12W). Such a route would keep us well clear of the Spanish coast and beyond the range of night fighter patrols from the Brest Peninsula.

The danger of an interception could not be understated. While we had been in North Africa, an unarmed DC3 of KLM had been shot down over the Bay of Biscay on its regular daylight shuttle flight to and from Bristol. It had hitherto served German interests to allow the aircraft to operate unmolested. Among the passengers was the actor Leslie Howard, and there was a rumour at the time that another of the passengers had resembled Churchill. Presumably the Luftwaffe had instructions to shoot down anything and everything if spotted over the Bay, on the off chance that somebody important could be onboard; Coastal Command aircraft on anti-submarine patrols, for example, had had a particularly difficult time in the area.

Fortunately there was little to trouble us. The engines were singing beautifully, and all was right with the world. Our steward, Shepherd, was dozing on his stool in the galley amidships when he was awoken by a growling voice. Starting out of his coma, the steward could see the PM's face, without his dentures, peering through the curtain and demanding soup! More than this, he wanted clear soup, and he wanted it immediately. Corporal Shepherd was no chef but did remarkably well in the circumstances. He only had an electric urn, rather like a samovar, to heat water but remembered that we had a primus stove for ground use and fired it up. He had no clear soup in stock, but had some thick pea soup and mulligatawny from the NAAFI. The PM seemed satisfied. When the captain later learned that Shepherd had lit a stove just under the main fuel tank, he was suitably horrified.

We approached the UK from the south west, still looking out for intruders. An expected escort of Spitfires failed to materialise until we were almost over Northolt, by which time it was almost too late, and we landed in beautiful sunshine at 06.00hrs.

Many lessons had been learned, and many more would have to be absorbed about the needs and habits of The Owner. Clearly some domestic modifications to the aircraft's interior were needed, but these would have to wait our return from the next trip. As it was, the PM hinted to Collins that we would shortly be needed for what was described as 'a very high level job'.

Speculation as to what this job could be led us nowhere however.

CHAPTER FIVE

BY ROYAL APPOINTMENT

Two days after our return to Northolt on June 7, the Liberator Commando (AL 504) was flown in from Dorval by Wing Commander Willie Biddell and parked alongside our York. This was the same aircraft that the prime minister had first used on his visit to Moscow in August 1942 and later to the Casablanca conference in January 1943. Then who should turn up but Group Captain Edward 'Mouse' Fielden, presumably to vet both aircraft.

Mouse Fielden was a station commander in Bomber Command. He was also an air equerry to His Majesty King George VI. With Fielden was the familiar figure of Group Captain Jeffs, the senior air traffic control officer at Transport Command. We drew our own conclusions. Commando left a day or so ahead of us with the secretary of state for air and his party.

Fielden had been for some time in charge of the King's Flight and was the Prince of Wales' personal pilot. The flight had been disbanded, however, in 1941 and so when the king expressed a wish to visit his victorious forces in North Africa in June 1943, there was theoretically no suitable aircraft at his disposal. At the highest level it was decided to use the York, at which the prime minister was overheard to say: "I have lent His Majesty my aircraft." He perhaps forgot that all RAF aircraft were nominally His Majesty's.

With our royal passenger confirmed, we were later briefed personally by the AOC-in-C Transport Command, Sir Frederick 'Ginger' Bowhill, who made us very aware of the great honour that was being bestowed upon us, and the very great responsibility that rested on our shoulders. This would be the first time, we were informed, that a reigning British monarch had left the United Kingdom by air, either in peace or war. Hitherto the honour of carrying His Majesty overseas had been given to the Royal Navy. It was up to us, he pressed, to show the navy that we could take on the task with equal efficiency.

Early in the evening of June 11, a number of vans arrived from the palace with mountains of luggage labelled 'General Lion' accompanied by two guardsmen batmen, Sergeants Jerram and Evitts, respectively His Majesty's chief valet and deputy sergeant footman. We were given what was to become a routine briefing on the weather conditions expected, as well as our signals instructions, and sat down to plan our route in more detail. The idea was to again head well out into the Atlantic before landing and refuelling in Gibraltar sometime in the early morning. We would breakfast on the ground before proceeding to Algiers where His Majesty would meet with the supreme allied commander, General Eisenhower.

Our passenger list was most impressive. As well as the king we had with us General Alexander, Lieutenant Colonel the Hon Piers Legh and Sir Alexander Hardinge, private secretary. Mouse Fielden was onboard, as was a Mr Cameron from Scotland Yard. Wing Commander Slee also joined the crew.

As forecasted, the weather was fine and smooth. His Majesty came forward to the flight deck once we had settled at our cruising height and took great interest in my astro-navigation methods. Clearly he remembered his star identification from his days in the Royal Navy. HM ships had been positioned in the vicinity of our two main turning points en route to act as rescue vessels should we be obliged to force land at sea. From 10,000ft, we had no chance of seeing either of the vessels, but were assured that they were there. For security reasons our communications plan was similar to all other RAF aircraft in transit from the UK to Gibraltar that night; only our route was different, to minimise the risk of hostile interception. In dire emergency we were told to head for neutral Portugal.

About twenty minutes flying time from Gibraltar, Jock Gallagher, our wireless op, received a general diversion message, sent to all RAF aircraft in transit, that because of fog at Gibraltar we were to land at the USAF base at Port Lyautey near Casablanca. Moments later, Jock received yet another message countermanding the previous instruction. Foggy conditions evidently existed there too, and the new diversion was to a place called Ras el Ma (near Fez) some way inland and therefore free of coastal fog. Jock queried these instructions using our allocated call-sign for the night, for we were only permitted to use the royal flight call-sign in an emergency. Since landing in fog at Gibraltar would be impossible, we had no option but to obey the instructions, along with all of the other aircraft flying that night between the UK and 'the Rock'.

Ras el Ma was a small RAF staging post, only recently taken over from the Americans, with none of the accommodation and handling facilities at a base such as North Front. Neither did it have the communications capacity in the local control to handle the sheer number of aircraft in the landing circuit at the same time. We had strict instructions not to disclose by R/T the identity of our VVIP. Evidently the secure radio link between Gibraltar and Ras el Ma was so overloaded with cipher traffic that no warning of His Majesty's imminent arrival had reached the CO. Furthermore, the Commando that should have reached Gibraltar or Port Lyautey ahead of us, with Group Captain Jeffs as ATC, was not on hand to alert the local RAF.

After circling several times with many other smaller aircraft, and notwithstanding our ample fuel reserve, we were obliged to request priority landing, for royalty could not be kept waiting while the RAF sorted itself out. The air traffic control officer had never seen a York before – but then neither had many others – and as we landed and parked on the temporary hard-standing he drove over to us obviously with the intention of giving us a piece of his mind. Seeing our passenger, he was somewhat stopped dead in his tracks, and scuttled off to alert his commanding officer.

With that touch of comedy farce that the RAF seems to specialise in and make a bad situation considerably worse, the staging post commander had enjoyed a particularly heavy party in the mess the night before. He failed to react especially quickly either to his batman's cup of tea or the urgent message that a royal aircraft had landed, and the king was on the hard-standing! He told the batman to go away. Indeed it was said that he thought that the whole thing was a wind up.

There is a variety of versions of just what level of panic ensued, but the officer eventually appeared, having obviously cut himself shaving, to find that his unexpected guest had decided to take breakfast on board the aircraft, rather than stand around waiting any longer. We stayed only forty-five minutes – sufficient time to refuel – and headed off for Algiers. We were intercepted over Oran and escorted by a flight of six USAF Bell P39 Airacobras and landed at Maison Blanche. This time His Majesty was properly received by the supreme allied commander as well as Admiral Sir Andrew Cunningham and Air Marshal Sir Arthur Tedder.

After two days in Algiers visiting allied headquarters (this was the time of Operation Husky – the invasion of Sicily), His Majesty was flown to Oran where he was met by General Mark Clark. The royal party had now been joined by Colonel Dermot Kavanagh, the crown equerry, and Sir James Grigg, the secretary of state for war. Clark had paraded part of the American Fifth Army for His Majesty's inspection, as we stood in the shade underneath the wing of our aircraft. As we stood, minding our own business, we were approached by a smartly dressed US colonel draped in cameras. Of course he demanded to know the identity of 'the big shot' we were flying. After being told that this was His Majesty King George VI of England there was a long pause, after which he solemnly said: "Gees, I guess that makes all you folks Dooks and Oils." It seemed a shame to have to inform him that we were merely the crew of his aeroplane.

On our return to Maison Blanche, the king spent June 15 and 16 visiting units of the allied forces and those ships of the fleet which were in harbour. We were invited to the royal reception at the Villa Germaine where His Majesty was staying, and enjoyed a most pleasant cocktail party amongst 170 other guests in quite splendid surroundings.

We were back in the air again on June 17, having exchanged one secretary of state for another, Sir James Grigg making way for Sir Archibald Sinclair, the secretary of state for air. This time we were visiting units of the Mediterranean Allied Coastal Air Forces under the command of the

famous Air Vice-Marshal Hugh Pughe Lloyd, the man who was widely credited with having saved Malta in its darkest days and who led the
fight back against the Italian and German air forces in the area. Indeed
a couple of days later we found ourselves at Castel Benito, the former
showpiece of the Italian Duce, where the plan was for the king to take
passage in HMS *Aurora*, to Malta to present the island with the richly-
deserved George Cross. We settled in for a comparatively long stay
while His Majesty departed to fulfil his official duties.

Our captain and Group Captain Jeffs, being of senior rank, went off
to stay in the senior officers' quarters. (Jimmy Jeffs had arrived ahead
of us to oversee air traffic control arrangements and prevent a repeat
of the previous shambles at Ras el Ma.) Bill, Jock, Jack and I were left
standing by our aircraft, waiting for transport to take us to our billets
and sceptical of what we might find when we got there. Then we
came in for a bit of luck. One of Montgomery's ADCs took mercy
on us and invited us there and then to stay at Eighth Army headquarters' mess at Zuara, some ten miles west of Tripoli, a tented camp right
on the shores of the Med.

The mess was basic but more than adequate, and the hospitality
extremely welcome. Well rested, we had the pleasure of being invited to tea at Monty's own mess one afternoon. The opportunity of
meeting in the flesh the man who was chasing Rommel and his
vaunted Afrika Korps out of North Africa was too good an opportunity to miss, and he described to us first hand his tactics for beat-
ing the Desert Fox. He also asked if we would like to witness the victory parade which was to take place as soon as His Majesty returned
in the cruiser from Malta. Obviously the answer was yes, so without
further ado an extra car was written into the operation order for the
day and we rode round the whole of the royal route in the 13th
vehicle of the cavalcade.

It was on June 24 that we finally left Algiers in the late afternoon
for Ras el Ma and home. It had been decided not to use Gibraltar for
security reasons, His Majesty's flight having received wide publicity in
the press. We made a smooth teatime flight and this time His Majesty
was expected and met with the pomp and ceremony that befitted his
status. The RAF had replaced the unfortunate staging post command-

er who had received us on our previous visit. We were on the ground for less than three hours for refuelling, weather briefing and flight planning while His Majesty was taken by the new CO for dinner at the Palais Jamai Hotel in Fez.

None of us wanted to hang around this rather desolate airstrip any longer than needed and we were away by 19.30hrs (GMT) with an expected arrival time at Northolt at 06.00hrs local time. Our planned route would again take us far out into the Atlantic, for all of the reasons previously stated. All went well, almost too well in fact. The weather was more benign than anticipated and the winds more favourable. It meant that by the time we turned from our northerly track towards southern Ireland on to a north easterly heading up the Bristol Channel to Lundy Island, it was clear that we were going to be early.

A few days previously, on the way from Tripoli to Algiers, we had arrived early for a meeting with General Eisenhower to everyone's embarrassment. Anxious to avoid another such incident, I suggested to our captain that we reduce speed, and perhaps dog-leg to lose time. The effect of reducing speed was to lower the engine revs and reduce the amount of noise in the cabin. Unfortunately, the change in engine note prompted Mouse Fielden to hurry forward and demand to know what was happening. He was not having any of it, and told us forcibly that HM did not wish to be in the aircraft any longer than he had to, and especially not for the convenience of a few waiting dignitaries. (We learned later that the king was not especially fond of flying and found the constant noise of the engines particularly trying.)

We were obliged therefore to resume our former course and speed and landed at Northolt well in advance of schedule – so in advance in fact that although the chief of the air staff (Portal), the AOC-in-C Transport Command ('Ginger' Bowhill) and the AOC-in-C Fighter Command (Sir Trafford Leigh Mallory) were ready for us, the prime minister was nowhere to be seen. Eventually he did turn up with signature black hat on his head and cigar in mouth, by which time the royal party was taking coffee in the officers' mess. He was somewhat irate to say the least. The Spitfire escort that should have intercepted us in the Bristol Channel eventually arrived just at the point HM was being driven across the airfield, dipping their wings as they swept over the runway.

We were all very tired, not just as a result of the long hours of flying (we had journeyed more than 5,000 miles in two weeks), but also because of the nervous exhaustion we felt from the sheer excitement of the past few days. Transport was arranged to take us back to Hendon, where I took the time to have a long soak in a hot bath.

I was barely out of the bath, however, when I was informed that all of the crew were expected at the palace by noon! Now I was anxious, because I did not have my 'best blue' to hand, and had to be smartened up by my batman as best he could. I had been to the palace before, of course, to receive my DFC but this was a considerably more intimate affair and we were led into a small drawing room to find His Majesty, Her Majesty Queen Elizabeth, and the air equerry waiting for us.

There were eight of us presented in turn: as well as the captain, Bill, Jock, Jack and myself, we were joined by Group Captain Jeffs and Wing Commander Slee, and our steward Corporal Shepherd. I noticed a small pile of boxes on a side table and immediately recalled that one of the 24 Squadron pilots who had flown the Princess Royal had been given a pair of cufflinks engraved with her crest, as a souvenir. My hopes rose at the thought of such a practical gift, although there was no way of communicating my excitement to my colleagues.

The king said a few words about the flight and the tour in general, and Her Majesty was similarly gracious and charming. Then His Majesty told us that he wanted to give us all a souvenir of what he called "a memorable flight". The 'souvenir' in question was to make us all members of the Victorian Order, with the seniority dependent on rank. In my case I was given the insignia of the MVO 4th Class (since re-titled Lieutenant of the Victorian Order). The Victorian Order is not a decoration or an award in the normal sense, but rather a personal gift from the sovereign for a personal service. Corporal Shepherd was presented with the Royal Victorian Medal in silver.

Then we were trooped outside for the inevitable press photo call before finally heading off to the Royal Aero Club in Piccadilly for a drink, a splendid way to celebrate the end of a most successful tour.

It quickly became clear to us that apart from the obvious task of getting our VVIPs from A to B on time and in comfort, the prime minister in particular expected a much higher standard of comfort – and particularly catering – than we had so far delivered. Once out of the UK we should have to rely on an embassy or local commander-in-chief's residence for top-class revictualling. Fresh, clean water was of course a must; we could carry only a limited quantity. The emptying and cleaning of three lavatory cans was also an issue, easy enough on an RAF staging post, but elsewhere, not so easy at all.

The RAF, even at home base, was ill-equipped to store the cutlery and china, the linen and blankets – and keep them clean and dry – in a Spitfire hangar. We had to resort to using the airing cupboards of the Northolt's officers' mess. In these early days too, a 2,000-gallon petrol bowser had to be specially despatched from Hendon for our use, for the Spitfires never needed fuel in such quantity. Gradually these problems were overcome and their solution became routine. But the provision of food – remembering that this was wartime Britain – was much more of a challenge, and its solution overseas was often unorthodox. Drink, on the other hand, was not such an issue as whisky and gin were in comparatively plentiful supply; as for wines, they had to be found from Number 10's own private cellar.

The galley of the York when she was first delivered had what we called a 'hay box' – ostensibly an apparatus that would keep pre-cooked meals warm. Whilst the design genius who had come up with the idea might have foreseen the needs of passengers in future generations, there was no way that The Owner was going to accept such sub-standard (in his opinion) catering. Thus as soon as the aircraft returned to base after the royal tour, urgent modifications were made to the galley. It was clear that a grill of some sort was essential; fast heaters were needed for hot drinks; a toaster was a 'must' – all within the capacity of the engine generators.

Alterations were also needed to improve the crew accommodation in the forward cabin, and more stowage was needed for my navigation gear, for Jock Gallagher's wireless gear, and Jack Payne's tools and spares. Another major modification required was the removal of the heavy wooden conference table from the main saloon to replace it with a much lighter, tubular aluminium folding-table and matching chairs. Our aircraft was thus returned to A.V. Roe at Woodford for the modifications to be made.

In technical aspects we were fortunate to find two friends, both experts in their particular field of civil aviation and of whom the Ministry of Aircraft Production and the bomber design teams in Manchester had hitherto ignored. They were GEC Aviation's division manager Frank Buckle, who had come up trumps with galley equipment made from sheet aluminium (provided by the RAF) and Lew Rumbold of Cricklewood who seemed to be the only manufacturer capable of making lightweight aircraft furnishings. Both were to play a big part in furnishing the interior of our later aircraft, the Skymaster.

Another good friend was the senior Rolls-Royce liaison officer to the RAF, Bill Lappin, who was on hand to learn of the behaviour of the Merlin engines in their transport role for the first time, with some of the York production earmarked for BOAC. Even then they had their eye on the lucrative post-war sales opportunities for their engines and were keen to keep the support of the prime minister. From then on we had a permanent Rolls-Royce representative available at Northolt, since they could ill-afford to have an engine failure.

At the front end of the aircraft it was soon obvious that the two bunks on the starboard side in the forward cabin would have to be sacrificed to provide accommodation for our flight engineer. Further space was also needed for the crew's accoutrements, for we were likely to be 'en route' for several days at a time between major bases. For navigation alone I needed to carry a quantity of maps and charts as well as ephemeral data in various navigation tables etc. Thus the forward cabin was to be used for the crew, except when we were obliged to provide a seat for the detective.

The aircraft was flown back to us at Northolt in the first week of August, with its galley redesigned and other modifications incorporated. We now also included a sergeant chef in the crew as well as a steward, both taken from the RAF officers' mess at Hendon. Corporal Shepherd, who was really our CO's batman, was returned to his normal duties. With the assistance of the PM's own valet, Sawyers, we now had a formidable 'cabin crew'.

CHAPTER SIX

VERY IMPORTANT PERSONS

The beginning of October found us serving several new masters, or at least borrowing The Owner's aircraft.

While our York was being refitted, the prime minister had sailed for Quebec to attend the Quadrant conference in Washington. One of the results of this conference was the appointment of Lord Louis Mountbatten as supreme allied commander-in-chief in South East Asia (SEAC). The PM's aircraft was to take him to Delhi to set up his new headquarters, and we looked forward to the flight with considerable interest. At the last moment, however, we received instructions that we were to proceed no further east than Tunis, and then return to Algiers at once in order to pick up another VIP for a conference in London, a friend of the PM.

I decided upon my usual precautionary route to Gibraltar, although not quite as far west as before. I had no wish to come face to face with a marauding Junkers 88 out in the bay, or indeed one of the longer-range Focke Wulf 200 Condors that had been known to attack lone aircraft straying across their path. The flight was rather bumpy, and two WRNS on Mountbatten's staff were ill, but conditions improved after we got to our cruising altitude of 10,000ft. We spent just a couple of hours at Gibraltar before heading for Tunis – a much clearer run in bright sunshine. At La Saballa we had a fast turn-around indeed. No further fuel was required and within twenty minutes we were off and back at Maison Blanche at 18.00 local time.

It had been a long night and day, and we would have liked to have been able to use the PM's weight once again to secure accommodation at the Hotel Aletti, but instead had to accept slightly less comfortable quarters at the RAF transit base on the east shore of the Bay of Algiers. These were more comfortable, however, than the accommodation found for Jack and the cabin staff, who were obliged to sleep on the aircraft.

The next morning we were ordered to return to the UK at once, having picked up our VIP who turned out to be the seventy-three-year-old South African leader Field Marshal Jan Smuts, en route to London for a meeting of commonwealth ministers. Smuts, whose sprightliness belied his years, had been flown as far as Algiers in a Lockheed Lodestar of the South African Air Force (SAAF) via Cairo. He was accompanied by Lieutenant General Van Ryneveld, his chief of staff, Captain Smuts Jr, the ADC, and the Rt Hon Harold Macmillan, then minister to the allied forces in North Africa, and John Wyndham, his number two. Sir Godfrey Huggins, prime minister of Southern Rhodesia was the final member of the party.

Although we had staged through Gibraltar with Lord Louis, our latest instructions ordered us to use Rabat on the Atlantic coast of Morocco, a former French airfield at Sale, just outside the town and now in RAF hands. It was excellently suited for VIP duties, being well away from habitation and secure in its isolation. It also had good wireless communications with the UK and other transport bases in North Africa. At a more personal level, I was delighted to find that the RAF station commander was none other than Group Captain John Sutton, 'The Maestro' himself.

The airfield was relatively empty when we arrived, and the weather briefing was good. Rabat was a considerable improvement on some of the airfields we had visited previously, especially Ras el Ma!

The field marshal was a charming passenger, appreciative of everything done for him and interested in anything we were doing. We left Algiers after lunch and made Rabat in three-and-a-half hours, via the Straits of Gibraltar instead of over the Atlas, flying westward with the sun sinking fast. We then followed down the coast of Morocco to land at dusk.

We had a relatively relaxed stop over; time for briefing and supper in the mess. Take-off was set for midnight UK time, with a flight plan of eight hours. It was a fine warm evening and we were undertaking our pre-flight chores before the passengers arrived. I opted to take a little stroll and make myself comfortable in the open air. As I did, a figure came and stood abeam of me; I assumed it was Jack with the same intention. I made some joke as one often does in such situations but instead of Jack it was a South African voice that responded "yes my boy, and a very good idea too!" The field marshal then went on to ask: "Do you know what the Duke of Wellington said to his officers before the Battle of Waterloo?" "No sir" I replied, guessing from the accent that he was our VIP. "To take all precautions before battle lest there is not another opportunity to do so!"

We left as planned and had a smooth run home. As soon as we landed, Smuts made a point of thanking the crew before being driven off to meet with his Dominion peers, the prime minister of Canada, Mackenzie King, and the prime minister of New Zealand, Peter Fraser. Not all of our VIPs would be so polite, or grateful, as we would later learn.

The newspapers were full of coverage the next day, although I was credited with being the pilot of the aircraft, which of course I wasn't. It was nevertheless pleasing to be described by one journalist as "one of the finest navigators in the RAF".

October was proving to be a busy month. We were given the task on October 9 of taking Anthony Eden to Moscow, or at least part of the way, for a foreign ministers' conference. He was accompanied by General Ismay from the Cabinet Office, William (later Sir William) Strang, Messrs Harvey and Pierson Dixon, Colonels Price and Dunn, and two others. The captain opted to fly direct to Algiers (we were confident by now of our aircraft's fuel consumption and endurance) and I planned the route accordingly. I estimated a flight of around ten hours, or perhaps a little less if the Atlantic sector winds were in our favour. They were. We arrived ahead of schedule with ample fuel reserves.

The trip, however, was not without incident. For the first time ever, the RAF police seemed to be interested in our aircraft before leaving

Northolt, and had been ordered to provide a security guard prior to our departure. The guard arrived mid-afternoon (we were intending to take off at 21.30) in their heavy boots, just as Jack and the cabin staff were at their busiest, loading stores and domestic items. Jack, never short of a sharp tongue when under pressure, was told he would have to open every container and have them examined for explosives. The request was ridiculous in the extreme, beneath the floor of the York we carried not only specialist items of spares, certain oils and greases in tins not obtainable overseas, but also emergency rations such as tins of bully beef, peas and even water. We were not about to open them all up!

Jack managed to fob them off while the police were taking tea. They had their revenge, however. The battery cart for the starter motors needed an airman on duty who also primes the Merlin engines from the undercarriage bays. In the interest of security, the police had forbidden anyone near the aircraft once the doors were closed. We therefore had no battery power to turn the starters, no priming, and no-one to pull the chocks away. Jack was obliged to get out of the aircraft and find the ground crew who were being kept back from the York by the police. A few choice words were exchanged, and we were at last underway, albeit somewhat later than planned.

It was a lovely flight, and from a navigational perspective there were all of the stars I could wish for. Even in 1943, when some of the more sophisticated electronic devices were coming into service to assist with navigation, I still had to rely on the stars and the occasional radio fix from Jock, assuming his W/T security procedures allowed for it. When Jock was able to extract a radio bearing from a neutral, or sometimes even an enemy radio beacon, these were of great assistance.

'Gee' and 'Loran' – hyperbolic navigation systems displayed on a cathode ray tube – were later installed and were of enormous help. The former was especially accurate over shorter ranges; the latter was useful over trans-oceanic distances. Both, however, could only assist in the areas they covered, and were of no help whatsoever over the Middle East or Russia. It was always preferred, therefore, to fly at night whenever we could, and obviously above cloud to use the stars. That meant flying with my oxygen masks glued permanently to my face.

As it was, we entered the Straits just as dawn was breaking and made a comfortable run to Algiers, landing half an hour after sunrise. We slept on the aircraft, and were ready for an early start the next day for a non-stop leg to Cairo. Again the flight was a pleasant one, and we were untroubled by any fighter escort or inclement weather. I set course inland to the south of the Algerian coastal range of mountains to Biskra, cruising at a comfortable 9,500ft. We then skirted the Mediterranean and flew south to Tripoli, where we headed for El Agheila – more famously known as 'Marble Arch' in Eighth Army parlance – and along the parallel of 30° N to Landing Ground (LG) 224. Referred to as 'Cairo West', this was the main RAF transport base for the Cairo area with large-scale maintenance facilities. We landed in the gloaming – late dusk, warm and smelling of Cairo.

At the time of leaving the UK we had high hopes of going all the way to Moscow, but we heard that the Air Ministry did not yet wish our York to be seen by the Russians. We were disappointed, then, to be told that the foreign secretary would fly on to Russia via Teheran in the RAF Liberator Commando, and we were obliged to return to Algiers to pick up a friend of The Owner, Sir Henry Craik, who was rather ill.

Happily we had our own friend in Cairo, one Wing Commander Teddy Smouha, who was head of the RAF air movements organisation in the Middle East. Teddy was quite a character, from a wealthy Anglo/Egyptian background, and although it was difficult to believe it by looking at him, he had once been a fine athlete, even winning a bronze medal in the 1928 Olympics in the 4 X 100m relay.

Teddy arranged it so that we were lodged in the Swiss-owned Hotel Metropole in the centre of Cairo, complete with its own skittle alley. We then spent an hilarious three days in the city, visiting all of the usual spots – Shepherds, the Turf Club and Groppi's – not to mention shopping in the souk. It meant that by the time we left Cairo, we were fully relaxed, so much so that after we took off on the morning of October 14, our captain retired to The Owner's cabin and slept soundly for three hours!

We were soon woken from our literal and metaphorical reverie, however, when the starboard engine began playing up. Until that point, we had suffered no mechanical mishaps of any kind, but a valve failure contributed to a minor engine fire of burning glycol. The pilot went through the usual safety procedures: the propeller was feathered and in fairly short order the fire blew itself out. We had little option but to return to Cairo and hope that the remaining three engines gave us no further trouble. We also hoped that a spare Merlin would be available for us when we landed. Just in case, I routed us north east towards the coast, instead of flying straight across the desert, so that the landing strips of El Adem and Mersa Matruh would be on hand if needed. Collins reduced speed and we landed back at Cairo West an hour after sunrise. Jack immediately set about trying to find us a new engine, working with the local RAF engineering team. A like-for-like replacement wasn't possible, so we had to make do with a different mark of Merlin from the RAF maintenance unit with all of the extra work that that entailed.

It took several days for the changeover to be completed, and the aircraft was ready for an air test on October 19. All went well, and we prepared for departure with a new set of local VIPs on board including the Rt. Hon Oliver Stanley, secretary of state for the colonies, and Rear Admiral Bromley, both of whom were awaiting passage to England. They would come with us as far as Algiers where they would have to make room for Sir Henry.

There were practical issues flying an aircraft with a different power plant. It needed different power settings in order to keep it synchronized with the other three engines. Jack and the captain worked together to ensure optimum performance and the York flew as well as ever, completing the trip to Algiers in nine hours.

An amusing incident occurred en route. During the night, when all was relatively still if not exactly quiet, Jack would take to walking aft just to check for any smouldering cigarette ends or other oddities, and have a chat with the steward. Whilst undertaking his nocturnal inspection on this particular journey, he heard a rattling sound that concerned him. He traced the source of the noise to a tooth mug in one of the forward toilets, and found that it had not been stowed properly in its holder. Picking up the mug, he threw its contents into the Elsan toilet, rinsed it out and returned it to its holder.

About two hours out from Maison Blanche, the passengers were roused, given tea and invited to dress for breakfast – always bacon and eggs. These would be served and cleared away before landing. While our new chef was cooking the food, the steward was accosted by a somewhat agitated admiral whose difficulty was immediately obvious – he had lost his false teeth.

Anything and everything that happened on our aircraft, with the exception of navigation, was reported to Jack. Even when The Owner's toilet became blocked with too much paper, it was Jack who was called upon to fix it, muttering as he did so that he was not so much flight engineer, more sanitary engineer! When Jock Duncan (our chef) explained the admiral's predicament, Jack immediately realised what had happened, the contents of the mug that he had thrown down the toilet must have contained the officer's teeth! There was nothing for it but to search in the can of Elsanol, and other fluids, with his sleeves rolled up. Jock Duncan kept the admiral distracted with more tea, while Jack managed to fish the offending item out of the mess. He then hustled to the galley to rinse them under the tap and dry them as best he could in a towel.

Rushing back to the admiral, Jack presented the teeth back to their owner, suggesting that he had found them on the floor behind the washbasin. A rather irate admiral promptly snapped them back into place. Jack was hardly able to keep a straight face, at which point it must have been obvious to our passenger just where they had been. Nothing more was said on the matter, but the story did eventually reach the ears of Number 10. We knew, however, that we weren't popular with the admiral, and I think all of us were pleased enough to part company in Algiers.

We eventually arrived home at Northolt with our invalid on board on the morning of October 21. Unusually we had climbed to more than 16,000ft at one point to get above the clouds, and ensure a less bumpy ride for our patient. He had been attended all the time by Colonel Richardson of the Royal Army Medical Corps (RAMC) – a gentleman who was familiar to us having also accompanied the royal tour of North Africa.

We were all very tired, but there was work to be done. The aircraft needed a new engine to replace our temporary 'spare'. We were offered one from a maintenance unit, a second-hand ex-Bomber Command engine that had been rebuilt by the Rover shadow factory. Jack refused to have anything but new, and so a factory-fresh Derby-built engine was soon delivered, fixed by a quick phone call to Bill Lappin in the London office of Rolls-Royce in Conduit Street. It caused quite a row with the Transport Command engineering team who were clearly miffed at us approaching the manufacturers direct and without their say-so. Jack Payne, as ever, referred his tormentors to 10 Downing Street, and within a handful of days we were fit and ready to fly again.

This time we would be flying into history for quite another reason.

In the first few days of November it became clear that a big VIP operation was in the offing. Our own Ascalon had been joined by two more York aircraft (MW100 and MW101) both built to VIP, if not exactly VVIP, standards. They were designed to carry eight passengers each in comfort relevant to their age and dignity. At first allocated to 511 Squadron at Lyneham, it was eventually decided to combine the three VIP aircraft in what then became known as the 'York Flight'.

The CO then ordered me to live in at Northolt and act as flight commander, though of course the actual duties of the aircraft and their respective crews were out of my hands. I became more of a domestic manager and focal point for any telephone enquiries. Later, when the last of the Polish Spitfires had departed for airfields closer to the south coast in preparation for the invasion, I had possession of all the hangar offices. This gave us much better storage, a briefing room and a passenger reception room. Hitherto there had been nowhere for the 'meeters and greeters' to assemble, nor a telephone for VIPs to use in any privacy.

On the world stage, events were moving rapidly. There was talk of a meeting of the 'Big Three' – Churchill, Roosevelt and Stalin – to settle the future of allied policy in conducting the war. Stalin let it be known that he would come no further than Teheran.

We were briefed to be at readiness and had been warned to expect a departure within the next ten days. The PM himself left the UK on November 12 by sea in HMS *Renown* for Malta. We assumed we would pick him up at Gibraltar.

The weather was appalling, and there was a series of delays over our own travel arrangements and cargo, but in the end we finally got under way just after midnight on November 16/17, with a very distinguished group on board: CAS Sir Charles Portal; the CIGS Sir Alan Brooke; General Bob Laycock who had replaced Mountbatten as chief of combined operations; and Colonel Boyle RAMC. The trip was bumpy and rather uncomfortable, not surprising given the conditions, but we made our landfall in good time, only to find that The Owner had left Gibraltar the day before we arrived. It was said that he had a heavy cold, and had decided to stay on board. His humour was not helped by news that Roosevelt had arranged for Chiang Kai Shek, the Chinese leader, to be part of the delegation so that the situation in the Far East could be discussed. Given that the conference was about the progress of war in Europe, it was an unnecessary and unwelcome distraction.

We remained on Gibraltar only long enough to take on more fuel, still fully expecting to rendezvous with the PM at some point, most likely at our next stop, Malta. This time nobody was late, and both our aircraft with our passengers and HMS *Renown* with its own VIPs arrived at the tiny island together. Again, however, there was a change of plan. Churchill had wanted to see Roosevelt in advance of the official conference, possibly so that they could discuss presenting a united front. The introduction of Chiang Kai Shek had put paid to that plan, and Churchill's continued ill-health and bad weather similarly spoiled his intention to fly to Naples and visit allied troops fighting on the Italian front. As it was, though we were on stand-by should he need us, in the event he decided to continue on to Alexandria on the *Renown*. In the meantime, one of the VIP Yorks (MW100) flown by Squadron Leader Tony Watson had arrived to take the CAS to Cairo via Tunis, and we were left for two days at Luqa before we continued our journey with the CIGS and Bob Laycock.

It was still cold and wet when we finally lifted off the runway at Luqa and settled down for the six-and-a-half-hour flight to Cairo.

Accommodation was difficult for visitors in transit through Luqa, regardless of rank, and we were obliged to sleep on the aircraft. We made our track direct to Marble Arch in the Gulf of Sirte, thence due east to Cairo, so keeping a long way south of Crete where the Luftwaffe fighter squadrons were still more than active. We skirted the edge of the great Qattara Depression before dusk and made a comfortable arrival in the dark.

If we thought Luqa was basic, the domestic arrangements this time at Cairo West were shocking. Because of the allied conference being held at the Mena House Hotel on the western edge of the green Nile valley (located between Cairo West and the city centre itself) all of the aircrew were to be restricted to the tented camp at the airfield. Conditions were very poor and even 'Dad' Collins, with his wing commander rank, was denied accommodation in the permanent mess. It meant an uncomfortable night beneath bug-ridden blankets.

We couldn't complain too strongly at the time. The resident squadron messes were simply 'out of bounds' to all transit aircrew, however senior. They were not built to accommodate a huge transient population requiring meals at all times of the day and night. Unfortunately, the problem was compounded because for once we could not sleep on our own aircraft on account of where it was positioned, on a hard standing, under floodlights and under guard. It was virtually inaccessible for any reason other than maintenance.

The next morning, after a disturbed night's sleep, our captain presented himself to the senior medical officer (SMO). He had been very badly bitten and asked the SMO to record that he had not slept properly owing to unacceptable local conditions. With signed medical certificate in hand, he then took the document to the station commander and requested that he convey to the ADC 'Tommy' Thompson that the crew was 'not fit to fly'. I doubt very much whether the station commander did in fact ever pass on the message, since it would in effect be saying that as a result of his orders, the PM's pilot was not available should The Owner wish to fly that day! The outcome of this demarche was fairly rapid: we were dispatched almost immediately to a decent hotel in the city without further ado. It was not the first, nor the last faux pas that this particular officer would make during our stay.

It was to be a further week before we were required for duty. In the meantime there had been much activity between Cairo and Teheran. The RAF was using Mehrabad on the south east outskirts of the city as a small staging post, whilst the Americans used the major base, with the Russians, on the west side of the city. An early start was ordained for all VIPs: Portal, Alan Brooke and Laycock joined Field Marshal Dill and Admiral Cunningham on the VIP York flown by Tony Watson; we took the PM, the two Thompsons, two secretaries, Moran, and Sawyers the valet. We also, for the very first time, had the PM's daughter, Sarah Oliver, on board, appropriately attired in her WAAF uniform as an additional ADC. Amongst the cargo we had a rather special gift from His Majesty that was to be presented to Marshal Stalin. It was 'the Stalingrad sword' – a magnificent blade designed and wrought by the Master Cutlers of Sheffield, and inscribed with the words: "to the steel-hearted people of Stalingrad, the gift of King George VI, in token of the homage of the British people."

Early morning fog delayed Tony Watson's take-off, much to the annoyance of the CAS who had been roused from his bed too early, given the conditions. It was obvious that no-one could take off in such weather, so why wasn't he left in peace for a little longer? The poor unfortunate station commander took the full brunt of Portal's displeasure; clearly the air chief marshal was a man who did not suffer fools gladly.

We got away ourselves at 05.30, the fog having lifted and given way to a beautiful Egyptian dawn, and soon after we had a clear view of the Nile Delta and the canal which we crossed at Ismailia. Our track lay towards Baghdad, cruising at a comfortable height of 8,000ft. As was now habit, the PM came forward not long after take-off to sit in the co-pilot's seat and enjoy the sights of El Arish and the Gaza Strip, the Dead Sea and the oil pipeline across the desert that linked Haifa to Kirkuk. He clearly had much on his mind for he stayed on the flight deck for much longer than usual, until lunch was served. Indeed lunch was a rather sumptuous affair: the PM started with turtle soup (quite an advance from the thick pea-soup Shepherd had managed on our maiden voyage), followed by hot roast chicken and/or cold ox-tongue and salad, accompanied by sauté potatoes and peas. Pears and jelly followed, with cheese and biscuits to round off the veritable feast. I recall the meal because Bill had taken the time to borrow my typewriter (I used it to type out the BBC overseas news headlines for the benefit of the passengers – a sort of in-flight Reuters!) and type it out on a blank menu card brought along especially for the purpose.

The flight was a memorable and a most enjoyable one. We crossed the three other great rivers of the Middle East – the Jordan, the Tigris and the Euphrates – their snake-like tracks providing clear signposts of our route and direction. After over-flying RAF Habbaniya we started to climb slowly from 8,000ft to 12,000ft to clear the Zagros Mountains, then past Kermanshah and Ramadan before steadily losing height and landing at Mehrabad in the mid-afternoon. The PM was met at the airport by Sir Reader Bullard, the British ambassador, and the commander of PAIFORCE (Persia and Iraq Force) with the usual pomp and ceremony, and was soon after driven away to the embassy.

For once everything was laid on and we were taken with the other RAF aircrew to the Darband Hotel situated on the northern outskirts of the city on high ground, in the cool. It was a former palace of the Shah and accommodation was luxurious. We stayed there for four nights, and for the last night we were quartered at the British military hospital, which was also the mess and headquarters of PAIFORCE. It was a most modern building, built pre-war, ironically, by a German contractor. The number of telephone lines installed in the various wards and rooms was said to be far in excess of what was needed for a hospital. Later we learned that this had been on the orders of the Führer himself. He had plans to turn the hospital into the military headquarters in Teheran, upon the juncture of Rommel's desert army and the hoped-for axis seizure of the Caucasus and Azerbaijan, prior to the invasion of India.

We were not privy, of course, to the detailed deliberations, agreements or arguments that stemmed from the Teheran conference, and had but a bit-part to play in its proceedings. (We only learned much later, for example, that the sword with which we had taken so much care in transporting thousands of miles was dropped during the presentation ceremony.) What we were very aware of, however, was the good humour with which the prime minister greeted us on his return. He was in fine form as we took off on the morning of December 2 to fly him away from the Iranian capital and back to Cairo. He was in even better form when served lunch, which this time comprised quail, courtesy of the local embassy, as were the fine wines which accompanied it. The route home was similar to the one taken out, and this time we had as a further guest the British ambassador to Moscow, Sir Archibald Clark Kerr.

The Owner took his usual seat in the cockpit, and for his pleasure we circled Baghdad so that he could enjoy the view. He was dressed, I remember, in his famous siren suit that had been bespoke tailored for him, and in which he was often photographed. Over his back was draped his RAF greatcoat, with the thick air commodore stripes clearly visible on each shoulder. His carpet slippers, comically embroidered with 'WC', completed his eclectic attire.

It was especially warm on the flight deck and as we were flying south west the sun was shining directly into our eyes. The Owner decided he needed both his hat and his sunglasses, and in stentorian terms, his trusty valet Sawyers was instructed to retrieve both, with his white panama being especially specified. Unfortunately, Sawyers' guess as to 'baggage wanted on the voyage' had gone badly awry, and the white panama was riding with the rest of the party's baggage in one of the supporting Dakotas. Poor Sawyers was called every name under the sun – quite literally as it happens! We felt enormously sorry for him. Trying to second-guess The Owner's needs for the many changes en route, especially when we had only limited baggage space on our own aircraft, was a thankless task. Mind you, had Sawyers had his own way then we should have had the whole aircraft full of luggage to satisfy the whim and fancy of his master. Stock regalia included the siren suit with a greatcoat of either a colonel in the 4th Hussars (his old regiment) or an air commodore (he was honorary air commodore of 615 Squadron). I don't remember him ever wearing it, but he also possessed a uniform as warden of the Cinque Ports that I think was reserved for naval occasions. It was not unusual for him to wear a combination of outfits as befitted his mood or comfort.

With Sawyers skulking at the rear, the flight continued serenely onwards, and by early afternoon, our landing ground at Cairo West was in sight, as was the end of this particular adventure. Another was soon to follow, the very next day.

Throughout the autumn of 1943, The Owner had been busy with a pet scheme of his to convert Turkey from mixed neutrality to join the war on the side of the Allies. The Turks had been prudently sitting on the fence, anxious not to be on the losing side and equally anxious about Soviet intentions in the longer term, at her back door.

Generally speaking, the Turkish army corps tended to be pro-German, having been largely trained and equipped by them, dreaming no doubt of past great ideas of a Kaiser and the Berlin/Baghdad axis. The officer corps within the small but efficient Turkish air force, however, was RAF-trained, and therefore decidedly pro-British. Indeed remnants of our training mission had lingered on after the outbreak of war in various ways, notably under the particularly energetic air attaché (and a small training mission) in Ankara, Bobby George (later the air attaché in Paris between 1945/46).

The US president and our own PM had evidently agreed to invite the Turkish premier, President Inonu, to Cairo for talks, at which the Russians would also be present. It was our mission to pick Inonu up from Turkey, and see him safely delivered to Egypt. We did not know at the time, however, that we would have competition for his affections.

Orders came through on the morning of December 3 that we were to fly to Adana which I had to look up on the map and found that it was in south east Turkey. It transpired it was a small civil airfield with no facilities whatsoever for large aircraft beyond a barely adequate tarmac strip. Our humour was slightly improved, however, when we were all issued rather ill-fitting sports jackets to wear with our RAF trousers by way of a 'disguise'. The clothes had been bought in the Cairo bazaar, and were unlikely to fool anyone, least of all an eagle-eyed German spy. Our arrival would surely be known in Berlin within hours of our landing; the aircraft, after all, had RAF roundels! We were also pleased to find that we would be taking a passenger, the PM's own son Randolph, as a sign of the high regard in which President Inonu was held.

I plotted a route through the Ismailia corridor of the canal air defences and around the coast of Palestine, over Gaza, Haifa, to Acre thence directly to Adana. It was only a short flight, around three hours, and when we landed we were warmly received by the few local Turkish air force officers present. Indeed a 'few' soon turned into quite a number as word got round that we had whisky on board and were liberally dispensing quantities of the stuff in Randolph's name. Being RAF-trained, as we suspected, they had an uncanny habit of homing in on the sound of a soda siphon.

It turned into quite a party, and our limited stocks were soon drained dry, at which point we had to move on to a local brew, raki, a Levantine version of ouzo but at aviation strength. We gathered it made a good disinfectant, and were careful not to spill any on our flashy new jackets.

We slept on board and woke early to find that we had had a visitor in the night. Parked alongside was Roosevelt's own personal aircraft, the Skymaster 'Sacred Cow'. We were curious, but not unduly concerned. We had no idea that the crew of the Sacred Cow was on a similar mission.

The benefit of the airfield was that it was positioned alongside the main railway line, and the remarkable sight of a VIP train with famous blue Wagons-Lit carriages against an otherwise barren landscape was one of incongruous splendour. What happened next, happened very quickly. The president, with his party, descended the steps of the carriages and was immediately surrounded by officials wearing all manner of uniforms. We were keen to get away and were not paying much attention. We didn't notice, therefore, that among those uniforms were a number of high-ranking Americans. We certainly didn't notice, either, that these high-ranking Americans were almost physically manhandling the president in the direction of the Sacred Cow.

As we continued our preparations for take-off, Randolph arrived in a panic, somewhat out of breath, to say that 'they' had nabbed 'our' VIP! It was a diplomatic farce of the highest order, and something had to be done. He decided that we needed to get a message to Cairo at once to alert the prime minister as to what was happening. Jock Gallagher, our Glaswegian wireless operator, poured cold water on the idea almost immediately. There was no way we could raise Cairo on W/T (we had no such thing as a long-range voice HF in those days) until we were airborne. The message would have to be in cipher in any case, and by the time that he had encoded it and Cairo had received it, decoded it and passed it to the prime minister (who might have already been en route to welcome President Inonu) we should ourselves have landed.

Somebody suggested a 'Plan B'. We were a slightly faster aircraft than the Skymaster and if we flew directly across the eastern Mediterranean and so cut the corner, we would beat the USAF aircraft into land and get to the prime minister to explain what had gone wrong. I worked out a route as quickly as I could and we bundled what few VIPs we had been left with on board. As well as Randolph, our consolation prize included the Turkish vice president, the British ambassador to Ankara, the Russian ambassador and our air attaché, Bobby George.

Despite all of our best efforts, we arrived in the circuit above Cairo West only marginally ahead of our foe, at which point the farce continued. The RAF air traffic control, assuming that we had the VVIP on board, gave us priority landing and marshalled us onto the place of honour where the PM et al were waiting. As we swung into position with the door facing the awaiting dignitaries, we showered the band with sand from our prop-wash. Then as the band struck up the national anthem, who should emerge from the doorway but Randolph, who was immediately asked by his father what he had done with the visiting Turkish president. As if this wasn't bad enough, the air traffic controller had marshalled the Skymaster onto a hard standing some way distant, and certainly some way from the admiring throng. And as there were no steps of Skymaster height available, the president was obliged to descend by ladder!

For once we thoroughly enjoyed the discomfort of officialdom from the level of the cockpit. We tidied ourselves away and took off for the hotel in downtown Cairo just as fast as we could.

This attempt to bring Turkey into the war failed; what part we had to play in that failure I dread to think. More likely, however, was our disastrous attempt to re-take Kos and Leros earlier in the autumn.

Whatever the outcome, the PM was determined that the president should return to Adana in a 'proper' aircraft, and the next time we met, The Owner had Inonu firmly by the arm as he steered him towards the door of our aircraft, with not a single American of any rank in sight.

We did our very best to ensure that our VIP enjoyed the finest hospitality the RAF had to offer. Somehow, no doubt through the good auspices of Teddy Smouha once again, we managed to serve some of the most delicate sandwiches I've ever seen, washed down with the finest champagne. This time there was no excitement, and the president, and the whole Turkish entourage, had a pleasant journey. He was obviously very happy, for after we landed he presented our captain with a gold wristwatch, and the rest of us received a box of 100 best Turkish cigarettes. Jock Duncan, our chef, seemed to come off best: he was given £20 in notes – a small fortune.

There were rumours that the PM wanted to visit the troops in Italy, having been thwarted in his previous attempt. We left Cairo on December 10 with, among others, the CIGS, who was planning his own tour of Italy before returning to the UK via Tunis. We were also carrying a rather splendid cake, a present from the RAF Movements staff in Cairo for the PM's birthday a week or so previously. It was set out on the conference room table for all to admire.

We knew when The Owner refused a piece early on, and indeed ordered that it be put away safely for a future occasion, that he was neither in the best of health, nor the best of humour. His daughter who was once again with us for the trip confirmed this to us. The PM, it transpired, had a heavy cold, and before take-off we had been instructed to heat the inside of the aircraft as best we could. This was easier said than done. The York's own heating would only take effect once the engines were warmed up, and we ended up borrowing an electric fire that we powered with a long lead through the airfield mains.

The flight itself was uneventful, remarkable only for the brilliant stars that twinkled in the night. Our destination was the airfield at El Aouina on the outskirts of the city on the road to Carthage. A quarter of an hour short of landing time, Jock transmitted our corrected estimated time of arrival (ETA) over W/T to receive the reply from Tunis ATC that El Aouina was closed to all traffic and that we were to divert to 'Whipsnade', the codename for an airstrip some ten minutes flying time away. Jock queried the instructions over W/T – we had to observe strict R/T silence – and we overflew the airfield with our undercarriage down to make our intentions clear. Tunis ATC, however, was equally adamant: El Aouina was closed.

We were obliged to do as we were told, and could only assume that there had been a last-minute obstruction or incident that would somehow place our passengers and indeed our aircraft in danger. We overflew the heads of the assembled VIPs awaiting the PM's arrival and headed off into the desert to what turned out to be a half-deserted landing strip inhabited by a local Beaufighter squadron. We were met by a scruffy-looking flying control jeep with an equally scruffy looking officer driving and knew immediately that something was wrong. Hasty telephone calls were exchanged and we established that El Aouina was indeed closed to all aircraft – except the prime minister's York!

The incident might have been funny had the PM not decided to leave the aircraft and sit glumly on a packing case, in the cold, whilst contact was established. There were angry words and some confusion. The sudden change from a warm cockpit to a cold winter's morning meant the damage was quickly done. Although we were in the air again within half an hour and arrived at the correct airfield ten minutes later, the PM's cold was already turning to pneumonia, in an attack that was actually going to last some time.

The visit to Italy was still in the plan, but was soon after postponed. The PM would actually spend more than two weeks in his sickbed, and only after the arrival of Mrs Churchill some time later did he show any signs of recovery. It was said that only she held the power to persuade him to take the medicines that were prescribed.

Whilst our Owner recovered in Eisenhower's 'Little White House', we were entertained most comfortably in a villa belonging to one of Eisenhower's ADCs in Sidi Bou Said. It was not until eight days later that we were dispatched to Cairo, although we had been dispersed the day after we arrived, on 12th, to Sidi Amor, another airstrip in the vicinity: the York in its standard UK camouflage was too obvious on the bare ground should a nosey Luftwaffe reconnaissance aircraft be searching out the PM's whereabouts.

The threat was all too real, and there were rumours at the time of a possible German commando raid on the PM's villa. The rumour was treated so seriously that a party of Irish guards was brought in to surround the building. A cover plan was also devised in which a VIP villa was rented and ostentatiously guarded by British troops on the outskirts of Cairo at Helwan. As part of this plan, the York was dispatched back to Cairo West with no attempt to conceal its arrival. We carried only Lieutenant Colonel Scadding, an RAMC doctor, and whose services were no longer required. The axis press and radio promptly reported that the PM was indeed in Cairo. It was good to think that as a crew we had some decoy value, because by now our comings and goings were associated with this unique aircraft.

It was Christmas Day when we were summoned back to Tunis to find that the PM was very much better. We had been invited to the Little White House for an evening party hosted by Sarah for all of the servicemen and women who had been involved in her father's stay there. It was a buffet supper drinks party with all of the 'family' and about five commanders-in-chief with their retinue. Churchill himself was in sparkling form, working the room in his dressing gown and slippers.

Although he was better, The Owner clearly needed time to convalesce. It was decided his recovery would continue in Marrakesh, and we would fly him there. To do so we had a choice: either we could fly westwards down the Mediterranean in and out of cloud over the sea all the way, out into the Atlantic through the Straits of Gibraltar and south to Marrakesh; or to fly inland south of the Algerian coastal mountains over the relatively low desert hills, over the Shatt el Hodna and take a chance that the predicted cloud was clear of the Taza Pass so that we could sneak through the Middle Atlas Mountains, rather than having to fly above them.

Our captain opted for the latter route, with the proviso that the BOAC Liberator, which had brought Mrs Churchill to Tunis, and which was carrying some of the entourage ahead of us, would radio back the weather conditions they found. The AOC-in-C concurred, flying over the Med at 6,000ft with all those convoys about was asking for trouble. Our York could easily be mistaken for a marauding Focke-Wulf Condor and the navy was known to be notoriously trigger-happy. Tedder decreed that we would take along his PMO, Air Commodore Kelly. It was unnecessary, and in the event, Kelly – and all of the oxygen equipment he insisted we carry on board – only managed to get in the way.

We took off at 08.15 on the morning of December 27. All of the Churchill family were on board, and we enjoyed a smooth flight at just under 6,000ft for the first few hours of the journey. We soon learned, however, that the Taza Pass was enveloped in cloud, and that the Liberator in front of us had come perilously close to high ground on its passage. The captain again was faced with a choice, and opted to climb for fifteen minutes and clear this section of the Atlas range at 11,500ft. At the point that he announced his intentions, the PMO nearly had a fit, but The Owner dismissed him, citing that the safety of the aircraft was more important than his own personal comfort.

While Kelly darted breathlessly up and down the aircraft asking questions of all and sundry, the PM seemed perfectly content with his brandy and soda, helped by the odd puff of air from the oxygen bottle. We arrived in glorious sunshine, the weather a perfect reflection of the PM's mood. For our own part we had a quick turnaround, leaving precisely twenty minutes later for the short hop to Rabat where we were instructed to pick up General Sir 'Jumbo' Maitland Wilson, his chief of staff Brigadier Murphy, and his ADC Colonel Chapman Walker and return them to the UK. Wilson's own aircraft, a Dakota named 'Freedom', had neither the range, nor our comforts. The flight home was uneventful until we started to let down 150 miles out from Hartland Point where landing forecasts made it obvious we would not make it in at Northolt because of thick fog. We were diverted to Lyneham, from where cars were organised for our passengers. We had to wait until midday before the weather had sufficiently cleared up to take the short flight to base.

And so it was that we got to celebrate a belated Christmas and New Year at home. Turkey and plum pudding, saved for us by the mess. We made sure that we celebrated hard.

New Year duties resumed for the crew of Ascalon on January 6 when we returned to Marrakesh with the same passengers we had brought in a few days earlier but with the addition of two other VIPs, Captain Manley Power RN, the chief naval planning officer on Admiral Cunningham's staff and who was an expert in amphibious assault, and General Sir Bernard Paget who was to be Jumbo's deputy. Two days later we were dispatched to Algiers to fetch the Duff Coopers. This time we took with us Brigadier Fitzroy MacLean, leader of the UK mission to Tito's forces in Yugoslavia, who would shortly be returning to said country by parachute. We made sure he was well catered for on the flight, with fillet steak and sauté potatoes. We didn't think he would see such fare with the partisans.

Having said our goodbyes to the brigadier, we were standing by ready for an 11.00hrs take-off when it became clear that there would be a delay. The Duff Coopers, it transpired, had had somewhat of a prang in their car, a rather splendid pre-war Citroen Light 15. When they did finally arrive, Randolph insisted that we broke with our usual rule of not serving drinks until after take-off, and made sure they were given some medicinal champagne – purely to calm the nerves. By the time we arrived in Marrakesh, and Mrs Churchill and her daughter had met them at the airfield, their nerves had been fully restored.

While we had been away, the prime minister had been recovering in his Moorish villa. Now he was fully rested up and in good spirits. We left for Gibraltar with Mr and Mrs Churchill and their daughter, accompanied by their friend Lord Beaverbrook, Lord Moran, and the two Thompsons. On landing, the VIPs went straight to the governor's residence for dinner, whilst the captain and I went to the met office and worked out a flight plan for a crossing that night of approximately eight-and-a-half hours to Northolt.

The PM was insistent that he should return by air, rather than at sea in what he referred to as 'the draughty battleship' (the *King George V*) that he knew to be waiting for him. What we didn't know, was that the Cabinet and the PM's medical advisers were being equally insistent that he would be taking a sea voyage whether he liked it or not.

With the ADC, Thompson, our captain was told personally to

report to the PM where he was quizzed on the weather, take-off time etc and the PM seemed most satisfied. Then it all started to turn sour.

On leaving the PM's bedroom, Collins was confronted by a rather angry C-in-C Med, Admiral Cunningham, and the governor, General Mason MacFarlane. They told him that on no account was the PM to fly home, whatever he might think. Even the AOC, it appeared, seemed to have been shanghaied into agreeing that the weather was unfavourable. Collins was told that he was not to attempt to fly at all that night, or even start the engines without express permission. If he did, he might find himself forcibly restrained. More than this, one of the York's engines was to be covered with a tarpaulin and stepladders placed alongside to simulate that the aircraft was u/s for the benefit of the duty spy who would have known by then that Churchill was on the Rock.

Jack Payne was most indignant. Our flight engineer took great pride in the serviceability of 'his' aircraft. We all felt as he did: that we were being bullied by the navy for whom it would be a loss of face if the PM returned to the UK by air. We thus had to 'pretend' that we couldn't fly, for the benefit of the Germans, and of the Royal Navy, until Churchill was safely in his cabin on the battleship and on his way home. This most unsatisfactory state of affairs continued until *King George V* sailed into Plymouth on January 17, when we were released from our orders.

We returned to the UK empty, and again had to be diverted, this time to Chivenor near Barnstaple. The weather was foul and we were parked on the most distant hard standing in some unfortunate Devonshire farmer's orchard. We were obliged to 'live in' the aircraft for forty-eight hours, the only lighter side being that we quickly made friends with our farmer after giving him some bananas for his children. He marvelled at our aircraft: "She's a big bugger bain't she," he said in his local dialect. "We didn't expect to see the likes of that thar on our archard."

I'm sure he didn't.

CHAPTER SEVEN

NEW FRIENDS AND OLD ACQUAINTANCES

For the next two months, Ascalon received a well-earned rest, and I was returned to more mundane duties on other 24 Squadron aircraft. It would be wrong, however, to think that The Owner would somehow lose interest in his flying yacht.

Northolt is conveniently located on the A40, and could easily be reached by car from Number 10. On one particular morning, whilst Jack was working on the Merlins with some of the engine fitters, the PM drove straight to the hangar. There had been no word of warning of his arrival, neither from the station commander (Group Captain Dickie Legg) nor even the guardroom (security was never as tight as one would have thought it should be on a serving RAF base). The Owner got out of the car to look around the York, which at that point had its engine cowlings off and various bits and pieces of its inner workings strewn across the grass. Without saying a word to anyone, he climbed back into his car and returned to Downing Street where he remarked to one of his secretaries that it looked as if someone had thrown a bomb at his aircraft. The comment was taken literally, and within hours a posse of RAF police had arrived to question Jack to find out who had 'bombed' the York. Jack managed to persuade them that all was well.

The PM called by again on another occasion, but this time security – and the group captain – were rather more on the ball. While Dickie was escorting The Owner as he inspected the York, the PM spotted one of the fitters standing on top of the main undercarriage wheel. He was reaching into the bay behind the inner engine, into which the wheel would retract in flight. "What is that man doing?" inquired the PM. Before Dickie had time to answer, he added: "Have him do it from the inside in future. It looks dangerous standing on the wheel."

The eight weeks that the York remained on the ground were well used. The reliability of the aircraft, and its engines, had been exceptional, thanks in no small way to the engineering excellence of Rolls-Royce and the care given to the engines and operating systems by our flight engineer and maintenance team. But after flying more than 21,000 miles amounting to some 100 or more flying hours in less than two months, everybody and everything deserved a rest.

It was not until April 4 that we were told that we would be leaving that night for Algiers to bring back one of our regular passengers, General Sir Harold Alexander, for urgent talks. Alexander was one of the most gentlemanly of passengers, and we were always pleased to have him on board. He always appreciated our efforts, especially those of the cabin crew, and enjoyed the comparative luxury and indeed the honour of having the PM's aircraft at his disposal. The landings at Anzio had stalled, and German resistance in Italy was beginning to build up rapidly. Meanwhile, planning for the invasion of France (D-Day) was continuing apace, and the whole future of operations in the Med was under discussion both in London and Washington.

We took off empty, and for once 'Dad' Collins wasn't with us. Bill Fraser was in command with a new co-pilot from 24 Squadron (Flight Lieutenant Stokes), and although we had no passengers, we had about half a ton of diplomatic bags and service mail. The next two weeks were spent ferrying 'Alex' from Algiers to Gibraltar and then back to Algiers, for which a different second pilot, Flight Lieutenant Stephen Clift, joined us freshly arrived from the Ferry Pool in Dorval. On April 18 we received new orders to proceed to Cairo to fetch another one of our favourite VIPs, Field Marshal Smuts, for a further Commonwealth prime ministers' conference.

'Janny' Smuts, as we had experienced previously, had that common touch that all true great men have. Indeed by way of example, after we had landed at Northolt and Smuts had been 'greeted' by the assembled VIPs, he was on his way out of the gate in his car when he remembered that he had forgotten to thank us for the flight. He returned to thank Bill in person. There are not many that I could think of that would have shown such concern.

The pace of activity was such that it was obvious that the longed-for opening of the second front could only be weeks away. On June 3 we collected General de Gaulle and his entourage from Algiers, returning to the UK via Rabat. By way of contrast to our experience with 'Alex' and the South African premier, there was not a word of thanks from de Gaulle, nor even a single word of courtesy from any of his entourage, not at the time or even second hand. We saw no more of him after he left the aircraft and learned later that he had returned to Algiers in a York of 511 Squadron from Lyneham. I hope he enjoyed his coffee and sandwiches, for it was clear that talks with the PM had not gone well if he was not prepared to lend him his air-craft for the return trip!

There was a most bizarre incident later that month, an incident for which the truth only emerged some time after the war and was made famous in a film. We were told that the York should be brought to readiness and prepared for departure for North Africa but without us, its regular crew. Jack, in particular, was unhappy about leaving his engines in the charge of another and we were all a little put out. Clearly something was going on. We were not invited to any of the usual pre-flight conferences over route and timing, and there was no information on the passenger list. It was clear that the PM was not included, and no special catering was being laid on. A crew from Lyneham flew in to take over our aircraft, flown by an acquaintance of ours, Flight Lieutenant 'Ozzie' Morris. On the day of departure, June 25, we were politely but firmly told to keep away from the flight office and tarmac and had to watch our aircraft leave from afar.

Sometime after we learned the truth. Our aircraft had been used as part of a deception plan codenamed Copperhead, to show off 'Monty's Double' in Gibraltar and Algiers. The idea was to deceive German agents into believing that the 'real' Montgomery was on their patch, and I believe the plan worked liked a treat. The PM had allowed Ascalon to be used by General Alexander and 'Jumbo' Wilson in the past, and Northolt would be the natural VIP departure point for this particular aircraft. It had, of course, its unmistakable square windows and bomber command camouflage; all other Yorks had round windows and a blue/grey colour scheme. The Germans were completely fooled, and the actor/impersonator Clifton-James who bore an uncanny resemblance to the field marshal won the plaudits he deserved for the film.

We spent a further two weeks in early July fetching and carrying General Alexander, as clearly there was some considerable acrimony between the British and US chiefs and discussions were taking place at the highest level. We headed for Rome at the start of the month, but sadly saw little or nothing of the Holy City but its distant domes from the airfield, Ciampino. (Today it is an international airport; then it was nothing more than two adjacent fighter strips joined together to make one long runway.) We were, however, warmly welcomed by the resident P47 Thunderbolt wing of the 7th US Air Force. They had recently 'liberated' a local distillery and had rapidly converted it to the production of a form of gin to drink with the plentifully available Italian vermouth. The label on the bottles proclaimed: "*7th Air Force Gin. The more you drink the more you sin.*" I quickly realised if not immediately then soon after that we were in Catch 22 country!

On July 11, we were ordered home. Another VVIP trip was in the offing, this time with a 'General Collingwood'. This time we knew him to be the king.

We looked forward to our second royal flight with confidence. We had learned so much in the year since we had last had the honour of a royal passenger, and now we had a proper RAF chef (Jock Duncan) and General Alexander who was to be His Majesty's host for the tour. HM Queen Elizabeth and their daughter the future queen, HRH Princess Elizabeth, came to see him off.

Take-off was scheduled for 22.30 on July 22, with our first stop to be the RAF staging post at Rabat Sale. A meteorological reconnaissance flight had been flown earlier in the day to confirm weather conditions en route. They seemed favourable. Just before take-off, as the party was standing by the aircraft some way from the nearest air raid shelter, and the king was commenting on some of the changes he had noted on the aircraft since his last flight, a V1 flying bomb (popularly termed 'doodlebug') roared over almost overhead. We then heard its motor cut out, and the bomb fell to earth and exploded, somewhere in the vicinity of Harrow. No one turned a hair. Her Majesty simply remarked that they had been sheltering from "those horrid things" all day.

We enjoyed a smooth flight in the long summer twilight, and as we climbed above the clouds and leveled out, His Majesty came forward to the flight deck to question me again on the main navigational stars I would choose.

This time when we arrived at Rabat we were not unexpected, nor was there any fog to delay our landing. The ever-present Jimmy Jeffs had flown on ahead to sort out matters of air traffic control and to keep an eye on any unforeseen diversions. He joined the aircraft for the onward flight to Naples which we took by routing ourselves via the Taza Pass to Oujda on the border of Algeria and thence to Oran. From Oran to Naples we had an escort of four RAF Beaufighters to our landing ground at Pomigliano.

Our York could not proceed north of Naples. Apart from the shortage of aviation fuel, it was too big for many of the airstrips on the itinerary. His Majesty was to visit a number of army and RAF units in the forward area and hold a number of battlefield investitures during a busy twelve day schedule. The royal party left us, therefore, to the delights of the RAF air transport wing headquarters' mess at Portici where we spent a pleasant few days exploring the newly dug ruins of Herculaneum as well as the better-known ruins of Pompeii close by.

The king was due to return to the UK on August 2, for which we were given forty-eight hours notice. All was set for an 11.00hrs departure when it became clear that something was awry. The king, who was usually very punctual, was late. When he did turn up, half an hour later, we discovered that His Majesty's RN driver had got lost. In trying to keep the monarch safe, the RN security men had tried to avoid the main routes by routing the car via the back streets. The result was actually to make the risk to His Majesty greater, and his transit much slower. We could easily make up the time in the air, so no harm was really done, and our flight schedule home bound had plenty of slack. His Majesty, however, made his displeasure clear.

From Rabat it was an eight-hour flight home, which we achieved without incident, albeit that the passage was a trifle bumpy. We didn't notice, but were told afterwards, that as we were in the circuit prior to landing, we narrowly avoided being intercepted by yet another doodlebug. It seemed somehow appropriate to be welcomed back in the way that we had departed.

This time there was no crew-call to the palace, and I could enjoy my hot bath without interruption. We received a letter later from the private secretary via our C-in-C that HM "was very pleased with the way that Wing Commander Collins and all members of his crew of the York carried out their duties during HM's recent visit to Italy."

It was no great problem for us to turn the aircraft around within seven days when the PM declared that he would, himself, be visiting troops in Italy. Revictualling and restocking of linen, towels etc had become almost routine, though wine was becoming rather scarce. Some routines were changing, however. German night-fighters were no longer based on the Brest peninsular, and this allowed me to shorten the route on our way to Algiers without fear of attack, and we could fly there non-stop with plenty to spare in the tanks. It was then a short four-hour run to Pomigliano.

We were to remain in Naples for seventeen days, the longest we had been 'marooned' anywhere. With The Owner's moods and requirements so variable, however, we were obliged not to stray too far from the base in case we were needed. When the call did finally come through, on August 28, we were to take the PM home, following the same route to Rabat for the first leg as we had done with His Majesty. All was fine until we reached the North African coast, but thereafter we flew in and out of thunderclouds, and whilst our captain did his best to avoid the worst of it, the passage was especially turbulent. Some of the passengers were ill, and after we landed we were told in no uncertain terms by Sawyers, the valet, that his master was not best pleased with us.

'Dad' Collins and I went straight to the airfield flight planning section to find out more about the route weather forecast for the night. It was far from promising with heavy thunderstorms expected off the Iberian coast, and in view of the PM's mood it was decided not to go any further that evening. Soon after, our captain was summoned to explain himself, which he did in forthright terms. Our captain was not one to be bullied by anyone, and the PM was obliged to concede the point. We understood his need to get back to the UK with all haste, and so it was agreed to fly in daylight the next day. The threat of Focke-Wulf Condors had all-but receded, and at 10.00 the following morning we were away and climbing to 5,000ft, happily without too much by way of turbulence. Occasional shots of the sun through the gaps in the cloud gave me some help, but I was very dependent on the radio beacons at Cape Roca (Lisbon) and Corunna for my navigation.

Half way across the bay we ran out of the high cloud and then had a smooth, and even pleasant, onward flight. Plenty of D/F bearings from UK control stations combined with sun position lines brought us up the coast of Cornwall to Chivenor and so on to Northolt in a shade under eight hours.

This was to be 'Dad' Collins' last flight as the pilot of the prime minister's York, Ascalon. He was now, officially, tour-expired as commanding officer of 24 Squadron and therefore due for a posting. It seemed only natural to us that Bill Fraser, the co-pilot, who had frequently assumed command when the PM lent his aircraft to others, should now achieve his ambition of slipping over to the left-hand seat. The PM, with a well-known dislike for new faces or change for change's sake, agreed. The proposition was put to the AOC-in-C and the CAS and approved.

On the change of captaincy of his aircraft, the PM wrote to Portal and asked for the following message to be sent to Collins:

"I wish to thank you for the efficient manner in which you have organised my flights and for the care and precision with which they have been carried out under your command. I am grateful too for the excellent arrangements made in the aircraft for my comfort and convenience by yourself and your crew."

I don't think that 'Dad' Collins received any outward recognition for his services from the RAF. Bill Van der Kloot, the American pilot for Churchill's early travels, at least collected an honorary OBE. I suppose that apart from our AOC-in-C ('Ginger' Bowhill) and his SASO ('Brackles' Brackley), few appreciated what Collins did to work up the private yacht environment that the PM so loved. He was a bit of a loner, and somewhat contemptuous of the relative inexperience of the RAF in long-range transport operations. He kept himself very much to himself, and did not attempt to court the lesser air officers at Command or group headquarters who were often keen to be 'in on the act'. Indeed many resented his entrée to Number 10. There were many critics of lesser abilities who hid behind official procedures when something urgent was needed or found. In the end it was 'Dad' who had to shoulder the responsibility, for no-one else could take the captain's decision whether a flight was 'on' or 'off'.

Now the burden of responsibility had shifted. Now it was up to Bill to lead us on our next adventure. And a whole new world.

CHAPTER EIGHT

WHEN TWO WORLDS COLLIDE

On a cold autumnal morning at the start of October 1944 I travelled into London with Bill to attend the Cabinet Offices where we were given details of a flight to Russia. It seemed that our next operation involved flying the prime minister to Moscow, to meet with Marshal Stalin. It would take an inordinate amount of planning, and we set to work almost immediately.

All RAF flights into Russia had to be made via Cairo, where delays were frequent while diplomatic clearance was obtained, communication and meteorological arrangements made, and navigational routing for defence identification laid down. And all this from one of our supposed allies! There was one piece of good news, however. Since Paris had now been liberated, we could fly directly over France to the Mediterranean.

We were airborne at 00.15 on October 8, crossing into France at Barfleur. The Owner was accompanied by Lord Moran and the ADC, Tommy Thompson, and of course Sawyers the valet. John Martin (one of the PM's secretaries) and Inspector Hughes of The Yard completed the party. A short while into the flight, when we had climbed to around 7,000ft, the PM sent for Jack (who else?) to have his personal oxygen turned on in his cabin. When Jack had adjusted the oxygen flow and fixed the mask so that the PM was comfortable, he went to leave but the PM demanded he take his pulse. Jack's medical knowledge was rudimentary at best, but he had no option but to grasp the proffered wrist. Not knowing much about pulse rates, or what was 'normal', he managed to put his head round the cabin curtain without the PM especially noticing and whispered loudly to Sawyers above the engine noise: "What's normal?" Sawyers mouthed the number '98', or some such figure, which Jack duly relayed to the PM. "Not bad for an old man," the PM retorted, and Jack was able to escape without his ruse ever being discovered.

We landed at Pomigliano just after dawn, and were joined by York MW100 which had taken off from Northolt just before us carrying Anthony Eden, the CIGS, 'Pug' Ismay and his deputy, Brigadier Jacobs. York MW101 would follow later. We stayed long enough to have breakfast and a brief rest before leaving for Cairo at 12.30hrs local time, with Eden transferring aircraft to our own.

The flight was very smooth, but sadly it all went rather awry at the end. It was the one and only time that Bill ever made a mess of a landing, though with extenuating circumstances it should be said. We had been directed to land at the little-used south-north runway at Cairo West that had a nasty hump at the point of touchdown. Bill misjudged his approach in the dark and we hit the ground with quite a thump. The York rose but not far enough that a burst of engine might arrest our fall, and we all but stalled onto the runway with a bang and a rattle. Bill was glum, but our passengers either failed to notice or were too polite to mention it.

The plan was to proceed to Moscow that night, on the assumption that clearances had been obtained. But there was a problem. Jack, on inspecting the undercarriage for any damage, noted that the oleo leg on the starboard side was leaking. This meant it would not stand the weight of a fully laden aircraft. Bill reported the news to the ADC, and because of the time it would take to effect the repairs, the PM would have to change aircraft. As it was, Squadron Leader Tony Watson had the privilege of taking the PM onwards into Moscow (in York MW100). We would have to follow on behind just as soon as we could.

With almost superhuman work by Jack and the local maintenance staff (led by a splendid Flight Lieutenant Ray), they off-loaded the fuel, jacked up the aircraft and exchanged the damaged oleo leg strut in record time. We were ready for the off by 02.00 (local time) – only four hours late.

We climbed to 10,000ft where we would get our best fuel consumption, and after Amman followed the Haifa pipeline to Ramadi, then over the Mosul to Lake Urmia. From there we continued on to Lenkoran, south of Baku, and reported our position to our man at Moscow control as we had been instructed. The procedure we had to follow was quite ludicrous, but we had no choice. Our RAF Moscow operator from our military mission had to sit alongside a Soviet operator who tuned the transmitter and receiver to the designated frequency. Jock Gallagher had quite a time of it trying to follow the ground operator, for the Russian allowed his frequency to drift.

My own challenge was to navigate over a country I didn't know and with maps that were of little use to a destination airfield of which we had only a vague description and for which there was no designated alternative. Radio navigational aids were zero, we had to fly in sight of ground (so that we could be visually identified) and had to report our position every hour. Given the very real threat of being shot down if we didn't, we stuck to our instructions most faithfully.

I gave Bill our course to follow the western shore of the Caspian Sea, turning north west for Stalingrad at Cherny Rynok where we descended to 4,000ft to remain under the cloud base. This was what they called 'Bradshaw' flying (after the famous Bradshaw train timetables), though sometimes without the railway lines! We were obliged to reduce our height still further to 2,000ft as the weather deteriorated, and although I was confident that we would not be running into any natural obstacles en route, there was always the danger of aerial masts or chimneys.

Without any large-scale maps of the area we literally zoomed towards the centre of Moscow, catching a tantalising glimpse of the shiny domes and cupolas of the Kremlin to port. We were worried that we might be fired at, and continued to fly as low as we dare so as not to lose contact with the ground. Our briefing told us only that Moscow Central airfield, our destination, lay on the northwest side of the city, on the west side of the straight main road towards Leningrad but still within the built-up area of the city. We had also been told that it lay beyond the unmistakable Dynamo Stadium. To put our mission into context, it would be like asking a Russian pilot to find Hendon, without any real navigational aids, and only telling him it was somewhere along the Edgware Road. Then we saw it, and our success was confirmed by a series of Very lights fired from the ground to say we had been recognised.

We had covered nearly 2,600 miles in twelve hours and forty-five minutes, and an average of 200 miles per hour. This was the longest flight we ever made in Ascalon, and there wasn't much left in the tanks. I admit there wasn't much left in my own tank either: I had now been without proper sleep for the best part of seventy-two hours since we left the UK, and I had to resort to the odd Benzedrine tablet to keep going for the last lap. This made you feel wide awake for a defined period, but there was always a downside, and when you did finally get to sleep and awake the following morning, it was like the worst hangover ever.

So this was Moscow. After we had clambered wearily from our aircraft and savoured the chance to stretch our legs, we were introduced to the Soviet air force engineer assigned to us, and who had already been working with the crew from MW100. Fortunately he had been with the RAF Hurricane wing in Murmansk in the winter of 1941, and therefore had a smattering of English. We soon discovered that we had easy access to the airfield by embassy car, pausing only to shout "Equipage Churchill" to have the gates opened by a bewildered armed sentry, complete with Tommy gun. It turned out that our air attaché had never been allowed inside the airfield boundary in the two years he had been in Moscow.

Accommodation had been arranged for us in the Hotel National, bang in the middle of town and listed first of all the hotels in Bradshaw's 1914 *Guide to Moscow*. It was perfectly acceptable, comfortable even, and amid the wartime gloom of the Russian capital, its Victorian-style faded red plush and weakly lit, dusty chandeliers looked positively attractive.

The receptionists, telephone operators and tourist guides all spoke English, and it was fairly evident to us that they had been drafted in especially, almost certainly by the NKVD (the forerunner to the

KGB). Our every movement was watched, and our conversations monitored, and we had a little fun between us going twice or three times around the revolving door in order to lose our 'tail'! We also placed an RAF greatcoat and cap upon a huge, stuffed brown bear that stood half way up the main staircase, much to our hosts' indignation.

The food in the hotel was nearly always the same. It started with caviar and vodka, and went on to include all kinds of smoked meats and fish washed down with copious amounts of wine. It was somehow incongruous to have all this splendour, when outside the streets – and the people – were grey and drab.

We took full advantage during our stay to take in the culture that the city had to offer. This included visits to the Bolshoi to see Swan Lake and Prince Igor. We went also to a command performance, given in honour of The Owner. Our box was the next but one to the prime minister and the Russian supremo, and we had a clear view of the man who was to bring terror to his people in their millions. He was surprisingly small, balding, and had bad teeth and a worse complexion, brought about from being constantly indoors. There was one amusing incident during one of the performances when the air attaché, Air Commodore David Roberts, who was sitting in our box, sat up on the back of his chair with his feet on the seat in order to get a better view. He was almost immediately told off by the obligatory secret policemen standing nearby that putting one's feet on chair cushions was not considered culturally acceptable in Russia.

As well as the ballet, we were also treated to a tour of the Kremlin, arranged for us by Tommy Thompson. The Kremlin was normally out of bounds to all foreigners, so this was a treat indeed, and we saw the famous Uspensky Cathedral and many of the magnificent rooms in the palace of the Tsars, including the fantastic white and gold St George's Hall.

On one of the mornings we took an excursion to visit the offices of the only British newspaper ever to be published in Russia called *British Ally*. It was extremely popular, and its popularity ended up causing its downfall in the end, but not before the editor, whose name was Laurie, took time out to show us around the local markets and shops and drinking dens of Moscow.

Back at the airfield, it is fair to say that the Red air force could not do enough for us. When Jack decided that the aircraft could do with a good clean and mentioned it to his hosts, a party of 'mrs mops' turned up within the hour, buckets and scrubbing brushes in hand. Jack nearly had a fit as they started to slop their water on the floor of Ascalon, and it was all he could do to prevent the aircraft from being flooded, such was the vigour with which they confronted their task. By the end, however, Ascalon was perhaps the cleanest she had ever been. The Russians also insisted that on refuelling the aircraft, all of the petrol was filtered (to remove any impurities) through chamois leather, lest something should happen to the PM and they should be accused of sabotage.

There was a story told to us at the time. It may have been apocryphal; it may have been true. During the Moscow meeting, Churchill had needed to consult with one of the British diplomats in the Middle East. Stalin offered to send one of his aircraft to fetch the diplomat and bring him to the Kremlin. The Russian pilot duly flew south, picked up the official in question, and started for home. As he flew over Russia, the weather closed in and he was soon in thick fog, and lost. By some miracle he managed to make out a railway line and, as all good pilots will do, decided to follow it. He flew so low, however, that he actually clipped a train coming in the opposite direction but again, by some miracle, managed to get the aircraft down in one piece without harm to him or his passenger. Stalin, however, was furious, and on his return, ordered the pilot to be shot for endangering the life of a British diplomat. The British protested, and the pilot got away with the defence that the train should not have been there as it was either on the wrong line, or ten minutes late. It might have been funny, had not Stalin then ordered that the train driver and engineer should be arrested and shot instead.

It was soon time for us to make plans for our departure, and Bill and I were summoned to Russian naval headquarters for a met briefing; the air defence of the Crimea was under the command of the Russian naval air arm. The plan was to fly from Moscow to Sarabuz in the Crimea in daylight where we would refuel. Our second leg would then take us by night over the Dardanelles and the Aegean to the familiar landing ground of Cairo West. The forecast was all but useless. The Russians did not want to give us any erroneous information, and their advice was punctuated by so many 'ifs, buts and maybes' that it was of little value. However, we knew that we were flying into better weather as we went south.

The two Yorks (MW 100 and MW101) left Moscow twenty-four hours ahead of us. We arrived in Sarabuz after four-and-a-half hours in the air, landing in light drizzle. The airfield was empty, save for row upon row of US-built fighters, Bell P39 Airacobras[4] rusting by the side of the runway. Given the lives that had been lost in convoys getting them there, it was a pitiful and rather depressing sight. The PM was met by the local admiral, and while they dined together we were invited into a somewhat primitive mess, leaving our aircraft to be guarded by some rather fierce-looking Soviet naval ratings. On the PM's return he was furious with us for not staying with the aircraft. We had seen the PM angry before, but on this occasion he was in particularly poor humour. We knew then, if we didn't know already, that the talks of the last few days had not gone well.

It was a pity that our last flight in Ascalon should end in such disappointment for The Owner.

---

[4] Bell supplied some 5,000 Airacobras and more than 2,000 Kingcobras to the Soviet Union during the war.

CHAPTER NINE

THE NEW MASTER OF THE SKIES

For well over a year it had been obvious to us, and most of all The Owner, that Ascalon had her limitations. We needed a bigger and better aircraft to meet the PM's expanding requirements, not least the ability to cross the Atlantic to see his friend the president at a moment's notice, without having to await the availability of a BOAC Clipper. There were limits to the York's range, and its basic military construction was simply too heavy to allow any development of its range and payload.

This is not to detract too greatly from an aircraft that had served us well, but even the beautiful Merlin engines had been designed to be thrashed in bursts at full power, as in a Lancaster bomber, without too much regard for fuel consumption, rather than long-haul cruising at low revolutions and economic power settings.

Our acknowledgement that we needed a new aircraft had coincided with our first look at the president's own aircraft 'Sacred Cow'. She was a Douglas C54 – in effect the military version of the civil DC4. The aircraft was in mass production at the Douglas factory at Santa Monica, and ten had been allocated to the RAF under lend-lease. In October 1943, Tommy Thompson sent a minute to the CAS, referring directly to the C54. In the early months of 1944, Bill Fraser, a gifted draughtsman as well as pilot, drew up some detailed plans for the interior, based on the successful layout of the York, that were subsequently discussed and approved at the highest level. By the mid-summer of the same year, the PM could say that Mr Roosevelt had given him an aircraft for it was decided that the first of the ten allocated to the RAF would be diverted for Churchill's personal use. So it came about that No 100 off the production line was delivered to us on June 10 by Wing Commander Willie Biddell of the Dorval Ferry squadron, to be registered EW999 in the RAF.

Although the aircraft was now in our hands, it was just as soon afterwards taken away from us. We delivered it to Armstrong Whitworth (the same manufacturers of the Whitley) at Baginton to be fitted out. Six weeks later, after the soundproofing had been fitted but before the furnishing had started in earnest, we gave her an air test so that noise levels could be carried out throughout the interior. Jack, who had been sent away to California for intense training on the new type, was anxious to see how 'his' new aircraft performed.

At the controls for the flight was Armstrong Whitworth's chief test pilot, Squadron Leader Charles Turner-Hughes. 'Toc-H' as he was known in the trade, made a great song and dance about flying the PM's 'plane. We declared ourselves satisfied, and left thoroughly looking forward to taking her over for good – and with our own pilot in charge. Of course it was not quite as simple as that, and there were many issues along the way and many delays, but the end result – finally – was what the PM was looking for.

We returned to Baginton on November 10, by which time the work had been completed, and spent four hours flying around the UK under Toc H's command. Back at Northolt, the aircraft was re-weighed and its centre of gravity determined for loading purposes.

On the evening of November 13, there was a party in the mess with Squadron Leader Charles Lancaster DFC & Bar and his York crew from Lyneham. The flight engineer, Alfred Enser, was a good friend of Jack's. The next day they were due to fly out with their own VIP, Air Chief Marshal Sir Trafford Leigh-Mallory, who had been appointed air officer commanding-in-chief South East Asia Command. Lancaster was ex-Coastal Command and had some four-engined experience but he certainly had no notable experience on Yorks, neither did the co-pilot who happened to be Leigh-Mallory's ADC. Their York was so new its paint was only just dry, and by way of training they had done little more than fly a circuit of the airfield. We knew the weather for the route they would be taking on the first leg of their journey was atrocious and all routine transport flights across France had been cancelled because of heavy icing. Leigh-Mallory, however, was an awful show-off, and since there was a great entourage there to see him off, he insisted they went. They crashed somewhere in the mountains near Grenoble, and everyone on board was killed.

No-one can state with any great certainty what happened, but we had our own theories when we heard that the York had gone missing. It may have been due to icing. The York had anti-icers, rather than de-icers, the difference being that the anti-icing chemical prevents ice from forming but has to be dispensed in good time. If the ice was allowed to take hold, the chemical simply washed over the surface and you could be in serious trouble. Another theory is pilot error through lack of experience. I know that in the official investigation, the lack of training provided was stated as a factor in the disaster. In thick cloud, Coastal Command pilots would instinctively head below the cloud, whereas the Bomber Command pilots would always try and get above it. The fact that they flew in at a height of around 6,500ft suggests our theory may have been correct. We blamed Leigh-Mallory himself, for he either couldn't, or more likely wouldn't, wait. After the event, 'Ginger' Bowhill insisted that any and all aircraft flying from Northolt, regardless of the passenger, had to come under his direct command to avoid such a tragedy happening again.

A few days later, we made a further air test in our Skymaster with the Transport Command signals staff to satisfy them that the new radio system worked as intended. We now had much more powerful American W/T transmitters that were to make Jock's duties to keep in touch with base considerably easier. We also had two American radio-navigation direction finders installed, far superior to anything Marconi could offer the RAF.

The Skymaster would give us an endurance of some twenty hours, as opposed to thirteen of the York, with a proper galley, cooker and refrigerator so that meals could be provided with raw materials from wherever the aircraft was supplied. There was also increased water storage and improved toilet facilities – including an electrically heat-

The Skymaster cockpit was much roomier than the York and easier for The Owner to access.

ed toilet seat, courtesy of GEC. From an operational perspective, we had a small on-board petrol generator to make us self-sufficient in electrical power so that, when on the ground, we were not dependent on local facilities to start our engines. Bill was especially happy with the enlarged cockpit, and a steerable nose wheel with differential toe brakes that would make taxiing and parking so much easier.

Accommodation was now in three 'classes': first class for the PM in his state room and en suite (complete with hot and cold water); second class for the immediate entourage laid out in the style of a Pullman sleeper; and third class for the detective and valet, Sawyers. Thus we could sleep up to ten passengers in comfort. As for the décor, the walls of the state room and its roof were in beige leather trimmed with sycamore wood and a grey Wilton carpet.

Unlike the York, the floor level of the Skymaster was 9ft 6 inches above ground level. A portable stairway was therefore built to fold away on board when not in use. Sacred Cow had an electric lift for Roosevelt's wheelchair. It also had a neat, Duralumin folding ladder that was raised and lowered electrically from within the aircraft. Not so our own. The Ministry of Aircraft Production (MAP) had laid down that all parts of a service aircraft must be stressed to withstand strain of 4G; we were thus obliged to carry round a staircase built for a battleship, a wooden monstrosity that had to be manhandled up and down by a system of blocks, pulleys and ropes. At first it was ordained that we should have a striped canvas awning that slid outwards from the aircraft as the PM appeared on the top step. This was certainly a step too far for Jack, who remarked that we should look like "a bloody ice-cream seller". Fortunately, as higher steps became available on destination airfields, this extraordinary contraption was only used when nothing else was available.

Bill, in close consultation with the PM's ADC, asked Number 10 for permission to take the aircraft across the Atlantic to Montreal to give her a proper work-out, and particularly to check its long-range performance and handling at full weight of fuel. Permission was granted, and on November 24 our crew, with Toc H and Walter Goodesmith, the MAP design authority, set off westbound via Iceland to Canada.

We made a daylight flight, cruising at 10,000ft, and everything worked as it should. My new radio navigation gear was a joy. I had to stand on a stool to take sextant shots out of the astro dome but there was plenty of room for my gymnastics and handholds for rough weather. The crew was situated well forward of the propellers; the exhaust systems of the Pratt and Whitney air-cooled engines were quite different from the Merlin cackle-pots, so our duties were less affected by fatigue induced by engine noise.

It went wrong when we landed. The nose oleo leg made an unhealthy banging noise as we taxied to our hard standing. Jack guessed that we had probably lost hydraulic pressure in the front shock absorbers, and that something was leaking. Examination on the ground proved that Jack's guess had been correct. (Much later it was found that the steerable nose wheel had been misused whilst man-handling the aircraft on the ground.) The difficulty was compounded by the fact that there were no spares available in Reykjavik, and very few in the UK for that matter. The decision was taken therefore to continue on to Montreal where the USAF could provide the parts we needed and the expertise to help us with the repairs. For the time being, Jack could fix the leg sufficient for us to take off, and assuming Bill landed gently at the other end, he was confident that we would get away with it.

Meanwhile there was another leak, this time as a result of the plumbing. Although Jack had pressed for copper piping for all domestic plumbing within the Skymaster, dural piping had been specified on account of its light weight, fed from a large header tank over the galley. Copper could be soldered by anyone; dural splits in cold weather, and in Iceland, with the temperatures below freezing, the pipes burst and leaked. We were obliged to live with it for the time being, but later, on our return to the UK, RAF tradesmen changed the most vulnerable pipes to copper.

The next day we set course for Montreal, and arrived without further incident. The leaking pipes had been isolated, and now being light of fuel, and with a deft touch, Bill was able to land and taxi without further damage to the leg. The USAF liaison officer was almost immediately on the case, and arranged for a fitting party to be flown in from the nearest C54 base.

On December 3, with a full fuel load and an all-up weight of 73,000lbs, we needed only 1,200 yards of a 3,000-yard runway to be airborne and settled in for our flight home of more than thirteen hours.

At cruising levels in a beautiful clear polar air stream the view of the night heavens was magnificent. All of the stars one's eyes could see were available for navigation and I felt completely in my element. As dawn approached, the sky brightened quickly as we headed eastwards and only the brightest stars and the morning planets remained. At sunrise I was able to repeat the 'old mariner's' trick of determining our longitude directly by noting the time of the appearance of the sun's arc and allowed a correction for the 'height of the eye'. A seaman would know the height of his ship's bridge; I had the latest radar altimeter, and so I too was able to measure the 'height of the eye'

left: What the best-dressed revenue officer was wearing in Moseley, Birmingham, 1939.

right: Happier times when war was a distant prospect. John is standing fifth from left
ng for the civil service RFC.

: Bombing and gunnery school at Aldergrove. John is seated second left on the second
Some volunteers had yet to collect their uniforms.

Top left: B Flight: John, Webb, Phil Harding, Hadley, Falconer, Gunn, Bartlett, Brown, Fleming, Robison Ford.

Middle: (From left to right): Ogilv Owen, Fennell, Hildyard, Crooks, Johnston (RN), Robison and the author.

Bottom: Briefings 1940-style were haphazard affairs. Identifiable in t photograph are John Sutton (with jacket) and 'the Colonel' (centre). John Bartlett is standing hatless at back by the map.

Above: Although not the author's aircraft, his Whitley looked in a similarly sorry state before she sank.

Left: The 'nose down' characteristic of the Whitley is clearly illustrated in this well composed official photograph.

Below: One of the squadron's Whitleys with the camouflage pattern of the time.

Top left: (from left to right) Falkingham, Christie, Coates, Clementi, and the author.

Top right: Chapman, station commander and Ken Smith, squadron commander, Linton, 1941.

Above left: A popular photograph used to promote the bravery of 'The Few' is acutally the 58 Squadron crew of 'A' Apple skippered by 'Dinty' Moore (left).

Right: Jack Kerry and Peter Elliot. Both went on to become distinguished pathfinders.

Left: 'Dinty' Moore gives the thumbs up from the cockpit while Peter Elliott looks on.

Middle: Ascalon lifts off from the USAAF base of Châteaudun du Rhumel, June 1943.

Below: A dramatic painting by Philip West of Ascalon in flight, complete with guards of honour.

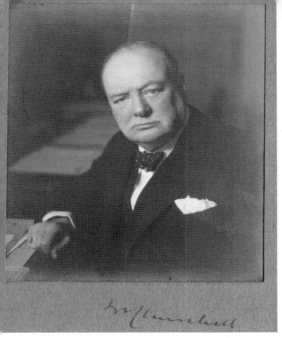

Left: Photo of The Owner given to John and all of Ascalon's crew.

Above: Churchill with Monty and CIGS Alan Brooke in an official photograph sent to John as a memento of their first flight.

Below: The Owner descends from Ascalon, helped by his son Randalph.

Left: Jock looking pleased with himself in the office at Northolt.

Below left: Bill in The Owner's banqueting suite (no passengers).

Below: Stephen Clift, Jock Gallagher and Bill Fraser on the flight deck of Ascalon.

Above: John, Bill, Jack, Wing Commander Jeffs, 'Dad' Collins, Wing Commander Slee, Jo and Corporal Shepherd after having been received by His Majesty.

Below: His Majesty takes to his staff car to inspect 8th Army at Tripoli.

Above: Ascalon proved such a curiosity to US ground crews that her take-off was delayed.

Below left: The author and Brenda on their wedding day, September 19, 1943.

Below: The crew making merry at Christmas, Hendon 1943.

Above: Wonderful head-on shot of the Skymaster.

Left: 'Sacred Cow' (nearest) and the PM's Skymaster at Saki - a very rare picture o the two aircraft together.

Below: Central Bombing Establishment (CBE) devel ment wing. Dickie Collard seated centre, the author is third from the left.

e: David Green (left) went on to become SASO 1 Group.
v: John Downey and the author (second and third from left) on the world flight at San
cisco.

Above: An evocative image of Aries in the fading light at Keflavik.

Below: 'Tubby' Vielle dwarfed by Aries which is herself dwarfed by the mighty Rock.

At midnight, Icelandic time, where daylight hardly ever ends.

m left and right: A new engine is fitted to Aries at Eielson airfield, delaying the author's
n from the Arctic.

Top: A party of Cranwell cadets at Luqa air[port] August 1949, on 'vacation training'.

Middle: Staged shot taken for PR purposes [with] the author standing centre and pupils seem[ing] engrossed in their work.

Bottom: The first ever course of the newly established RAF Flying College, 1950. The author is top row, far left.

RAF FLYING COLLEGE.   No I COURSE.   JAN: 1950

BACK ROW: S/LDRS; MITCHELL. GREEN. FELL. HAWORTH. COUNTER. MACKAY. HOY. SWAN.
CENTRE ROW: W/CDRS. TACON. FRANKS. HAIG. SKEILLS. BINKS. BOAST. COOPER. BURNETT. SINCLAIR. BILLETT.
FRONT ROW: LT/COL. LAW. W/CDRS. COULSON. HATFIELD. FROGLY. LT. COL. PERRY. W/CDRS. EDWARDS. HANAFIN. LT. COL. KNOBLOCH. W/CDRS. KEAN. MCCONNEL. W/CDR. MITCHELL. LT. CDR. SIMPSON.

Top left: Stafford Coulson (left) and Lt Col Perry (right), listen attentively in class at the RAF Flying College.

Top right: Conducting one of many inspections while Director of Recruiting.

Middle: Another one for the publicity men - planning the polar outing by a map of Iceland.

Bottom: At the Boat Show supporting colleagues with their high-speed air sea rescue launch.

Top: Mrs Ghandi and the author talk Canberras!

Bottom left: 'Chilly' Chilton (former C-in-C Coastal Command), Sir John Grandy (CAS) and the author at the end of course dinner at Manby.

Bottom right: A recent photo of the author.

accurately. It was then a case of subtracting the time of the sunrise on the Greenwich meridian (as tabled in my *Air Almanac*) from the time of the local event and hey presto I was left with the longitude. It was simple yet satisfying, but not very accurate navigation.

We had been in the air for thirteen hours and ten minutes by the time we landed and still had some seven hours of fuel left in the tanks. We were back at base with the prospect of Christmas at home, and could report to Tommy Thompson that we were now ready for his master's pleasure.

We did not have long to wait.

While we had been in Montreal, testing our new aircraft, the PM had been fretting about the situation in liberated Greece. The communist rebel movement (ELAS) was determined to unseat the shaky provisional government and prevent the establishment of a democratically elected parliament. A civil war had virtually broken out in the capital, and whilst the Americans at best turned a blind eye to Greece's problems, the PM was determined not to let the communists take control, and took it upon himself to find a solution to the crisis.

The possibility of Christmas at home with my wife, who was by now heavily pregnant with our first child, quickly evaporated when Bill and I were summoned to the Cabinet Office and told we would be flying to Athens within twenty-four hours. Considerable secrecy surrounded the flight, although there was feverish activity around Northolt as the aircraft was loaded with its provisions, including new, specially designed lightweight china and glassware. Our briefing was thin on detail. We knew only that our destination was the airfield at Hassani (now the international airport) which at the time was home to a squadron of Spitfires and Beaufighters, as well as being a staging post for transport support operations. The CO was none other than Wing Commander Cecil Lewis, the First World War pilot who achieved fame as the author of the acclaimed WWI story, *Sagittarius Rising*.

We perhaps hoped that the inaugural flight for Skymaster might be more high profile, and less urgent. In the event, we were only informed late on Christmas Eve 1944 that we would be leaving at dawn the following morning to stage at Naples (Pomigliano) with the

PM and his party, which this time comprised Lord Moran, Anthony Eden, John Colville, Pierson Dixon, two secretaries, Marion Holmes and Elizabeth Layton, a detective, Sergeant Davies and the omnipresent Thompson and Sawyers.

The prime minister revelled in his new aerial yacht whilst Sawyers fussed about, because for once there was ample space for his master's clothes, and he no longer had to decide what might be needed 'on voyage' and what could follow behind. I too was rushing around prior to take-off, first to visit the hangar loo and then after being summoned to the CAS to answer questions about my intended flight plan. As I hurried across the dimly lit hangar, I stepped on a nail which went through the sole of my shoe and into my foot. It hurt like hell, but by now it was too late to report sick, and I had to make do with a first aid pad inside my sock to stem the flow of blood and offer at least some modicum of comfort.

With the pain in my foot, we were airborne shortly after 05.00, taking what by now was the standard transport route across France. The PM came forward to the flight deck an hour or so into the flight and took his usual seat in the cockpit. He was thoroughly enjoying himself, and especially the better view forward and abeam. This time his access to the cockpit seat did not have to be interrupted by inadvertently putting his hands on some lever or switch.

A little later into the flight there was a change in engine note as Bill increased the power to get above cloud. The PM sent for me and enquired our height and position. I explained about the high ground just abeam of our track, but he remembered that I had brought him this way (we were over the Ligurian Sea) before, and at 7,000ft, at which point he asked me to account for the different altitude. He seemed happy with the explanation I gave, and I left him marvelling at his own memory for detail.

Our aircraft was met at Pomigliano by Admiral Sir John Cunningham and Air Marshal Sir John Slessor, but we were not long on the ground before we were off again for Athens, the PM enjoying an excellent lunch on the way. Bill went straight in to land without hanging around, as we were warned by local RAF control that the communists had taken to firing pot shots at inbound aircraft.

The Skymaster was used as a mobile conference room as the PM conferred with the ambassador, Rex Leeper, and General Scobie the local GOC. 'Alex' and Harold Macmillan, who had arrived separately from Italy, were also present. My main memory was simply that it was bitterly cold. Elizabeth Layton, one of the secretaries present, was also cold – so cold in fact that her fingers struggled with the typewriter. Later the PM transferred to HMS *Ajax*, anchored off the port of Piraeus, to have talks with Papandreou and the Orthodox Archbishop Damaskinos.

The RAF staging post was a bleak spot to spend Christmas, and local morale was low, not helped – I'm afraid to say – by their CO who did not appear to be a good manager of men. Even a firkin of beer that we had brought with us failed to inject any noticeable festive spirit as the officer was teetotal. (We had trouble opening the barrel, as we had no tool for removing the bung, and then had no spigot. A resourceful engineer removed a brass tap from the kitchens and this sufficed.) Not only was the staging post cheerless, but it was also potentially dangerous. Gunfire was frequently reported, although on one occasion it was some fool messing around with a Sten gun – a far from stable weapon at the best of times. A bullet made a hole in our undercarriage doors, which we decided to keep quiet. There was no point in unnecessarily alarming our leader.

Politically it transpired that the PM had made good progress, and Bill and I were summoned to the embassy in the centre of the city to discuss our plans for departure. No armoured car for us however, we were driven into town on the back of an open-topped RAF truck, escorted by an evil-looking local desperado with a ubiquitous Sten on his lap that in my mind could have gone off at any second. The vehicle was bouncing horribly, and I can safely say that I was more frightened of being accidentally shot by our guard than by ELAS terrorists!

It was not until December 28 that we were again on our way, the PM's business having been successfully completed. We had only meagre rations, having failed to secure any attractive foodstuffs from our local embassy beyond ouzo and olives. After an overnight stay in Portici, our final leg took us the seven-and-a-half hours to Northolt, although in the event we had to divert to the USAF base at Bovingdon, near Amersham in Buckinghamshire. The PM seemed satisfied, although complained about the noise of the ticking clock in his state room (he wouldn't have been able to hear the clock in a York) and the temperature of his heated toilet seat. He ordered that it be disconnected at once.

Our Owner was acclaimed as a hero for diffusing the Greek crisis. We were delighted because we were back in the UK, and had driven the forty minutes or so to Northolt in time for tea and a splendid pre-New Year's Eve party in the mess. Soon after I was able to go home and see my newly arrived son, after we had ferried the Skymaster back to its base.

It was wonderful to enjoy a few days leave with the family, especially now that we numbered three. We knew that an end to the war in Europe was in sight, and didn't doubt that we would soon be busy.

Although victory could only be a few months away, pilots and crew were still being killed over the night skies of Germany, as I was to learn from bitter experience when told that Kenny Lawson had been reported missing. I had come to think of Kenny as indestructible. He had completed two tours as an observer, and then fulfilled his burning ambition to become a pilot. He was nearing the completion of his second tour when he was shot down over Nuremberg. Two of his crew managed to get out, but not Kenny. Wing Commander Kenny Lawson, DSO & Bar, DFC was on his ninety-eighth trip. He had pushed his luck once too often, and paid the ultimate price. He would have been my son's godfather, had he survived.

The call we expected surely came when we learned that another 'Big Three' conference was in the offing, code-named Operation Argonaut. Stalin would not leave Russian soil whilst there were still Germans on his land, and so we would once again be going to him. At our preliminary planning meeting in Westminster, we discovered that as well as our Skymaster, the four aircraft that now comprised the York Flight would also be used, including Ascalon which was now under the command of Squadron Leader Ozzie Morris and his 511 Squadron crew out of Lyneham.

Our destination was to be Saki on the west coast of the Crimea. Because of the size of the allied airlift, the RAF had provided in advance the necessary infrastructure to ensure things proceeded as smoothly as they could, including air traffic control, met office and a radio navigation beacon. It was with some confidence therefore that we set course on the evening of January 29, 1945 for the first stage of our journey to Malta. We were supposed to leave at midnight, but poor weather obliged us to take off three hours ahead of schedule to avoid predicted snow at Northolt.

The earlier take-off would make our estimated arrival time at Luqa around 04.30 local (03.30 GMT), where it would still be dark. The ADC had signalled General Ismay (who had flown on ahead) to inform him of our change of plan, and that the PM would remain asleep on the aircraft until 08.00. The instructions, therefore, were that there was to be no band or VIPs to greet him, and to keep the noise to the minimum. The instructions, of course, never got through, and when we landed we arrived to discover a guard of honour, a band, the island governor, the C-in-C Mediterranean, 'old uncle' Tom Cobley and all, who had actually been standing in the cold for more than an hour having confused our ETA. It was, as you can imagine, acutely embarrassing, especially as the prime minister failed to emerge and remained resolutely in his bed.

Lord Moran remained asleep during the whole incident. Some hours later, after the PM had finally disembarked, he popped his head out of the curtains from his upper bunk and asked a rather tired Fraser how far we were from Malta. Bill, with a completely straight face, retorted: "nine feet six, sir." Suffice to say his lordship was not amused.

This was not the first time Lord Moran had fallen sound asleep in an RAF aircraft on the ground. When the PM was flying home in the Liberator Commando back in early 1943, the aircraft developed a fault in one engine, obliging it to delay take-off and remain overnight. The passengers left the aircraft while the local ground crew looked to effect the necessary repairs overnight, but somehow missed the fact that his lordship was still on board. It was only later that they discovered that he was missing, and had actually been locked in the aircraft all night.

Getting some twenty-five VIP aircraft punctually away from Malta at ten-minute intervals carrying over 500 passengers in all was quite a task. Tragically, one of the 511 Squadron's Yorks flown by Flight Lieutenant Eaton Clarke crashed into the sea off Lampedusa, out of fuel, while en route to the island. A number of army and RAF officers perished, including Captain Barney Charlesworth, the CIGS' ADC, who had been on his staff since Dunkirk. The reason for the crash was never satisfactorily explained.

Our flight to the Crimea took us in broad daylight over Samothrace and on to Alexandropolis and Midye, having a fine view of the Dardanelles and the Bosphorus which to our starboard. It was a smooth flight, but increasing cloud obscured the Crimean coastline. Jock has no problem in picking up the Saki radio navigational beacon but our fighter escort leader (we had six P38s keeping us company) was having difficulty making contact with the fighter controller at his own destination airfield, Sarabuz. Without such contact he was effectively 'lost', and he radioed whether we could help give him a steer when in sight of the ground. We told him to follow us as we let down through the overcast, and pointed him in the right direction. He must have had some maps of the Crimea to hand, because we later heard that he made his landfall without further incident.

The Sacred Cow, with 'new' more powerful engines and modified to carry additional fuel in her wings, landed shortly behind us, and from our vantage point in the cockpit we saw the president lowered to the ground in his wheelchair via the purpose-built lift, and greeted by Molotov and Vyshinsky. It was clear to all of us that he was a very sick man indeed.

Saki was yet another basic military establishment, and we were pleased to find our own, albeit rudimentary, staging post that had been set up by the RAF in advance of the trip. While I was counting myself fortunate, Jack was behind in the aircraft, assessing the local conditions. In his judgment, the wet and dirt of our surroundings would soon make a mess of our interior, and the damp would turn our linen mouldy. He was far from happy, especially at the prospect of spending ten or more days on the base. In chatting to the Sacred Cow's pilot, Colonel Otis Bryan (the ex-TWA chief executive), we discovered he had already made arrangements to fly back to Cairo for the duration of the conference, on forty-eight-hour call. Bill quickly sought out the ADC before he left with the party for Yalta, and a similar dispensation was granted to us. Jack was now happy again.

It was dark when we landed at Cairo, and the unexpected arrival of the PM's Skymaster caused quite a stir. We had with us Brigadier 'Pop' Hill, ex-30 Mission Moscow, and Pop bore a passing resemblance to the great man himself. Indeed so great was the resemblance, especially in the half-light, that when Pop emerged from the aircraft, cigar in hand and fur hat on his head, the deception appeared complete. As is so often the case, accidental deception is often more effective than a planned event. Indeed I have often compared what happened next with the efforts extended in the famous 'man who never was' episode, for the Germans were completely taken in. Berlin radio announced the following morning that the PM had arrived in Cairo and the 'Big Three' were to meet in Luxor.

In Cairo, Bill Fraser had been forewarned by the ADC to contact the AOC of 216 Group, for The Owner might wish to visit Alexandria on his return from Yalta. A suitable airfield had to be found, and Whitney Straight very kindly laid on his own aircraft (a Beechcraft Expeditor) and his personal pilot. Having visited a number of airstrips and ruled them out, Bill decided upon the RAF flying boat base at Aboukir with the associated maintenance unit. It had only one runway of 1,000 yards, and local officers were concerned about crosswinds, but Bill seemed satisfied. The aircraft when we got there would be light of fuel, and Bill assured the local commander that his strip would suffice.

After ten days in the Egyptian capital, we were ordered to return to Saki. Unaware of the close relationship the crew enjoyed with the ADC, the RAF had thoughtfully added another forty-eight hours to the safety margin we had allowed. When we landed, late in the evening of February 8, we had in effect at least another four days of kicking our heels before the prime minister would be ready to depart. In that time we were billeted in bungalow-style accommodation that looked as if it might once have been part of a hospital or sanatorium. Made of wood and plaster, the hut was surprisingly warm, heated by traditional wood stoves. Around us was the all-pervading smell of burning wood and Russian cigarettes.

The local people said little. Some shapeless women occasionally came in to tidy our rooms and to stoke our fires. For food, we ate our own tinned rations and drank whisky and beer that had been specially imported. We slept on iron-framed beds that were functional rather than comfortable, with blankets that I noted had been supplied courtesy of the Canadian Red Cross. It was a most curious camp. There was a communal bathhouse which, like ours, was wired for sound, and loudspeakers kept up a never-ending barrage of Russian music that we could only switch off by cutting the power leads. But it wasn't all bad news. On the day before the main departure, February 10, the Russians organised a 'flyers party' to which we were all invited. It started in the early afternoon and descended into a drunken orgy, with bodies lying around everywhere in various states of drunkenness, some sleeping it off in snow-filled ditches. A good deal of souvenir hunting went on, and I managed to secure a Russian soldier's hat badge without too much trouble. One or two came away with medals in exchange for a few RAF buttons. It was reckoned to be an enjoyable party by all who took part.

There was some uncertainty as to our exact date of departure. Bill bumped into Otis Bryan who told us that the president was leaving on the 13th, and so guessed we would be leaving at much the same time. The Americans gave their Skymaster a quick air test to ensure all was well. It wasn't. As the pilot came into land, we could see smoke billowing from one of its engines. A con rod had snapped on one cylinder, and the engine would have to be changed. With customary US speed and efficiency, a spare was delivered from Payne Field, the US Cairo base, within seven hours in a Curtiss C46 'Commando' freighter. By the morning, the new engine had been fitted, and the Sacred Cow got away on February 13 as planned.

We decided that we too would conduct a brief air test. Whether we had been spooked by the American experience I cannot say, but what happened next was a most unpleasant co-incidence. Only a few minutes into the flight, one of our engines also developed a fault, and started to belch thick black oily smoke. Jack switched it off and Bill undertook a perfect landing on three engines. Jack was up a ladder with the engine cowlings off soon after, and discovered that a rocker box axle had come adrift and mangled up the exhaust valve on one of the cylinders – number one cylinder, as it happened, and therefore the master cylinder for the magneto timing and the worst of all to replace. Not that we had any replacement parts, of course, or spare engine near to hand. Then Jack had a brain wave: he could take a good cylinder off the dud engine from the Sacred Cow that the Americans had thoughtfully left behind.

Jack worked all through the night and in the rain, with the aid of a small Russian floodlight, to remove the ruined cylinder and replace it. This was Jack at his very best; the master craftsman at work. All we could do was provide moral support, hot drinks and food. By midday the following day the work was completed, and the engine ready to start. It burst into life without even the slightest sign that anything had been wrong with it, and after yet another brief air test later in the day, we were at last ready for the off. The PM with his VIP party boarded the aircraft promptly on their arrival the following morning, and we were airborne shortly after noon.

We were pleased to be underway, and after lunch had been served, The Owner came forward and sat in the co-pilot's seat. He was joined by his daughter Sarah. For once, he was quite talkative, and as we flew in sight of the Gallipoli beaches, and the scene of one of the greatest military blunders, he reflected on what might have been if only the commanders had exhibited the same courage as their troops.

We stopped just the one night in Athens where peace now reigned, leaving 'Alex' to make his way to Italy in his own aircraft, and taking in his stead Randolph Churchill who always seemed to be on hand when there was free drink and cigarettes on offer. It was said that he was not popular with the more senior VIPs – he was, after all, a mere captain and they thought him indiscreet. The PM, however, loved to have his family around him, and to that end he was of little concern to the crew.

Our onward journey passed without incident, and at Aboukir Bill proved that the local commander's concerns were unwarranted as he executed a perfect landing, using up only half of the 1,000 yards of runway at his disposal, to the astonishment and I think pleasure of the greeting party. We had barely had time to check into our RAF accommodation when we were told to return to the aircraft. There would be time only to join the president for lunch at sea off Alexandria, as he was hurrying homeward. It was, in the event, the last time the two men would meet; a few weeks later, the president was dead.

We would not then remain at Aboukir but continue to Cairo the same day. Sawyers was not best pleased and had to re-stow all of the PM's belongings, perhaps a little haphazardly. We left Aboukir after tea, reaching Cairo in the dusk.

After four days in Cairo, we left on February 19 to fly non-stop to the UK over-flying Luqa and Marseille at a comfortable cruising height. Fog at Northolt necessitated diversion to Lyneham where Mrs Churchill had been warned and was waiting for him with his train for London. We returned the aircraft to its base the following morning.

CHAPTER TEN

SWANSONG FOR A PROUD LADY

By early March, the allied forces had advanced beyond the Siegfried line and were massing for the Rhine crossing. The PM was anxious to be in on the action, and on March 2 we left Northolt with him, the CIGS, and 'Pug' Ismay (plus the usual entourage) and headed for Melsbroek on the outskirts of Brussels, accompanied by an escort of Spitfires. It was but a short stay over before we proceeded on to Juvincourt (designated A58) near Rheims. The PM was to visit Eindhoven, Julich and Goch by train and car to witness the Rhine crossing. We waited for the PM's business to be concluded before flying back to Northolt.

Arriving home on March 6, we found a much larger than usual line-up of 'meeters and greeters' waiting for the PM's return. The secrecy of our flights in previous years seemed to have finally gone by the wayside, and everybody clearly wanted to be in on the act and claim their little place in history. As The Owner reached the bottom of the steps, he turned to his ADC and asked to see the pilot, keeping the dignitaries waiting. Bill, who had been flying in shirtsleeve order, struggled into his tunic, rushed down the steps and was shortly by the PM's side. The PM led him by the arm to one side, and said: "My boy, they are going to make you a squadron leader." Bill replied with as much respect as he could muster that he had actually been a squadron leader for two years. Unperturbed, the PM simply said: "Well then, it must be wing commander. I am very pleased," at which point he turned, waved briefly to the crowd, climbed into his car and was driven away.

Much of the PM's flying over the next few weeks did not require a long-range aircraft such as ours, and his needs were ably met by the Dakotas of 24 Squadron. This was fortuitous, for the Skymaster was on notice to take Mrs Churchill to Russia where she had been invited in her capacity as chairman of the British Red Cross 'aid to Russia' fund. Specifically she had been invited to Rostov-on-Don to see various items of hospital equipment that her fund had provided. Our party would comprise Mrs Churchill and her secretary Grace Hamblin, General J.E.T. Younger of the British Red Cross, with Mabel Johnson, secretary of the fund, and Professor Sarkisov from the Soviet embassy in London.

Despite the progress of the war, we were confronted with the same issues with regards routing and planning, and could still not approach the country from the west for fear of being intercepted and shot down. The PM was there to see his wife off, announcing to anyone in earshot that "she will be safe with my crew". We flew non-stop to Cairo, a comfortable flight that we undertook never higher than 10,000ft. We knew that Mrs Churchill did not like flying, and it was a great undertaking for her to make such a long journey without the company of any of her family. Accordingly we gave the best service we could, and did everything to make her feel at ease.

She stayed two days in Cairo as a guest of the resident minister of state, Sir Edward Grigg, and celebrated her 60th birthday. We were off again on April 1, taking the now familiar passage over the Dardanelles. We were obliged after crossing the Crimean coast to make our presence known, which we did both by rocking our wings and reporting our position to Moscow Control via radio. Our track then lay over Melitopol to Kharkov, past Tula on our starboard beam and on to Moscow Central. As usual I had no radio navigation facilities to help me, even though we had specifically requested them to disclose what beacons they could to assist with the radio compass.

We approached Moscow as before at rooftop height in a downpour, but this time with slightly more confidence, as the geography of the city outskirts was more familiar. Bill landed without incident, and a large delegation was there to greet Mrs Churchill, with no fewer than three ambassadors including our own, Sir Archibald Clark Kerr. We too received a warm welcome from our Russian hosts who were most keen to have a closer look at our Skymaster.

We were instructed to return to Northolt without any embassy passengers, to be on stand-by for the prime minister, returning later to fetch Mrs Churchill on May 7.

Leaving Russia by air is considerably easier than entering it, and when the time came to depart on April 4 we simply flew south to the Crimea at an altitude that made visual verification possible over given checkpoints, and left the country at Saki. We had on board with us a most interesting character in Major Dick Rossbach of the US Army. Rossbach had been in a prisoner-of-war camp overrun by the Russians and had somehow made his way independently to Moscow, which was no mean feat given the circumstances and obstructive approach that the Russians were adopting in regards to repatriating POWs. I was to meet Dick Rossbach again. We also had Tom Brimelow[5] and his fiancé Jean, both from the British embassy, who were on their way home to get married. Jack, in one of his more mischievous moments, insisted that once we were outside of Russian territorial waters, our captain could perform the ceremony for them in the aircraft, and afterwards they could use The Owner's state room as the bridal suite! Brimelow's fiancée declined.

We made our landfall at Malta after just over eleven hours flying, and stayed overnight, returning to Northolt the next day.

I went on leave on April 9, and travelled up to my parent's home in Pembrokeshire. I had been there a few days when the local bobby called at the house with an air of tremendous secrecy. He told me it was most urgent that I made contact with my base and spoke to the station commander which I did. The station commander similarly pressed upon me the urgency of returning to base. I had no option but to obey his instructions to make for the nearest RAF station

---

5. Later Tom Brimelow rose to become ambassador in Moscow and was raised to the peerage after being permanent under secretary at the Foreign Office.

(Carew Cheriton in this case) and, with the minimum of disclosure, request a lift to London by air.

I had tuned into the BBC that morning and heard that President Roosevelt had died, and guessed therefore what was on the cards: that The Owner needed the Skymaster to go to the US for the funeral. I raced over in a local taxi to Carew Cheriton where the commanding officer was most obliging, and allowed me to hitch a ride in an Anson to Northolt in the guise of a navigational training exercise.

I arrived to find preparations in full swing, but it was apparent that there was indecision at Number 10, for while the PM was anxious to go to Washington, the Cabinet was equally adamant that he should stay. Sir Alexander Cadogan describes the incident in some detail in his diaries, and we remained ready to go at a moment's notice. In the end, The Owner didn't go, and Eden went in his place. He was to regret the decision both for his respect for Roosevelt, and for an opportunity to have an early influence on Truman.

Mrs Churchill, during this time, was still in Russia, and our orders were to rendezvous with her in Moscow on May 7 and bring her home. We left Northolt on May 3 with 1,000lbs of mail and no passengers. A direct route was not on, as there had been some seven days of bad weather over the south of France with cold fronts and icing conditions. Instead, we opted to stage at Rabat, albeit a long way round, and then after refuelling, fly direct to Cairo. There we waited for the mandatory but still tedious clearance from the Russian authorities for our proposed route, this time directly north over Turkey via Nicosia to Saki. Mrs Churchill had clearly generated enormous goodwill among her hosts, for our clearance was given as proposed and without argument.

The weather forecasts were as hopeless as usual, but at least the winter weather was now fast disappearing, and we finally arrived over Saki on a lovely clear morning once again to waggle our wings to announce our presence. Unfortunately the weather deteriorated the closer we got to Moscow and we ended up flying at 3,000ft below a solid cloud base. We had made good time, however, but despite our efforts, it was actually to be another four days before Mrs Churchill was ready to depart, and as a result, we found ourselves in the Russian capital when we heard that the war in Europe was finally over.

It is very difficult to describe how we felt, but I recall the main feature of our own VE Day was a call to attend the British embassy where we were all able to hear the PM's voice making the historic announcement that fighting was at an end. This was followed by a very moving service of thanksgiving held in the ballroom of the residence. It was conducted by a RNVR padre who had been visiting Moscow from the British naval headquarters at Murmansk, where the movement of the much under-publicised arctic convoys was supervised. Many members of the various allied missions were present including Edouard Herriot, the French statesman and his wife who had recently been released from German captivity. He said that the last time he had heard Churchill's voice was in 1940 at Tours making an impassioned plea for the French to hold out and not surrender. He had wept then in defeat; now he was weeping unashamedly for joy.

The Russians did not sign the formal surrender documents until May 9, so we ended up with two days of victory celebrations. We were urged by our embassy to be visible in the streets in our RAF uniforms, and were soon mobbed by jubilant crowds and hoisted upon their shoulders. After we had been positively identified as part of 'Equipage Churchill', we were tossed into the air as a local sign of their approval and goodwill. I found the whole affair pretty alarming, and was obliged to dive into the occasional drinking hole to escape further attention.

The next day we were given tickets to the Bolshoi where we had the privilege of seeing the great ballerina, Semenova, take the leading role in Swan Lake. When she came to take her final curtain, she graciously turned the applause towards the former royal box and the whole cast and audience applauded Mrs Churchill. That night we watched a magnificent firework display from the warmth and comfort of our hotel.

It was almost a pity to leave, such was the hospitality, but we were all keen to be home and celebrating our survival with our families. I sent my wife Brenda and Clive a cable, a copy of which I still possess. Take-off was set for 08.00 GMT (10.00 local time), but before that there was considerable farewell activity. A large number of dignitaries came to say their goodbyes, including the foreign minister Molotov – a very great honour indeed. We had quite a few boxes of souvenirs to load, plus the inevitable official mail and diplomatic bags, which taxed our stowage capacity. This capacity was stretched to the limit by one item in particular, a massive portrait of Stalin that was a gift for the prime minister. We only just managed to get it on board. At one point we had so many well wishers on the aircraft that the weight threatened to tip us up. Fortunately, some quick thinking by the two stewards averted what could have been an embarrassing incident, the tail strut having already been removed for take-off. We were soon safely on our way to Malta.

For the remainder of May and June, the Skymaster remained in the hangar but for occasional air tests and training flights to keep our hand in. I fulfilled routine duties with the Hendon squadron aircraft. There was an air of anti-climax around the station, now that the war was won, and our own future was in doubt. At the beginning of July, we went to Berlin to inspect the RAF facilities at Gatow for the forthcoming conference. The PM was to have a few days' break at Biarritz, before proceeding onwards. As it was, I returned to Northolt with very obvious jaundice, and was admitted to the hospital at RAF Uxbridge. The navigator from Ozzie Morris' crew (now on Ascalon) took my place.

My days with 24 Squadron, the Skymaster and her magnificent crew had finally come to an end.

CHAPTER ELEVEN
TO WASHINGTON AND BEYOND

When I finally emerged from hospital, Bill, Jack, Jock and the rest of the crew had gone, as had all of the aircraft, away in Berlin. I also had a new station commander, Group Captain Ford, who had taken over from Dickie Legg. Before Dickie's departure, however, he had told me that he was being posted to Washington as air attaché. This was most fortuitous for me, because he asked whether I would be interested in joining him as his assistant. It was an easy decision, and by the end of July I was posted from Northolt to the Air Ministry in a supernumerary capacity while I was 'prepared' for my next job.

I was excited by what the future had in store, but saddened to hear of the sudden demise of the Skymaster and the VIP Flight just a few weeks later. Churchill, to his intense frustration and profound shock, lost the post-war election to be replaced by Clement Attlee. Attlee, a Labour man and staunch socialist (despite, or perhaps even because of, his public school upbringing[6]), had no time for the trappings of wealth or ostentation, and the Skymaster took its last VIP flight on August 2. The aircraft had, of course, only been on lease-lend to the British government, and therefore had to be returned under the agreement. This was primarily to protect the three major airlines –

[6.] Attlee was an old boy of Haileybury as, coincidentally, were a great number of famous wartime RAF senior commanders including Sir Trafford Leigh-Mallory, Sir John Slessor, Sir William Dickson and Sir Brian Baker.

Pan American, American Overseas, and TWA – from unwelcome competition from BOAC. Much later it was damaged in a landing somewhere in China where it had been allocated to General Marshall, by now the US ambassador in Peking. It had been abandoned – a sad and rather depressing end to what was once the queen of the skies.

Meantime I prepared for my return to the US. I was lucky to have had Dickie as my 'sponsor'. We had become friends while I was the living-in local flight commander. As well as being our own home station, Northolt was the main base of a famous Polish Spitfire wing of Fighter Command. I had joined a small fraternity known as the English speaking union representing the small number of resident RAF officers amongst the more numerous Poles. By virtue of my connection with Number 10, I came to see considerably more of my CO than others of similar rank, and got to know him rather well. Dickie had been pre-war RAF, from the single-seater world, and had for a time been the adjutant of 603 (City of Edinburgh), one of the auxiliary squadrons. When war came, he found himself in Athens as assistant air attaché for Turkey (the air attaché himself was based in Ankara), and when Greece fell he managed to make his way back to the UK. He wanted to get back into the fighter world, but never did, being posted firstly to Sharjah before taking over as station commander, Northolt. He was a gentleman in every respect, and I liked him enormously. I also got to know his wife who was only slightly older than Brenda. It was a happy, and in my case most fortuitous relationship.

It was wonderful to be in the US again. I was of course based within the embassy, where the work of an air attaché was essentially representational with other foreign delegates in the capital. With the USAF itself it was largely a liaison job, with a friendly air force already well known to us through the close co-operation we had enjoyed during the war. We even had our own aircraft – an Avro Anson 19 – with which to show off British products. It was a wonderful old crate, a post-war passenger development of the basic version that had served the RAF so well in training. Wherever we went we were teased about how many turns it took to raise the undercarriage by hand, and were quick to point out that we now had modern hydraulics.

On one occasion we flew it, in stages, to Havana to negotiate with the Cubans for facilities that could be used by the embryonic British South American Airways (BSAA). BSAA was attempting to establish routes to Central and South America but competition was fierce. We already knew that we would be dealing with Juan Trippe and PanAm who were firmly in the saddle in the region. Taxiing up to the main terminal building with a flat tyre, I recall, did not enhance our arrival in the Cuban capital!

The RAF worked tirelessly to promote what might now be termed 'Brand GB' across the globe, and particularly the Americas. One of the first ever pathfinder units, 35 Squadron, paid us a visit in the summer of 1946 in their wartime Lancasters that had been especially painted all white for the tour. They had tremendous fun renewing old acquaintances. They were followed later by 617 Squadron, which by then had exchanged their Lancasters for the newer Lincolns. Alongside the Boeing B29 Superfortresses, which were now in abundant supply, our old tail-down aircraft looked positively ancient.

Representational duties took Brenda and me all over the US. I found that my previous experience of a more mundane daily life in an average working US household where I lodged near the Link factory was valuable background to the more exotic life of the Washington diplomatic round. We met numerous high-ranking officers on our travels, perhaps none more famous at the time than General Carl Spaatz, who had been commander of the US Strategic Air Forces in Europe and later, the Pacific.

I had the very great honour of receiving from him the US Legion of Merit for my contribution to the basic training of air force navigators and for my efforts at the Binghamton factory developing the CNT simulator. I remember the award ceremony quite clearly. It was in Spaatz's office in the Pentagon, and as Dickie and I entered, the general – who knew Dickie very well – exclaimed: "Gee, Dick, if I'd have know you were coming, I would have had my pants pressed!" My citation was signed by no less a man than President Harry Truman.

The Americans could be queer fellows. On the one hand, they could be very friendly and informal, and put you instantly at your ease; on the other, they were almost Teutonic in their ruthlessness and inflexibility. Regulations could not be challenged. That's not to say that we didn't make friends while we were there. I was particularly good friends with an air force liaison officer, Colonel MacDonald[7]. Charles MacDonald had flown P38s during the war and served alongside the world famous aviator, Charles Lindbergh, while Lindbergh had been working for Lockheed in the Pacific teaching pilots how to get the most out of the aircraft for range. The Americans were famous for having only two throttle settings: fully open or fully closed!

As well as high-ranking military men, we also met various high-ranking politicians, among them Ham Andrews. Congressman Andrews was a Republican from Buffalo, New York, who, not withstanding his own party membership, was chairman of the armed services committee. Through him I was able to visit Capitol Hill on more than one occasion and learn something about how the US government worked. I was actually in the chamber on the day that the act was debated and passed, creating the United States Air Force (previously the US Air Corps of the US Army) of which Spaatz was appointed its first chief of staff.

Ham was a charming man, and took quite a shine to Brenda and me, inviting us to the most magnificent parties at his country estate. Here we found ourselves socialising with many of the country's most powerful men of that time, including such names as General Ira Eaker, one time commander of the US Eighth Air Force, and General Hoyt Vandenberg who was to succeed Spaatz as the chief of staff of the USAF.

It was a marvellous time to be in the US. The currency of the RAF, so soon after the war, was at its peak, and we were made welcome wherever we went. It could on occasions, however, become a little crowded. As well as the air attachés attached to the embassy, there were various missions and a separate RAF 'delegation' commanded by Air Chief Marshal Sir Guy Garrod, who was also the RAF member of the military staff committee, United Nations organisation, New York. While Sir Guy was no bother, the same could not be said for his deputy, Sir Victor Goddard, who took umbrage that Dickie

---

[7] MacDonald commanded the 475th Fighter Group and was the third ranking ace in the Pacific during the Second World War.

had a rather splendid Packard for official duties. Sir Victor, an air marshal, could not understand why a mere group captain had his own car. He decided that he, and not Dickie, should be the air attaché, prompting Dickie to seek the advice of the ambassador. It was quickly sorted, and Sir Victor was told in no uncertain terms that air attaché appointments were nothing to do with the RAF delegation.

The ambassador to Washington in the early days of my posting was Edward Wood, an austere gentleman better known as Lord Halifax. Halifax had of course gained some notoriety before the war for supporting Chamberlain's policy of appeasement (a policy that was subsequently shown to be fatally flawed). He had been in Washington since 1941, and ran what would best be described as a 'traditional' embassy from the beautiful splendour of the Lutyens Building on Massachusetts Avenue. To be invited to the embassy was on a par to being invited to Buckingham Palace, and a significant honour. They arranged, for example, formal investitures (a number of the senior US military commanders received honorary KCBs and KBEs) in which I invariably had a role to play. Halifax had been born with a withered arm, but made up for it by having incredibly strong fingers. Pinning medals to an individual's chest was not a problem for him, but he struggled when the honour being conferred meant putting a ribbon around somebody's neck. He therefore worked out a system. I would present him with the ribbons on a cushion that he would take with his good hand and place both ends on the recipient's left shoulder. I would then hold one end while he deftly completed the task, and the 'formality' of the occasion was maintained.

We had some quite brilliant ministers and secretaries on the embassy staff, including the first secretary, a rising star by the name of Donald Maclean. He was later head of chancery – a powerful position – and a most engaging character with an impeccable background. I found him perfectly charming, if a little smooth, but there was not even the slightest hint of his communist leanings as one of what would later be called 'the Cambridge five'. The only notoriety he gained while I knew him was for his taste in flowery waistcoats!

Halifax returned in May 1946 to be replaced by Sir Archibald Clark Kerr, recently returned from Moscow (and an early VIP passenger on Ascalon). The Americans had been most impressed with Halifax as he was, in their minds, a 'real' member of the nobility, a real 'oil'. Sir Archibald had only recently been elevated to a peerage, as Baron Inverchapel. The style of Inverchapel could not have been in greater contrast to that of his predecessor. Perhaps it had something to do with his Australian/Scottish parentage. He was friendlier, and considerably more democratic. On one occasion I was sent for and he asked me to sit down – something that you never did in the ambassador's presence. He then pointed to a silver tray with a decanter of whiskey on it and said: "Help yourself, boy." (For some reason he always called me 'boy'.)

Inverchapel managed, unwittingly perhaps, to upset a number of his hosts, especially those that were most conservative or right wing. The Americans were scandalised, for example, that he brought with him from Moscow a Russian valet as part of his personal retinue. Ambassadors were privileged to bring in their personal staff without question and to secure visas for them, but to give a visa to a Russian was not a popular choice.

My time in Washington was fast coming to an end, and I faced the prospect of returning to the UK and a somewhat uncertain future. Before I had left, it had been patently obvious that general duties (GD) pilots were more favourably placed for promotion than GD navigators by reason of command opportunities, having had the chance to display their leadership qualities and operational knowledge in charge of an aircraft, flight or squadron. In Bomber Command, a few outstanding navigators had been in command of squadrons, but they were the exception that disproved the rule. There was pressure, therefore, to get on a pilot's course as soon as possible, not just amongst we navigators, but also from all GD branches – wireless operators, flight engineers et al.

There had been some provision for engineers (including some signals specialists) and doctors to be given flying training, and then their wings. Some had proved outstanding as test pilots and flying doctors, with excellent career prospects. Others never proceeded beyond the FTS stage, but nevertheless wore the coveted pilot's wings and thereby qualified for advancement. I felt I was in danger of being left behind.

The air council were well aware (which we were not at the lower levels) of the coming enlarged requirement for navigators with the advent of the jet bombers, particularly the 'V' force. Understandably, they did not want highly experienced navigators to become highly inexperienced pilots. But it was simply not enough to keep them in the Service with the promise of a permanent commission (which I already held) but little prospect of promotion.

It was against this background that I sailed home from New York in October 1947, bringing my family with me, enjoying the comfort of a new Cunarder, the *Media*. Docking in Liverpool, we were met by my younger brother, Geoffrey, who was by now a first officer with Cunard. He had had a most eventful war, having had two ships torpedoed from under him. On the first occasion he had been on a Fyffes banana boat, and spent several days adrift in a lifeboat before being spotted, by pure chance, by a passing Blue Star meat boat en route to Argentina. He and his comrades were landed at Buenos Aires, and taken in by the local seaman's mission, where they were given clothes and accommodation. Disgracefully, his pay had been stopped the moment he came ashore. On the second occasion, he was torpedoed in the channel by an E-boat – a fast German motor torpedo boat.

Geoff had also been junior third officer on the RMS *Queen Mary*, and part of the crew on the day in October 1942 when the massive liner collided with the cruiser HMS *Curacoa*, cutting her clean in two. Only just over 100 of her complement of 440 men survived, and the *Queen Mary* could not stop to pick up the struggling men in the waters, for fear of enemy submarines. Although he was not on watch, my brother clearly remembers a shudder as the two ships came together. It was a terrible tragedy.

After a few days on leave, I found myself posted on a Spec.N refresher course at Shawbury (Salop) where I quickly realised how out of touch I was with the latest wartime developments in electronic navigation. Having spent two years flying with Churchill and other VVIPs and two years in Washington, I had lost touch with RAF station life, having led a somewhat sheltered and some might say exotic life since the spring of 1943. Having satisfied the instructors and myself that I was still fit for purpose, I was posted to the Central

Bomber Establishment (CBE) at Marham.

The CBE had formed at Marham towards the end of 1945, and to all intents and purposes mirrored its sister unit, the central fighter establishment at West Raynham, the principal difference being that our role encompassed the testing and proving of new bomber aircraft (rather than fighter aircraft) prior to their deployment within front-line stations.

The unit was divided into two: the tactical wing commanded by Group Captain Sydney Bufton; and the development wing led by Group Captain Richard Collard. I was to get to know both men well in the coming months, and admired them greatly.

'Sid', as he was known, had served with distinction in the war, receiving the DFC at much the same time as I received my own. He was the man largely credited with helping to create the elite pathfinder force, and became great friends with the group's first commander, Donald Bennett. Later he had been director of bomber operations, and was therefore admirably equipped for his new role.

Dick Collard was also a true gentleman, who had needed every ounce of his calm demeanour and diplomatic skills to survive nearly three years as a prisoner of war, often as the senior British officer (SBO) in the camps in which he was held. He had kept his men together including a number of Norwegian officers (he had also been awarded the Norwegian War Cross) in the face of the Russian advance, and threatened the Germans that they would be tried as war criminals if anything happened to them that contravened the Geneva Convention. He had been awarded the DSO and DFC before being shot down over Duisburg flying Wimpey IIs with 12 Squadron in 1942. (Dick later joined Handley Page and tried to get me to go with him but I declined. Had he been working for De Havilland or Rolls, I might have considered it, but Handley Page was not a company I aspired to join.)

The commandant of this prestigious outfit was none other than 'Crack 'em' Staton, now an air commodore. Staton was a veteran of the first war, and later CO of 10 Squadron, who as I recalled earlier had dropped his bombs 'safe' on the *Tirpitz*. Like Dick, he had had to endure three long years as a prisoner of war, but this time in the hands of the Japanese. Physically he had suffered considerably, having all of his teeth removed for refusing to answer questions under interrogation, but he was still a man of imposing size and character. He was also obsessed with shooting, especially revolvers (he later represented the UK in the 1948 and 1952 Olympics), so much so that he appeared to spend every waking moment practising on the range.

I was attached to Dick Collard's development wing, as navigation officer. There was plenty to keep us busy. When we took delivery of the Skymaster in my days with 24 Squadron, the aircraft came with a handbook the thickness of the Oxford English dictionary. British aircraft arrived with little more than a thin pamphlet of pilots' notes. It was down to the CBE to put more of the proverbial meat on the bone, conducting such things as high altitude trials and take-off runs with different loads for which we took full advantage of Marham's new 3,000ft runway. There was a mixed assortment of aircraft, notably the Lincoln but also the impressive B35 and PR36 variants of the Mosquito.

Trial flights took us as far afield as Shallufa in the Canal Zone and Khartoum, testing how the various aircraft performed in extreme weather conditions. I lost a great deal of weight working through the hottest part of the day, but it was good for my tan. I also got to see quite a bit of Khartoum town, spending time at the Sudan club and enjoying dinner at The Grand, overlooking Omdurman. In the Lincoln trials, we also got as far as Nairobi – a city that was little more than an overgrown country market town run by extremely lazy English settlers – but managed to make a detour to photograph the crater of Kilimanjaro and Mount Kenya, both of which had snow on them.

For ballast we used wartime unfused 1,000lbs bombs, some of which were inclined to go off 'bang' on impact when jettisoned over the sea, especially those that had been left out in the desert ammunition dumps. They were notoriously (and understandably) unstable.

On some of these occasions, especially when flying the Mossie, my skipper was David Green, one of the flight commanders. David was quiet yet assured, and a highly competent pilot. Once when we were flying together in a B35 Mosquito he demonstrated a dead stick landing. Approaching the runway, he cut both engines and then immediately shoved the nose forward until the aircraft had the speed and the position over the airfield for landing. Then just as suddenly he hauled back on the control column and executed a perfect three-point landing. David was another with the DSO and DFC, who had been stooging around in Hampdens with 44 Squadron while I had been trying to find targets in my Whitley. (After he left us he went on to command a Canberra squadron and then one of the first Victor squadrons. He was SASO 1 Group until his retirement as an air commodore in 1971.)

I was at the establishment when the first Berlin crisis was at its zenith, which in turn led to the rather accelerated deployment to the UK of the 35th Wing of the US Strategic Air Command that arrived with three squadrons of B29 Superfortresses, one of which flew into Marham in June 1948. They were capable of carrying the US atomic bomb, but whether they brought any of the things with them I never knew. Whatever the Soviets thought, or knew, this rapid deployment certainly helped to relieve the pressure on communications in and out of the city at that time.

The speed with which we welcomed our American friends was recognised in an official notice from Colonel S.T. Wray, OC USAF detachment to Marham to Air Commodore Staton, CB, DSO, MC, DFC. The notice read:

> "I desire to express the appreciation of General Hoyt. S. Vandenberg, chief of staff, US Air Force and Lieutenant General Curtis E. Le May, commanding general, US Air Forces in Europe for the manner in which personnel at RAF station Marham prepared for, and received, US Air Force personnel.
>
> "The courtesy, efficiency and willingness with which the US personnel were met, processed and cared for, imposed as it was as an additional burden on top of normal activities, and at the sacrifice of two weekends, reflects the highest credit on the personnel of Marham.
>
> "The efficacy and unity of purpose with which the US Air Force has enjoyed in joint operation with the

RAF is a matter of record and the treatment accorded to us on this occasion further cements these bonds uniting the two air forces. It has given me much personal pleasure to have been associated with Marham personnel on this occasion and I wish to thank all ranks for their indefatigable efforts in this regard."

Having aircraft the size of a B29 on our station meant that space on the airfield as well as in the mess was at a premium. We had been squeezed up in every way, but being well aware of USAF ways, in the air as well as on the ground, I felt much more in my element and believe I was instrumental in smoothing the operational workings of the base. I also managed to wangle a few flights in the Superfortresses, as well as their hack B17 that they maintained for casual communications duties.

It was in November that Dick Collard told me he wanted a word. A most prestigious posting had come up, as senior navigation instructor at the RAF college, Cranwell. Having spent a hectic twelve months learning about RAF bomber operations and the future Command, and the chance of moving on from being a navigation specialist, I now found myself having to pack up and move to a totally new environment as the first non-Cranwell graduate to join the staff.

I was in for a bumpy ride.

CHAPTER TWELVE

A TESTING TIME

I drove over from Marham, full of anticipation, and stopped for lunch in the little village of Swineshead. On arrival at Cranwell, I was directed to the station mess where I would live for the first three days before I could transfer over to the college mess proper.

My formal appointment was as senior navigation tutor, in which capacity I was responsible to Patrick Johnson, the ex-vice chancellor at Magdalene College, in his new role as director of studies. Under him were two senior tutors, one for humanistic subjects, the other for science and engineering. I naturally came under the latter. In addition, I also had allegiance to the chief flying instructor for the conduct of the cadets' navigation exercises. I was to take an active part in college activity.

I found myself in the cradle of the pilots' empire – Lord Trenchard's baby – amid the crisis going on about the academic level of entrants aspiring to permanent commissions, a crisis that was to affect both the army and the navy. Fewer and fewer ex-schoolboys were opting for the armed services. They wanted a university education, believing that a graduate had a better chance in life. Could the three service cadet colleges be upgraded to university status and thereby offer degrees?

From the outset there was conflict. The RN questioned whether a long-haired graduate could ever have the necessary fighting (Nelsonian) spirit. The army was better placed having long since upgraded its gunner and sapper (ex-Woolwich) entrants in this way and believing it would be relatively easy to assimilate the signallers, for there was always the need for technically literate officers in such corps.

The RAF too needed technically able officers; the future of the jet engine, rocket weaponry and propulsion required a technical brain, and there were a few (such as Whittle) that we had already recruited. But for the GD branch they must have the potential to fly. In practice, after a year's attempt at Cranwell, it proved impossible to combine the academic freedom of a university course with the discipline/regularity of flying training.

Thus the RAF abandoned the idea of a degree-awarding Cranwell course in favour (eventually) of an ex-university entrance for all PC officers via the already established route of the university air squadrons. In this way the potential officer had to prove his ability to fly by undertaking elementary flying training during the long vacations. The failures could be weeded out, or diverted into ground branches, before actual enlistment. (All this was to come to my desk in 1970, when on return from two-and-half years in Moscow, I was made director of RAF recruitment.)

Cranwell, the first military air academy in the world, had opened in 1920 under the command of Air Commodore Longcroft. By the time I joined the staff, at the tail end of the era of ex-schoolboy cadet entrants, the college commandant was Air Commodore George Beamish. Beamish had recently taken over from Air Commodore Dick Atcherley who, like his twin brother, was said to be as mad as a March hare (the stories about them are legion) but by all accounts a most effective leader and inspirational commandant. Beamish was very different. One of a famous family of RAF officers, all of whom distinguished themselves in various ways, Beamish appeared to have only one ambition: to beat Sandhurst and Dartmouth at rugger and cricket. He had the tell-tale cauliflower ears of a rugby player, and a broken nose that had clearly been kicked and punched into shape. But then having been capped for Ireland, and being chairman of the RAF Rugby Union, his passion for the game was perhaps understandable. It was just a pity that flying training in those days appeared to take a second priority to sporting prowess.

Taking almost the exact opposite approach, and someone at Cranwell that I got on especially well with, was the CFI, Donald MacDonell. Donald was a strict disciplinarian, but whereas others were impressed by sport, Donald never lost sight of the fact that his pupils were there to fly. At one time when I was there he had a dreadful row with a parent for wanting to throw the son off the course. Every student at Cranwell, however, was carefully selected, the crème de la crème, and not 'allowed' to fail. Donald insisted upon the highest standards, and managed to win that particular battle.

After my own experiences on the outside, I found the college very claustrophobic and almost self-satisfied. There was an impression that only Cranwellians counted; the cadets were a long way from learning that the majority of aircrew then serving were by no means Cranwellian, but rather volunteer reservists such as myself. The system had developed a snobbism of its own and on my arrival the assistant commandant (Group Captain 'Doggie' Oliver[8]) impressed on me his ideas that they were trying to make officers and gentlemen from the background no longer so stratified as pre-war society.

In the long vacation the cadets could go sailing on the college yacht in the summer (a German windfall – war loot appropriated from the Luftwaffe Yacht Club at Kiel), skiing in the winter (at the RAF Germany survival school) and a variety of other sports all-year round. Gentlemanly pursuits were encouraged such as beagling and the local hunt would meet once per season at the college mess. Gliding was also available on the airfield, not that this was particularly gentlemanly but it all helped to broaden their outlook. Life in the college mess would ensure their table manners were taken care of and suitable members of staff (which let me in) had to dine-in with the cadets to set an example.

My offices were in the magnificent college building, and the lecture rooms were effectively laboratories – well equipped and spacious. My main problem was trying to re-orientate myself; to stop worrying about the future navigation of jet aircraft, or Bomber Command's policies in the immediate future. Instead of enjoying the thrill of despatching aircraft all over the world (I calculated I had flown more than 35,000 miles in nine months at Marham), I now had

---

[8.] J.O.W. Oliver CB, DSO, DFC – former CO of 85 Squadron during the Battle of Britain.

to concentrate on cadets – teaching them navigation and, above all, teaching them to be officers.

I felt straightaway that the cadets had something lacking in their education, beyond the academic, and should see something of everyday station life, to prepare them for the 'real' world after Cranwell. I therefore decided to use my initiative (on reflection a rather naïve thing to do) and went ahead with very provisional plans (without permission) for volunteers from the senior entry to go on an overseas navigation exercise in vacation time, using Lancasters borrowed from the Empire Air Navigation School at Shawbury whose CO, a very clever Anglo-Swiss by the name of Air Commodore 'Tubby' Vielle, I happened to know rather well (he was a Spec.N pilot and had been my chief instructor at Port Albert).

By flying a triangular route to Malta and Gibraltar, the cadets would get a glimpse of 'overseas'. The plan was to undertake the trip in the summer leave for the then senior entry-to-be, but when I offered it to Doggie Oliver for his approval, I was roundly castigated for having the nerve to involve 'outsiders' without his permission. I must admit that the whole incident left a rather sour taste in my mouth. I felt I was being paid to show initiative, but was now being rebuked for having done so. The trip was saved, however, when I pointed out that far from being 'outsiders', the CO of the EANS was ex-Cranwell, as were the AOC Malta and AOC Gibraltar!

Doggie relented, but I was always to bear in mind that these cadets were slender plants, and not yet fully fledged 'officers and gentlemen'. They should not be exposed to the brutal life of the common airmen until they had graduated.

I ran two of these overseas exercises in successive leave periods. Both were intended to give the cadets training in flight planning and cruise control, navigation techniques, general crew training and overseas flying conditions, and involved round trips of around 3,600 miles. The first, in the spring of 1949, went off without a hitch.

The second was slightly more eventful. Our party of twenty or so cadets spent three very pleasant days in Malta, where we toured Luqa airfield, visited the aircraft carrier HMS *Triumph* (her captain had been the naval attaché in Washington), and had a good look over the local radar installations and control stations. We also had the chance of swimming in St Paul's Bay and Comino, and were ready for our flight home, as the local newspaper reported it, "sun-tanned and happy". Unfortunately, having left the sanctuary of Malta for Gibraltar, the weather was such that we were diverted to Tangiers, of all places! I had the awful fear of 'losing' cadets in downtown Tangiers but fortunately the weather cleared quite quickly and so we were soon away. It was only a short hop across the Straits into True Blue territory where they were all safely entertained by a suitable programme of visits around and into the Rock of Gibraltar by the AOC's staff.

The social round at Cranwell was hectic, and soon after taking the post I found suitable accommodation on an estate of typical pre-war houses in nearby Sleaford, which meant that Brenda could come and share the load. By now my second son, Neil, had arrived, and the departure of his nurse to get married meant Brenda being lumbered with the housework as well as the two boys. Whereas our home life was comfortable, I was never easy with my appointment at Cranwell, and it was by sheer good fortune that I found myself selected, with a number of other senior experienced navigators, for the first course of the newly established RAF Flying College at Manby.

This was an amalgam of the three 'Empire' schools for flying (EFTS), navigation (EANS) and air armament (EAAS), creaming off the staff and aircraft, as required from each these schools. Each of the schools was subsequently downgraded to group captain commands, whereas our own college had an air commodore as commandant, in our case Air Commodore Andrew McKee.

'Square' McKee, as he was affectionately known, was as tall as he was broad as he was wide. He had enjoyed a good war, being highly decorated, and was enjoying an even better peace. As a leader, he was incredibly keen and very well liked and at one time commanded 75 Squadron, the New Zealand Wellington unit. One of his particular traits was his inability to remember anyone's names, with nearly always amusing consequences.

The purpose of the flying college was to train GD all-rounders who would be suitable, on promotion, to command the emerging strategic bomber force. Times were moving fast, and we needed the right people in the right place to command the new nuclear-armed V-Bomber force, and stations that combined surface-to-air missiles with manned all-weather fighter interceptors, carrying air-to-air weapons. It was essential to broaden out the students' education, getting away from the single-minded attitudes in Fighter and Bomber Commands.

The year's course at Manby, with its satellite and better runways at nearby Strubby, was designed to include a good background in aerodynamics and modern jet propulsion (completely new stuff for me), and for navigators an express provision that we were to be taught what it was like to be at the controls of a jet aircraft. In fact, due to kind friends who were QFIs, I was trained to fly solo in the college's Harvard trainer, as well as to have some hours in the dual jet trainers (the Meteor 7). I was able to satisfy myself (and others) that I could fly!

As students we heard most erudite talks from top designers, such as George Edwards of Vickers Armstrong, and the scientist Sir William Penny on what makes an atomic bomb detonate and how to make an H-Bomb. However his lecture went well over the heads of most of us. In the world of armaments we became more intimately acquainted with the effectiveness of weapons (or ineffectiveness, perhaps) which some of us had blithely distributed over the Third Reich.

In the piloting world, all of the pilots had to qualify on jet aircraft, regardless of previous experience. This made for some interesting exhibitions of flying, especially by those from the bomber or flying boat worlds in the cockpit of a tiny jet fighter for the first time.

Wing Commander Stafford Coulson was one such pilot who struggled to make the transition from four-engined bomber to single-seat jet. 'Staffy', the life and soul of any party and a confirmed drinking partner of mine, was an accomplished pathfinder (the former CO of 582 Squadron) more comfortable with throwing a Lancaster around the night skies of Germany than a nimble Meteor. To be flying with Staffy on interception exercises and listen to him curse as he tried to bring the camera gunsight to bear on the target was always amusing, especially afterwards when we were invited to a post-flight viewing of our results.

Wing Commander Percy Hatfield was another mad-type whose landings were worthy of note. Percy was a flying boat pilot, ex-95

Squadron, and attempted to put his Lincoln down on a runway in the same way he used to plop his Sunderland down on water, with often hair-raising results. In fairness to Percy, he hadn't flown a land-based aircraft for the better part of twenty years.

Others had no such difficulties. Lieutenant Commander Desmond Law RN, for example, one of our two naval pilots (the other was 'Willie' Simpson), converted with ease. Dickie Law, as he was known, had flown all manner of aircraft in the Fleet Air Arm and had previously thrilled — and to a certain extent terrified — crowds in the US with an aerobatic display in a Sea Hornet at Idlewild airfield in New York, (now JFK). I believe he later became a top rep with Hawker Siddeley.

'Liaison' flights were very much a feature of post-war flying, and in the autumn of 1950 we took the definition of training to new heights. Six aircraft were to fly more than 100,000 miles and visit no fewer than seventeen countries — both to practice our long-range navigation and to exchange information with our commonwealth and USAF colleagues.

The first three aircraft took off from Manby on October 18: two for Canada and the third for Australia and New Zealand. Over the next two days, three more aircraft departed: one for Alaska; one for the United States; and the final aircraft, on which I would be one of two navigators, was to fly around the world. In all, the aircraft were carrying seventy-five members of the staff and pupils from the college including three Australians, two Canadians, and two officers from the USAF. None was to visit his home country.

The lead aircraft, a Hastings, was flown by Group Captain George Lott. George was yet another airman with only one eye, having been blinded on the eve of the Battle of Britain. I recall that he blamed the navy for it, having been operated on by surgeons at the famous Royal Naval hospital at Haslar. His Hastings was bound for Australia and New Zealand by way of Malta, Iraq, Pakistan, Ceylon (Sri Lanka) and Malaya. It was due to complete its five-day, 9,000-mile journey to Darwin in fifty hours of flying.

Lott and his crew were wearing tropical kit, whereas the crews of the two Lincolns that left for Canada a short time after were clad in arctic clothing. These aircraft were captained by Squadron Leaders Robert

Radley and Ernest Tacon. Tacon was formerly of the King's Flight and one of our Kiwis. The two were to fly firstly to Keflavik in Iceland before proceeding to Goose Bay (Labrador), Ottawa, Edmonton, Trenton, and Summerside. They were to return by way of the Azores.

Two further Lincolns were scheduled to take off the following day, one for Alaska, and the second for the United States – a fact that seemed to amuse the press. The former aircraft, captained by Squadron Leader Peter McKeand, got off without a hitch to visit various US Alaskan Command bases. The second, a rather well known aircraft called Thor II, went u/s, and had to be replaced. As it was, the pilot, Wing Commander David McKinley (who had achieved fame for a polar research flight in 1945 in the original Aries aircraft with another friend of mine from the Spec.N world, 'Andy' Anderson) and his crew were delayed a further twenty-four hours before they could finally get away. His outward journey was to be a non-stop 2,100-mile flight to Labrador.

Our own aircraft was a Lincoln II, serial RE367, and taking the name Aries III. (For a short time it was known as a 'Lincolnian' but the name never caught on.) It was a standard Lincoln but for a few crucial modifications. All of the turrets had been removed and additional fuel tanks built in to the nose cone and bomb bay. We therefore carried 4,600 gallons of fuel – considerably more than the standard frontline aircraft at that time – which gave us a still-air range under optimum conditions of about twenty-two hours, or approximately 4,000 nautical miles.

The crew comprised four highly experienced pilots: Squadron Leader John Downey – who had joined Manby from EFTS where he had been one of the very best QFIs; Squadron Leader Alan Frank – who had flown Battles in France and later went on to become AOC 5 Group; Squadron Leader John MacKay – a Canadian with the DFC; and Dickie Law. As for the rest of the crew, there were two navigators, Squadron Leader Trevor Thain and myself, two signallers, and three craftsmen – a crew chief/fitter, radio fitter and instrument repairer/electrician.

With John as our chief pilot, we were in safe hands as we set off from Manby at 22.00 on October 20. We were to fly 9,000 miles in three hops: we landed first at Khartoum, from whence we made our onward flight to Mauritius, landing finally at the Royal Australian Air Force (RAAF) base in Pearce, near Perth, Western Australia.

The flight was not without incident. On the hop between Mauritius and Pearce, (which was undertaken at 11,000ft on oxygen all the way) a short while after we became airborne the artificial horizontal gyroscope failed. Effectively this was one of the pilot's most important blind–flying devices, and John had to make a decision as regards whether to turn back or go on and chance that we could manage on primary instruments alone. Fortunately, our instrument 'basher', Sergeant Rowden, had a spare instrument in his toolbox and within two or three minutes the gyroscope was exchanged. It was a remarkable piece of work, and enabled us to fly on normally.

We landed at Pearce, absolutely exhausted, after a journey of more than sixty hours in three days. I believe we were all thinking the same thing at that moment: we needed a beer. But it was not to be. We were met by a rather supercilious medical officer who demanded to see our inoculation certificates. They also nearly had a fit when they realised we had oranges on board – or rather the remains of the peel. With clearly no concept of what we had just been through, we were not allowed to move until the aircraft had been sprayed, and we had ourselves been decontaminated.

The stops at Khartoum and Mauritius lasted five hours and seven hours respectively. Apart from making the journey in very short time, the aircraft was also the first to make the east to west crossing of the Indian Ocean non-stop by a land plane. We also made the fastest point–to–point flight from London to Khartoum – a journey of 3064.28 statute miles in fourteen hours, twenty-three minutes and ten seconds – a fact later confirmed and certificated by the Royal Aero Club of the United Kingdom.

After our initial introduction, we received a more formal – though considerably more friendly – welcome from the officer commanding western area, RAAF, Wing Commander Ford, and the local newspaper – the *West Australian* – was on hand to capture the moment for posterity. We then spent a most pleasant week and a half being entertained by a hospitable nation, including a personal invitation by the team manager of the MCC to watch their match against Western Australia. Some of our crew had the opportunity of renewing old acquaintances from the war, among them my co-navigator, Trevor Thain, who was photographed in the *Perth Daily News* reminiscing with a former colleague, Squadron Leader G.F.D. Allen, about their time at 99 Squadron at Waterbeach. They had not seen or corresponded with each other for eight years, but Allen had recognised George in an official press photograph, and the station arranged that they should meet.

I too took a little personal time out to visit a cousin in Rottnest, Charlie Mitchell, who ran a local salt concession. To make the visit possible, RAAF Pearce flew me over in one of their Wirraway trainer aircraft, and I spent a most pleasant few hours with Charles catching up on family news.

From Pearce we flew down to Melbourne, landing late-morning for a stopover of four days further rest before our onward journey. Keeping to schedule we flew to San Francisco (Hamilton air force base) via Fiji (Nadi) and Honolulu (Hickham AFB), and thence back to Britain via Bermuda. Between Fiji and Honolulu, which we did non-stop in sixteen-and-a-half hours, we crossed the intertropical front (where the trade winds turn around and start blowing in the other direction) with comparative ease. Apart from some thunderstorms in South Carolina, our flight from San Francisco was also uneventful.

There was some embarrassment in Bermuda (Kindley AFB) when we realised that our English currency was of little use on a base that only took US dollars, and we had to use all of our guile to revictual with the rations required.

All six of our college aircraft made it home safely to worldwide acclaim, the plaudits being led by the AOC-in-C Training Command, who sent a message to the commandant that appeared on the station notice board on November 22. It read:

> "Delighted to hear of the safe return of your many and varied world-wide flights. Please convey to the captains of aircraft, their aircrews and maintenance personnel, and all connected with the organisation of these flights, my appreciation and congratulations on their success. Also a

special word of congratulations to the captain and crew of Aries on their record non-stop flight from Mauritius to Perth. This all goes to show what can be achieved by good organisation, skill, initiative, and good team work. Well done."

It was a fitting finale to the end of the course.

Our record-breaking around the world flight was not the only significant long-range expedition that I undertook in my two years at Manby.

In April 1951 we, that is Group Captain David McKinley, John Downey and myself, organised a weekend training exercise to Bermuda in Aries. Officially, it was to give some of our pupil aircrew valuable experience in long-range navigation and pilotage. Unofficially, it just so happened that the dates chosen for the exercise coincided with the weekend that Dickie Law and his fiancé Patricia had decided to get married, in Pembroke, Bermuda! We routed to Bermuda via Goose Bay, but flew back directly – a non-stop flight of some seventeen hours. It was worth every minute.

A slightly less gratuitous opportunity came our way in July. In the field of navigation we were in the forefront of what was known as high latitude flying; the idea of a Soviet bomber attack 'over the top' was much discussed. Manby, and EANS Shawbury, had a proud record of undertaking flights over the geographic and magnetic north poles. They had started in May 1945 with David McKinley's first polar research flight in Aries I, the converted EANS Lancaster. Numerous flights were then completed between 1947 and 1950. And then came our turn.

We were again to be part of a much wider navigation training operation involving five aircraft (six if you included the Hastings that flew on ahead with the ground crews) and again we would be using Aries III because of her enormous range. Keflavik in Iceland was chosen as an advanced base for all of the aircraft. Four (commanded by the recently promoted Wing Commander Alan Frank, and Squadron Leaders John Lawrence, Robert Radley and John Downey) were to fly a 2,478 circular course from Keflavik to Shannon Island, off the west

Tour party to Bermuda for Dickie Law's wedding with
John Downey (third from right) and David McKinley (seventh
from right). The author is second from left.

coast of Greenland, and back to Keflavik. Aries would fly from
Keflavik to Eielson AFB via the North Geographic Pole, twenty-six
miles from Fairbanks, and should have an ample reserve of fuel in her
tanks. This route would cover a distance of 3,090 nautical miles, and
take around eighteen hours and thirty minutes of flying. Homeward it
was planned to fly direct from Eielson to Manby – a distance of 3,600
miles, over the North Magnetic Pole. The guiding principle in the
selection of these routes was that they should offer the maximum challenge to the crew, whilst not impinging on safety. They would also give
maximum practical distances in high latitudes, and include a long
flight over areas of low horizontal magnetic field strength.

We had yet another highly experienced and highly decorated crew.
The captain and first pilot was Wing Commander Robert Frogley, the

former CO of 50 Squadron during the war. He had two co-pilots, Wing Commander Philip Heal and Wing Commander Andrew Humphrey, later to become CAS. With regards to navigators, there were three of us. On this occasion I was the first navigator, with Flight Lieutenants Jillings and Grocott lending support. Two radio operators and two other specialists completed the crew of ten, and we were joined by Mr Jackson, a correspondent from Reuters.

Before the main event, we undertook a ten-hour 'shake-down' flight to Iceland and back, the only air training we thought necessary during which crew drills were practiced.

The conditions we needed for observation of the sun and the moon meant the flight from Iceland had to be taken between July 24 and July 28, and it was on the morning of the 24th that we took off from Keflavik, fully loaded, and climbed to our ideal cruising altitude of 11,000ft. It was soon clear, however, with the cloud build up and weather forecast ahead that we would have to climb higher. Even at 14,000ft, we could not completely escape the clouds, and ice quickly began to form. Frogley achieved another 2,000ft but at the cost of alarmingly high fuel consumption. Fortunately the weather cleared and we were soon able to reduce our height until glimpses of the polar sea were clearly visible. Thousands of small blue lakes of thawed water potted the surface of the ice. We fixed our position over the pole as accurately as we could at 10.30GMT, and half an hour later made W/T contact with Eielson. It was somehow incongruous flying in Arctic conditions in shirtsleeves on the flight deck; as it was hot and sunny.

Despite concerns about our fuel consumption earlier in the flight, we needn't have worried. It was soon evident that we would have sufficient fuel in the tanks with some to spare. The weather, however, closed in, and as we progressed towards the coast of Alaska we flew through sleet and rain and were obliged to fly in and out of the clouds, well above the Brooks Range. I could see little of the ground below, but could identify the Colville river as we began to let down. We arrived in Eielson in just over eighteen hours, about an hour-and-a-half longer than we had estimated.

Our return was somewhat delayed. An engine problem, a coolant leak, meant we had no option but to wait for a new powerplant to be delivered and fitted, and that meant having to wait for one to arrive from the UK. The ground crews did a remarkably quick job given the circumstances, but it meant that we were unable to commence our flight home until early August, and that meant that the moon was not available to us for providing a fix.

Our time on the station, however, was far from wasted. We could not speak too highly of the friendliness and co-operation shown by the local USAF personnel, and we managed to make a number of flights in the weather variants of their B29 Superfortresses, making us honorary members of their 'society of pole vaulters'.

We also borrowed some rods and tackle and flew down to Lake Minchumina in a Dakota to do some pike fishing. The aircraft transporting us suffered a burst tyre as it came into land, veering off the runway and into a ditch. No-one was hurt, and it didn't affect our enjoyment. The air force simply sent another Dakota to pick us up.

The return leg started at 18.03GMT on August 3, and we climbed to 11,000ft through layered cloud and rain. By Fort Yukon the weather began to get better and by the time the Richardson Mountains were reached, the skies were brilliantly clear. Our radio team could make only spasmodic and unsatisfactory contact with various ground stations but managed to speak to the operator at Alert Bay radio, the most northerly Canadian airstrip, on HF who seemed delighted to hear us on air and especially pleased with our most British of callsigns, Mike Mike Uncle Baker William!

The expected tail wind helped our journey, and Aries was holding up well. Conditions were clear up until Ellesmere Land, and we decided to climb before running into cloud and threatening our fuel consumption. It was possible to see the Wolstenholme Fjord on the Greenland side of Baffin Bay, and Cape Dunsterville to the north, a distance of some 150 miles. Visibility in Baffin Bay was also excellent, and the brilliant sunshine turned the icebergs and other floating ice into blues and greens of every shade. Keflavik was in easy range, and after another few hours we at last began to descend in and out of strato-cumulus cloud with the first visual pinpoint of the British Isles at Cape Wrath. Weather checks were made on various airfields by voice radio until at last we were in touch with home base, and landed, in the rain, after a flight of nineteen hours and thirty-five minutes. We had sufficient fuel left in the tanks for a further one hour of flying.

The flight was a tremendous success. In my report published in the *Polar Record* afterwards, I said that the aim of the exercise was to develop our polar navigation techniques, and that we had achieved what we set out to achieve. We became aware of the development of NORAD, the radar defence line across Canada and Alaska, providing early warning of the approach of Soviet bombers, and of course missiles, aimed at the North American continent. Officers at Manby not only increased their knowledge and confidence of putting theory into practice, but also developed a wider conception of intercontinental military aviation. Surely the end of 'Mercator mentality' in the RAF, as Trenchard called it. Our crew's knowledge of the physical geography and meteorology of the polar area was widened enormously. We brought back a good many photographs that we shared with the Scott Polar Research Institute.

At the end of my course (by which time we had a new commandant in the form of another one-eyed senior officer, Air Commodore Sid Ubee), I was retained on the staff as the senior navigation instructor, with the prospect of further widening my experience in every respect – except in the world of piloting, for I had already had my 'allowance' of hands-on experience. Indeed I was specifically told that my pilot training was to be taken no further.

The cost of running the course, each year, in flying time and in employing such a number of instructors and students for a full year drew adverse comment from the financiers at higher levels of the RAF. Furthermore, the Lincoln was looking decidedly old-fashioned next to the English Electric Canberra that was now coming to the fore.

I amassed some 450 hours in each of the two years I was at Manby. Not long after I departed, in 1952, the course was shortened and, sadly, the far-ranging flights were largely curtailed.

I left on promotion to wing commander at the end of 1952 and was delighted, in the New Year's Honours list of 1953, to learn that Her Majesty had approved the award of an Air Force Cross (AFC). It meant another trip to the palace for the investiture, to which I took Brenda and my sister with me. A photograph taken at the time

Outside Buckingham Palace with the author's sister and Brenda to receive the AFC.

appeared shortly after in my local newspaper in Croydon.

In my new role I had been posted to Air Ministry in the directorate of operational requirements. This was a three-year stint dealing with installing the latest 'electronic navigational gear' into the V-Bombers and we had started thinking of future requirements for a proposed supersonic bomber that was later cancelled by Duncan Sandys – Winston Churchill's son-in-law – in favour of missiles.

The posting, a desk job, gave me the chance to buy a house and commute every day. It was concerned with the new aircraft being ordered for the RAF, and with future developments. It was a most interesting and busy time. I came into close contact with project designers and development engineers and this involved visiting Farnborough as well as the Radar Research Establishment at Malvern and Pershore. Not only was side-scanning primary radar being developed with fixed aerials along the fuselage for the future, but radar measurement of drift and groundspeed at the RRE was also almost ready for production. The first of these promised to give us extremely high definition radar; the latter, with suitable computers, provided the navigator with his DR position on counters from accurate measurement of drift and groundspeed. This was a step towards automatic navigation not to be truly achieved until sat nav appeared some years later.

Tempting invitations to leave the air force and join one of these up and coming instrument firms came my way on a regular basis, with the attraction of a company car and an expense account. One in particular came from Harvey Schwartz, the charismatic leader of Decca who was actively trying to promote his Decca navigator system to the RAF and wanted me to sell it for him. But with the responsibility of two young boys at boarding schools, and the knowledge that one's worth to a particular company might quickly fade, I had no real nerve for the outside world – at least not at this stage. Besides, my career seemed to be developing more widely, and although theoretically 'flying a mahogany bomber', I actually managed to get in a number of flights, especially at the weekends, both with research establishments' aircraft and on a variety of service units.

On one occasion, for example, while I was on leave, I wangled a trip to Bahrain delivering a new Mosquito, returning by BOAC. On another, I managed to fix a trip with the RCAF on their scheduled transatlantic service to Dorval, and then on to Vancouver and back – all this in twelve days 'escape' from the office. This was in the military version of the DC4M, powered with Rolls-Royce Merlin engines. My zeal for travel was at the expense of time with the family, I realised later, but I was still selfish for flying.

While I was at the directorate I was invited to fly supernumerary with a BOAC Boeing Stratocruiser transatlantic flight to Dorval and back, exploring the use of jet streams. These aircraft, which were effectively B29s married to a new bulbous fuselage (not dissimilar to the relationship between a York and a Lancaster), were operating regularly at altitudes that I had not flown at previously (they had a service ceiling above 32,000ft).

I also managed to attach myself to a signals unit at Watton, in Norfolk, where I indulged a variety of aircraft, including the RAF version of the B29, which we called the 'Washington', on various 'research' assignments. In these many and varied ways I gained experience in further 'types' and augmented my navigational knowledge as well as adding a useful 300 or so more hours of flying in my logbook.

The three years went rapidly by. But I was not yet to leave my office chair, finding myself posted to the Joint Services Staff College at Latimer, Buckinghamshire. Latimer is a wonderful spot in the Chess Valley on the Herts/Bucks border where I made a great many new and interservice friends. If I am honest, I was rather idle, but there was always the advantage that I could get home easily at weekends. This was to be only a six-month escape from the navigation world to which I was promptly returned, to a post at the Royal Aircraft Establishment (RAE) at Farnborough. There was again compensation in that I could rent a large house in nearby Cove, with space for all of us and a large garden to boot. I was once more close to flying.

My work, however, in the instrument department (IAP) was not to my liking, being concerned with the theoretical design of a navigation and bombing system for the manned, supersonic bomber of the future. The system was intended to release, at the appropriate moment, the RAF's first 'stand-off' flying bomb. Everything was in the research phase and the project was ultimately cancelled in a great burst of 'cuts'.

Although I worked in the 'factory' as opposed to the 'flying' wing of the RAE, I was extremely lucky to find my overall RAF commanding officer was Group Captain David McKinley, under whom I had already served at Manby and in the Air Ministry. Once again I was able to keep up my flying hours away from my immediate 'factory' job. I was able to fly the met research flight's Canberra for a number of trips – they were always pleased to have an extra navigator for their long and sometimes rather boring high-altitude flights – and I also got involved in the sale of a number of Canberra light bombers to the Indian Air Force. This was a deal pushed through by the zeal of Mrs Gandhi who I had the great honour of meeting at a reception at the Indian High Commission and discussing the advantages of the Canberra over competition from the Russians. She didn't want the IAF to buy the Russian Ilyushin IL28s (Nato code-name 'Beagle'), an inferior aircraft in almost every respect but being almost 'given away' by the Soviets anxious to exert their influence over the air force that was very much on their side.

This gave me an opening to navigate a delivery aircraft from the English Electric factory at Warton to Agra, not very far from Delhi, flying with Captain John Hall, a company test pilot. I spent a pleasant few days at Agra, as a guest of the commanding officer of a transport wing of the IAF, Group Captain Jaswant. I remember Jaswant for the day he volunteered to fly me to Bombay to meet a connecting flight (I was returning with a first class ticket by an Air India Super-Constellation), he was incredibly hung over after a busy night in the mess. We flew down in one of his station's aircraft, a twin-boom cargo aircraft (a Fairchild C82 Packet), and his physical condition was reflected in his landing.

The return leg itself was not without incident, for I did not know that in boarding the Super-Constellation, a civil aircraft, we would be staging through Prague which at the time, of course, was firmly behind the 'Iron Curtain' and strictly forbidden territory for an RAF officer. Fortunately, the Czechs took little interest in transit passengers in civilian clothes and I was mightily relieved to be ignored.

I 'escaped' from the RAE after some eighteen months (and 100 or more very interesting flying hours) with some 'outside' help and to the relief, perhaps, of my very senior scientific officer-boss, who clearly needed some mathematical heavyweight at his beck and call and not a flying navigator with limited mental ability. I was appointed to a joint staff job on the planning staff of the new Ministry of Defence, in the Cabinet Offices, in October 1957. This was not exactly a nine-to-five job (for we worked all hours) but it did necessitate wearing a bowler hat rather than a scruffy trilby.

Furthermore, I now had my first RAF quarters on the newly built estate at Bushey Heath, near Stanmore, whence I commuted to Whitehall.

The corridors of Whitehall were a new world for me. I joined the Middle East team not so very long after the Suez debacle and the UK

defence policy was being reshaped. We – that is to say an RN commander, an army major and me – reported to the next tier, deputy
directors (all three four-ringers) who in turn reported to the three
service directors of plans. All of us were on our respective service pay
rolls, but in an inter-service structure of the ever-expanding MOD.
(By the time I returned to London from Moscow in 1967 the service intelligence staffs were similarly integrated.) The three services
were steadily being downgraded to operating departments in their
own elements. But for the present, I was to enjoy my new challenge.

As was now habit, I managed to escape to fly whenever I could,
but in a slightly more formal way than usual by persuading friends to
take me flying to Australia with the Comet squadron (216) then at
RAF Lyneham. We flew in stages to Adelaide and back in a week,
which was certainly a mind-broadener.

A year later my RN deputy director, 'Jock' Hayes[9] very kindly
organised my week's leave on the aircraft carrier, HMS *Centaur*, under
the command of Horace Law, which was then serving in the waters
around Malta. This was a totally new experience, especially when I
managed to be catapulted off in a Fairey Gannet aircraft for rocket firing exercises (steam catapults and arrestor cables had been added in
1958 for the carrier to handle jet aircraft). They also allowed me to
be 'jack-stayed' (transferred in a somewhat flimsy chair by rope and
pulley from ship to ship) across to our escort frigate HMS *Sole Bay*.

On the social side I accepted the challenge after dinner one night
to accompany the duty engineering officer on his inspection of the
ship's rear bearing for any leakage. This meant I had to crawl to the
very stern section on hands and knees (this for a bet) and in full mess
kit. I'm pleased to say that I won my bet, but climbing up the verti-
cal steps nearly finished me off. I returned to UK the same way as I
went out to join the ship – in a slow Beverley heavy transport aircraft
('stopping at all stations') from Abingdon. This was a very valuable
two-week exercise that broadened my joint-service outlook that had
already been well developed from JSSC Latimer.

---

[9] Later vice-admiral.

My two years at Whitehall finished with a flourish when I was appointed as temporary ADC to the Turkish chief of the defence staff, one General Mustafa Erdalhun, who was on an official visit to the UK. The military in Turkey held the power base, and the UK was keen to maintain cordial relations with a country that could best be described at the time as 'volatile'. (Later Erdalhun was involved in a coup and sentenced to death, but was subsequently pardoned.)

Mountbatten was his host for the visit, and my orders were to look after the general, for which I was told to draw sufficient funds from the Government Fund Hospitality Office to provide him with whatever creature comforts he desired. This meant I might have to negotiate with a specified 'Madam' to produce the right girls as fitted his individual taste. In truth, the general was not especially enterprising. He did not wish to go out in the evenings and we spent very little of this money.

He was very polite and well mannered, but compared to the stories shared with other ADCs, my own experience was pretty tame. I did, however, enjoy escorting him on visits to the army at Southern Command (we went by helicopter), to the RN at Eastney Barracks, and flying up from Northolt to visit Scottish Command (in an RAF Devon) to witness the Tattoo in Edinburgh Castle where he took the salute. Our last formal engagement was a farewell dinner hosted by Mountbatten at the Honourable Artillery Company (HAC) in London.

It was a fitting end to two years of hard, but most enjoyable joint-staff work.

My escape from the navigation world continued with my new posting to the new Near East Command in Cyprus as secretary of the joint intelligence committee (JIC) which now served a very much-reduced area.

In addition to the three service intelligence officers (group captain equivalents), the command still retained its civilian agencies on the committee (see page 170). These departments collected and reported to London in their own right; each had their own staff. We were also served by a royal engineer (sapper) mapping squadron who produced very high-grade cartography of all kinds for our operating area. I was not overworked and the resources of the joint command provided for our off-duty interests. The sappers built a golf course on the Akrotiri peninsula, maintained three inter-service sailing clubs (with boats kindly provided by Lord Nuffield) and, in season, the ski lift on Mount Troodos!

I had been promised before leaving London that I should take over from the present incumbent of the post, on completion of his tour, and be promoted group captain after six months. The six months came around quickly, and I at last managed to attain this exalted rank. The 'scrambled egg' on my hat was complemented by access to an ex-officio married quarter at Paramali, in walking distance of my office. My family had already joined me and we moved from our temporary rented accommodation in downtown Nicosia.

I enjoyed myself very much and came to know my AOC-in-C (Bill MacDonald) and his SASO (Ginger Weir) very well, as well as the senior staffs of the other two services. As the AOC-in-C was to become the air secretary in due course, he had a direct influence on my later appointment to Moscow as the defence attaché. (Who was it told me that a job in the attaché world was the kiss of death in a GD career?)

When I arrived at the headquarters of Near East Command in November 1959, military operations against the EOKA terrorist/freedom fighters had ended earlier that year and peace had effectively broken out. A treaty was signed for the establishment of British sovereign base areas (SBAs), in each of which separate garrisons were housed. In the east was Dhekelia, with an army brigade, and the west at Episkopi housed the new joint headquarters and had the large RAF base at Akrotiri nearby. In both areas we had adequate access to scarce water sources on the island, carefully surveyed and included within very irregular shaped boundaries.

The headquarters staff were what remained of the old GHQ Middle East (note the important difference in title) in the Canal Base from which we had been compelled to 'withdraw' after the Suez crisis and the revision of our treaty with Egypt. In taking over as secretary to JIC (ME), there was only a small residue left behind of a much larger organisation that served the old organisation. Nevertheless, it still consisted of representatives of those civilian bodies – GCHQ, MI5 (for internal security intelligence within Cyprus as it affected the SBAs), MI6 and the JIB, each with a considerably reduced staff but still the same status of their chiefs. Our chairman remained in Foreign Office hands (now the Foreign and Commonwealth Office) in the rank of minister. The army and RAF were represented as usual at colonel/group captain level, with the naval commander reporting to flag officer Mediterranean in Malta.

Very many of the JIC's responsibilities regarding the perceived Soviet threat in the Middle East were held in London so I was not likely to be overworked. Furthermore, coming from the joint planning staff of the Ministry of Defence, I was familiar with the set-up and its parent organisation, the JIC in London. That wouldn't stop the jockeying for position and the privileges of rank and, most important of all, appropriate accommodation. This was in short supply, made worse by the Mountbatten-designed joint command organisation: one supremo – (in our case to be a four-star general) as well as the existing single-service commanders at three-star level.

We were thus grossly over-ranked in every department.

In my own particular bailiwick, the Foreign Office chairman, a minister, reckoned he ranked on parallel with, but by no means subordinate to, the three-star officers. Arriving with a large family (from two marriages) of six children, he needed – and secured – two quarters. The Nubian manservant he'd brought with him had to sleep in one of his garages.

The high commission in Nicosia was still a Commonwealth office, in no way subordinate to the FO representative, and there was constant acrimony over the right to fly personal flags on their respective official vehicles – only on duty, of course. As our minister had no territorial rights (as it were) he should only fly the appropriate FO flag when he drove in his large white Jaguar down to swim on the local beach (within the limits of the SBA). That he did so when touring around the island got to the ears of the high commissioner, who was suitably incensed. (The high commissioner's car flew the defaced union jack when he made his rare trips outside the capital, Nicosia.) It really was comic opera, generating much personal animosity. To make matters worse, and within my immediate purview, we dealt with intelligence material at a much higher security level than was accorded to the high commission. That at least put us one up! It was long after I left – in 1962 – when the whole ridiculously over-ranked organisation was cut down to size and the role of Nicosia vis-à-vis Episkopi settled by newly created 'FCO'. The old Commonwealth office had long since been disestablished.

Notwithstanding the personal squabbles that did not directly affect me, my job was enjoyable and not overly stressful. I bought myself a car and I could commute between the headquarters, the sailing club and the various lovely swimming beaches; we started work early and generally finished at lunchtime.

I'd always wanted to travel and exploit any opportunity to get out of the office and go somewhere new. In this job I had both the time and the means at my disposal. In our command we still had a resident transport squadron based at Nicosia as well as a small communications flight. We were about to pull out of Nicosia airfield and hand it over to the newly independent civil aviation authority – and move its assets to RAF Akrotiri, which continued to expand.

I took the chance of visiting the outposts of our command area by flying via El Adem (in Tripolitania) thence to Khartoum and Aden (Khormaksar), continuing to Bahrain by way of Sharjah. Then returning the same way to Cyprus, the whole trip in a piston-engined aircraft took seven days. It gave me some idea of distances and the extent of these staging posts as well as the deserts. With my change of allegiance from a MOD organisation back to the RAF again and being the RAF representative on the JIC (NE), I was more directly involved with the RAF planning and operations staff.

The Middle East, of course, remained predictably unstable. British efforts to build on its influence in Iraq with the creation of the ill-fated Baghdad Pact as a means of defending the whole area from Russian influence were thwarted by the overthrow of the royal regime and the murder of King Feisal. The British embassy in Iraq was sacked with considerable embarrassment over our inability to do anything about it, notwithstanding our garrisons of army and RAF in Cyprus. Arab nationalism was strong and Iran was to follow next.

But before that happened, I exploited our routine support flights to visit Teheran and went to stay with the air attaché. An RAF team was then helping with the installation of a full air defence radar system, built and sold by Marconi. I was able to revisit the Derbavend Hotel, once in the countryside but now in the northern suburbs of the ever-spreading capital, where I had stayed on the occasion of the 'Big Three' Teheran conference in 1943. The Shah was still on his throne, but only just. US policy, intent on getting a bigger share of Persian oil, was not exactly on our side, being intensely anti-monarchist. But the western diplomats successfully conceived the Central Treaty Organisation (CENTO) Pact, to work as an extension of NATO with the intention of continuing the containment of Soviet Russia. At least that was the hope. The Americans could safely join this body and at least agree to co-ordinate with us some of our air force target plans. Iran and Turkey now became vital for our military air routes to the Gulf and on to India and the Far East for we could no longer overfly Iraq. There was plenty of our own work, and more planning with CENTO meetings in Ankara and Naples.

After our withdrawal from Suez there followed a strong Russian influence within Egypt and Syria whose forces re-equipped with Soviet aircraft and ships at bargain prices. This naturally threatened our many interests more locally. In Israel I made liaison visits to several IAF bases and to Jordan where we still had a small RAF training mission. We provided an aircraft and a pilot for the king, whose life was saved on one occasion when Syrian MIG aircraft encroached on Jordanian air space in an attempt to shoot him down. His RAF pilot dived almost to ground level and the MIGs declined to follow.

Living in a married quarter on camp meant commuting was minimal. Social life was very pleasant and easy. The two boys, both at boarding schools in the UK, could fly out for holidays sometimes managing an indulgence passage (free) and sometimes paid for on BEA to Nicosia. They too could enjoy sailing and tennis with their contemporaries on holiday. I managed to take all the family on a visit to the Holy Land and on to Petra, flying down to Ma'an in a Jordanian air force aircraft, to see the Rose Red City.

Amongst my travels was a formal visit to the local Turkish governor of Mersin, a newly developed commercial port on the south coast. This was in the command's RAF high-speed air sea rescue (ASR) launch. It was all rather interesting, flying a group captain's flag on the small mast. The launch was there in case an RAF aircraft should find itself in trouble in the eastern Mediterranean, and my visit to the governor was to clear the way to use his port facilities if required in such an emergency. I was received with great courtesy.

Later, with another couple from the headquarters, my wife and I took leave and journeyed to Istanbul 'coastwise' in a small commercial vessel of Turkish Maritime Lines. Occupying the only two double cabins, we left Cyprus from Famagusta and called first at Iskenderun where we stopped long enough to take a taxi to visit Antioch: then on to Mersin (carrying a mixture of passengers and freight – often as deck-cargo) and so successively calling in at Alanya, Antalya and Bodrum to Izmir – a very busy port and NATO base, and so finally through the Dardanelles to Istanbul.

We tied alongside not long after sunrise, and marvelled at the way that the rising sun caught the minarets of the famous mosques. It was an incredible sight. After several days sight-seeing, going up the Golden Horn and staying in an old fashioned hotel with hydraulic lift – the famous Pera Palace – we flew to Ankara where we enjoyed seeing all of the personal relics of Ataturk, reverently preserved and displayed. We returned to Cyprus by air, our minds much enriched by the visit.

Before my tour ended I was informed that my next job would be as SASO of 25 Group with its headquarters at RAF White Waltham. This was the training group under an air vice-marshal that was responsible for the basic training of navigators and wireless operators, and overseeing the university air squadrons, which were to become an important element in the recruitment of permanent commission officers for Cranwell. We had plenty of time to arrange our passage home, attend to the despatch of our heavy kit (fortunately by air freight) and take some leave. We also had the certainty of a married quarter that went with the job that was located on the western outskirts of Maidenhead in Berkshire.

We opted to go overland, driving the car, which we shipped with us on an Adriatica Line vessel from Famagusta via Piraeus and the Corinth Canal to Naples. The car went as deck-cargo and because the ship could not come alongside, the car and ourselves went out in a lighter. Seeing the car lifted by crane into the lighter from the dockside then again by the ship's crane did not inspire me with confidence. However, all went well and in due course we were off-loaded in a more conventional way on to the Naples wharf.

We drove home via friends in Rome, then on to Munich where we had arranged with the Mercedes factory for the car to be thoroughly overhauled and cleaned after its rather arduous first two years driving all over the Cyprus mountain roads. Our onward journey took us via Luxembourg to the Channel and over to Dover where the AA had new number plates ready and waiting for us.

So I found myself back in the world of navigation, though in a more rounded role. Within our little command we had the initial training school for direct entry officers, two navigation schools and one for air signallers, all equipped with purpose-built training aircraft – the Varsity – with the range to reach Malta or Gibraltar in one hop. We had a standing agreement with the French air force for staging at French bases, if need be, to make overseas flying a worthwhile exercise for the final stages of their course. In this I had scope for my continued flying, both as a working navigator (in a supervisory, that is to say a 'safety' role), and at the same time becoming familiar with the workings of the schools concerned. Many of these exercises took place at weekends. This also gave me the chance to get to know the various station commanders and how they ran their respective stations.

In addition we were responsible for the administration and flying efficiency of the university air squadrons. These were used to give elementary flying instruction on the Chipmunk light aircraft to preselected students, also flying mainly at weekends. They were based and maintained in most cases at civil airfields, by contract.

I was working for a charming two-star chief with whom I got on extremely well. I had a staff car, which I generally drove myself, and we had the group communication flight on the airfield.

I had been in the job only a few months when I found myself invited to accompany the AOC-in-C Flying Training Command on a liaison visit to the RCAF and USAF navigation training schools overseas. The AOC-in-C was no less a man than Air Marshal Sir Gus Walker, a

famous rugger 'Blue' and an international cap, who had been seriously injured in the war, attempting to warn a crew that a bomb had fall-
en from their aircraft while taxiing for take-off. The bomb exploded,
and he was lucky to escape with his life, albeit minus an arm.

In planning this sortie, the AOC-in-C was taking full advantage of
the annual tour arranged for the RAF specialist navigation course,
now located at RAF Manby. We had a 216 Squadron Comet at our
disposal for the trip, from its base at RAF Lyneham, and were accompanied by 'Splinters' Smallwood, now an air commodore and the
commandant at Manby.

We were away for three weeks in all, visiting first the RCAF headquarters in Ottawa (via Keflavik and Goose Bay) and then west to
Winnipeg before going to the USAF equivalent school at Mather
Field, outside San Francisco. It was interesting to see American tech-
nical developments in navigation instruments and radar at various
manufacturers in and around Los Angeles, and we spent time also at
the USAF experimental establishment at Wright Patterson Field near
Dayton, Ohio – a kind of cross between our Farnborough and
Boscombe Down – before finishing at USAF headquarters in
Washington, DC.

It was a wonderful and refreshing experience of the New World,
and extremely useful in getting up-to-date with the latest developments in the navigation sphere. Everyone liked Gus and everywhere
we went we had VIP treatment. Gus was always fully briefed before
landing at each venue by his ADC, and used this 'intelligence' most
effectively in endearing himself to our hosts. We flew home via Goose
Bay and then direct to Lyneham.

Back at my desk I found we were heavily involved with the UAS
and the proposed expansion of the scheme. The AOC-in-C himself
was a university graduate (Cambridge) entrant as was my AOC, Air
Vice-Marshal Paul Holder, who graduated with a BSc from Bristol.
It took some time to convince the treasury that university graduate
cadet entrants had not only developed intellectually from the school
boy (as was patently obvious) but by learning to fly at least to private
pilot licence standard in vacation time and becoming immersed in
basic RAF lore, we should have weeded out those with no aptitude

for flying. Some of these could still be diverted to other RAF branches, and some even to navigation. By using this route, the failure rate
of pilots at the FTS stage was considerably reduced.

Using our Anson aircraft we could oversee the various flying facilities that had to be organised for the UAS aircraft, some on RAF stations (including St Athan and Valley for the Welsh universities), others
at contractors' airfields such as Marshalls for Cambridge and Faireys
at White Waltham for the colleges of London University. In the
course of our visits one got to know some of the academic staff who
were sympathetic to RAF recruitment. Professor R.V.Jones, then professor of natural philosophy at Aberdeen University, was a great supporter. I was to come across the UAS organisation again in the years
ahead when concerned with recruiting policy in the Air Ministry.

From my logbook I see I made regular trips, sometimes with
Topcliffe aircraft giving sprog W/T operators some overseas experience to Malta, staging outbound at Orange but homebound via the
civil airport at Nice, which in those days was not as crowded as it is
today. Later, in the autumn of 1963 I accompanied a Topcliffe aircraft
to Wildenrath, an RAF airfield in West Germany, and before the year
was out I accompanied a Stradishall aircraft on a navigation exercise
with students to Malta, staging again at Orange, but this time both
ways. Winter weather over the Massif at our cruising altitudes (around
10,000ft) could be extremely unpleasant.

Throughout all this time I had the support of an excellent staff. On
the flying side – for the airfield operations in general, as well as on the
instructional side for the training of air signallers and navigators – I
was well served by staff officers who knew their business. Indeed they
knew more than I could of individual school workings and their
training results. There were passing out parades to attend and parents
to meet, justifiably proud of their newly commissioned sons.

It was a good posting from every point of view. If I was destined
to remain in the navigation world, it did not seem unreasonable that
I might have a chance to achieve my ambition of a station command.

But then events took an unexpected turn.

CHAPTER THIRTEEN

BEHIND THE IRON CURTAIN

In the spring and early summer of 1964 I was able to fit in two more overseas trips, one to Malta and another to Gibraltar.

Out of the blue I got a call from the staff officer to the air secretary (the RAF's chief appointments officer) who, by now, was my ex-AOC-in-C from Cyprus, Bill MacDonald. I was report to his office the following day. I found the whole thing intriguing, especially as the message had not come through 'usual channels'.

In the interview that followed I was offered the chance to go to Moscow as the defence/air attaché, with the acting rank of air commodore. It seemed that my earlier experience of diplomatic life in Washington and my fairly recent involvement in Middle East air intelligence had counted in my favour.

I was to tell no one but to go home and consult my wife, for no one would be appointed (or have his name put forward) for a job behind the Iron Curtain – which existed in those days 'with knobs on' – if their partner were unwilling or declined to accompany them. My wife thoroughly enjoyed foreign travel and readily accepted the challenge, so the machinery was set in motion under wraps of confidentiality. Not only did my face have to fit with our FCO, but it also had to be acceptable to the host country. It also needed to be approved by the palace.

I was to have nearly eighteen months before assuming my appointment. This was largely taken up with language training and with briefings about my work. In parallel, my wife and I had much to do on the domestic front, for whilst we should be provided with suitable accommodation, its present furnishing left a lot to be desired, and we would need to provide such things as our own table silver, and much of the glass.

We were briefed extensively by a recent occupant of the job and his wife, who were friends. This was a great help: for whilst a group captain (and his wife) might be expected to possess a certain amount of 'furnishings' to entertain at his rank, a diplomatic appointment needed very much more. Dinner parties for up to twelve or fourteen people were the norm in a Grade I embassy such as Moscow. Even larger cocktail parties were also a common requirement, a convenient way of meeting 'all sorts and conditions of men (and women)'.

Suitable basic rations had to be ordered from the UK. This sounds rather strange now that the shops of Moscow and St Petersburg are as good as the West End of London. But this was emphatically not the case in Cold War Soviet Russia where, typical of those days, there was the one 'dip' shop which stocked certain scarce 'luxury' items, at a price, even when duty-free. We could apparently, and did frequently, buy quantities of the best caviar at a reasonable price and the local bread was good, but we couldn't get milk or good meat. We, or should I say the wives, would quickly learn what bargains were currently in stock, but a lot of basic cooking requirements would have to be ordered in bulk and shipped out ahead. We could order through a special department of the NAAFI or from export departments of big stores such as Harrods, or in Helsinki and Copenhagen. (Our fresh milk would come to the embassy in a bulk order by train from Helsinki, and in the winter months the milk froze solid.)

My language training was supposed to take place at the joint services language school, then at RAF Tangmere. This was an excellent course but designed for young, graduate National Service entrants who already could show proficiency in at least one other European language. It comprised twelve months of concentrated study, by which time they should have reached 'linguist' proficiency. It was not, however, for a forty-five-year-old who had been long since divorced from classroom study. Furthermore, the school lost its 'jointness' just as I arrived. The three services went their respective ways: the army to their school of education at Beaconsfield; the RN remained as self-contained as ever; but the RAF sent their Russian students to RAF North Luffenham, a signals technical training unit. It was made quite clear to me that they could not cope with a senior officer wanting a crash course in conversational Russian.

To make matters worse, I was told to abandon these studies for the moment, as I was required to go on urgent detachment to the staff of the RAF inspector general in London. The inspector general was Air Marshal Sir Pat Fraser, lately SASO to Air Chief Marshal Sir Basil Embry, who as well as being a former test pilot and unit commander at RAE Farnborough, had also been the UK representative on CENTO. He had been instructed to investigate urgently a supposed leak of top-secret documents from the office of the AOC-in-C Germany in Rheindahlen. This made visits to that headquarters essential, for several days at a time. My Russian language training would have to wait.

This disorganised my preparations somewhat, but did not last long. The subject was a tricky matter at the highest political level, made the more embarrassing by the fact that it followed so soon after the Macmillan Government had been humiliated by the Profumo affair and Christine Keeler. It also came on the back of the belated discovery that an ex-clerk to the naval attaché in Moscow, one John Vassall, a known homosexual to the KGB but not the RN, was being blackmailed in London, when he had joined the staff of the junior naval minister of defence. To add to this the possibility of the RAF losing a secret operational document from the headquarters in Germany, which was constantly on alert for Soviet troop movements affecting the status of Berlin, would be acutely compromising if it became known to the press. So we started our enquiries in London and then stayed in Rheindahlen, gathering information and inspecting premises and facilities before writing our report. The document had not been actually lost, but mislaid. A number of people were severely criticised over related security issues and nothing about it ever reached the newspapers. I returned to my studies.

I was fortunate to know my predecessor-but-one in the job who was now serving in the UK. We met up with our respective wives and discussed what we could expect. They proved to be an enormous help with the domestic preparations and practical considerations such as clothing. We learned much about our future accommodation and the Russian staff. By way of some little compensation for the disruption of my totally unsuitable course at North Luffenham, I was sent to Paris for a month to live with a White Russian émigré couple. This was comic opera, but I did learn a great deal about the few remaining, very elderly White Russians still living and was once taken to their club (or headquarters, they liked to think) from which the old regime would one day organise their return to a royalist Russia. A number of their members had been murdered over the years by the overseas arm of the KGB.

In due course, our preparations were completed. My appointment was confirmed and formally announced once the agreement had been received from Moscow. Our passage was originally booked on a British boat of the Baltic Line sailing from the Surrey Commercial Docks, but the company altered its sailing to Hull which was not convenient. We eventually took passage on the regular Russian Baltika Line boat from Tilbury, complete with a good deal of our impedimenta, to Leningrad where we would be met by one of my assistant air attachés (there were three on my staff, as well as a number of airmen clerks).

Service attachés are, in effect, the ambassador's military staff and their duties vary from embassy to embassy depending on the UK's relationship with the host government. A NATO capital clearly is very different from a potentially hostile state. They are also the point of liaison between the Ministry of Defence in London and the host country's forces. They should therefore become as well acquainted as possible with these forces. This does not mean that they are in any sense spies or run any network of agents; what it does mean, however, is that they are expected to use every overt opportunity to further their knowledge and report their findings to the appropriate body. (We invariably carried a camera with us wherever we went and were trained how to use it. The lens was so long that taking pictures out of the window of a moving vehicle proved to be a challenge, not without its amusement.) We took only tourist pictures, of course!

At that time there was precious little liaison, but we did meet suitably vetted Soviet officers at embassy receptions and National Days. In such a widespread country as the Soviet Union there were often vast distances to be travelled, and this often proved difficult. The Russians are historically wary of strangers. The Soviet regime made them more so, and at that time they were fiercely hostile to the capitalist West. This was an attitude that was fostered by the regime in all walks and levels of Russian society. But it would be wrong to typecast them all like that. My Russian driver, Dmitri, was extremely friendly, as was our cook/maid, though needless to say they were obliged to report to their 'employers'. The state hairdressers I regularly visited were positively large and jocular.

Since the Soviets expect their service attachés in Western capitals to be accorded all manner of travel facilities and invitations to military exercises and displays, they very grudgingly had to reciprocate. So travel we did, to the Arctic North, the Far East, to the many national states on the southern borders, mainly Muslim. We visited the resorts of the Crimea and the Black Sea; we travelled by car, by the civil airline – Aeroflot – by train and even by boat – across the Caspian to reach Teheran via Bandar Pahlavi. We usually travelled as a foursome, taking our wives. This privilege gave us the comfort of a companion (also so she wouldn't be left worrying back in Moscow on her own) and so we conveniently filled a four-berth sleeper coupé. It also gave the Ministry of Defence another pair of eyes and an extra driver – for free, as it were. Of air displays, there was only one in my time, a vast affair at the new Sheremetyevo airfield (now the main Moscow international airport) in 1967.

We stayed in all sorts of accommodation, ate in a variety of establishments, some more revolting than others. To give ourselves a degree of independence (service in Russian hotels was notoriously slow) and our preference for western food, we picnicked in our hotel rooms, cooking with a variety of devices, ranging from the Tommy Cooker (a solid fuel heater dating from the first world war) to powerful electric immersion heaters that sometimes had damaging effects on the hotel's electric wiring!

We were obliged to give forty-eight hours notice of our intention to travel beyond the Moscow city limits and since all our bookings (for travel tickets and hotel accommodation) were made by the embassy to a designated Soviet agency, the KGB knew all about our plans (and could guess our interests). That meant our plans could easily be thwarted by the excuse that no seats/rooms were available on the days we wished to travel, or the hotel in which we wanted to stay was fully booked. Nevertheless, travel we did and some of our most interesting trips involved visiting neighbouring capitals that, by designated and approved routes, the authorities did not usually deny.

I had the chance to fetch a new staff car from London (having flown home) to drive it back to Moscow via Vienna, Budapest and the Ukraine, with my wife. This avoided the tortuous shipping, as deck cargo, via Leningrad. We also drove a private car home, belonging to a friend who, similarly, wanted to avoid having to ship it from Leningrad, mid-winter. Our route took us through Warsaw to Prague and Southern Germany to the Channel port in the autumn, just keeping ahead of the snow and a continental winter!

We entertained a great deal and enjoyed the return matches (one had to be punctilious about social matters). These events were not without incident. One evening, while dining with the Japanese defence attaché, there was an embarrassing gap between the starter and the main course, and our host became very angry with his wife for committing such a social faux pas. (He and I actually later became good friends.) The same happened to us on the occasion (just once was the rule) that the ambassador – Sir Geoffrey Harrison[10] – came to dine. Harrison was decent enough, although a touch arrogant, but his wife Mimi was a positive dear. She simply turned to Brenda and said: "Oh you mustn't worry about such things, they happen all the time."

Although we could occasionally be met with kindness, we were more often viewed with suspicion, and the authorities could be particularly beastly to my wife and indeed all wives of embassy officials. There were the small things they could do to make life unpleasant,

---

[10] Sir Geoffrey Harrison was retired from Moscow having been seduced by his Russian maid Galya.

such as sabotaging our washing machine or removing our cook with the excuse that she was 'sick'. Then there were more serious incidents including being forced off the road in our car whilst driving past a well-known military base. Wherever we went by car, we invariably had a 'tail' and they made their presence well known.

The KGB knew everything about us – our character, our habits, our relationships – etc before we arrived. In my case, that didn't amount to much, and there were no indiscretions that they could use against me. This was not the case with one of my acquaintances whose wife was blissfully ignorant of an affair that he was conducting back in the UK. His wife may have been ignorant, but the KGB certainly was not, and subtle (and later not so subtle) remarks at dinner parties and receptions began to take their toll, until she could not take their sustained campaign of harassment any more. In the end, both she and her husband were obliged to return home.

We were well-travelled after our two-and-half-year stint. The boys came out occasionally on their holidays at our expense, unless a fortuitous visiting service aircraft had available space. We were visited by family members and could show off the sites; my staff car (black shiny Humber Snipe) with my faithful Dmitri – our driver – was a valuable perk.

Suffice to say we were not sorry when our tour came to an end. Our official duties could be burdensome and they included two state funerals. The one I remember in particular was for the Russian cosmonaut and hero of the Soviet Union Yuri Gagarin, the first man in space. All of the foreign service attachés were invited and congregated at the House of Unions. Gagarin was lying in state in an open coffin adorned with flowers. Having paid our respects, we were given red armbands to wear as a mark of respect, and as the funeral cortege assembled, we ourselves gathered in rows a dozen or so abreast to slow march to the strangled strains of Chopin's funeral march. From the House of Unions we marched along the Ulitsa Okhotny Ryad until we wheeled to march across the Manezhnaya Ploshchad and then up the slope to Red Square. I kept my dressing with the Indian military attaché, a fine looking Sikh in the most fantastic cavalry officer's uniform. Looking around him at the others in our ranks, he turned and said to me: "We'll show them how to march." And so it was that the slow march at Gagarin's funeral was led by representatives of the British Empire!

It was, on reflection, a historic occasion in which to be involved, even on the fringes. It was also very emotional. Gagarin left a widow and young family. He was the hero of the moment, and it was as if the whole country was genuinely united in grief.

I elected to return by sea, bringing as much luggage and accoutrements 'in the hold' as possible. By having our packing done by the embassy contract packers we could be sure of avoiding export bothers at the frontier (diplomats were often accused of smuggling out antiques and icons), the team always including one 'goon' (KGB man). Americans always did their own in-house packing and frequently found their belongings had been interfered with, en route.

We sent our heavier luggage ahead to Leningrad to be loaded on the new Sovmorflot transatlantic ship, the *Nadershnya Krupskaya* – named for Lenin's wife, which would call at Helsinki, Tilbury and Cherbourg for Montreal. We took the night train from Moscow direct to Helsinki, with limited cabin baggage, and stayed one night with the resident air attaché. This avoided any exit hassle at the frontier and we could join the ship in comfort.

We were at last home where we started, with the family waiting and the reality of our new lives dawning as a tatty RAF J2 van accompanied us with our luggage. The RAF later delivered our heavier boxes to my new quarters which I had been allotted at Stanmore. I was once again destined for an Air Ministry desk, after a long disembarkation leave.

I was posted to a newly created position of Director of Recruiting, within the manning department, a field I'd never been involved in. Our chief concern was the ongoing problem of attracting suitable recruits for the various categories of aircrew. This problem was made greater still by the numbers game: how many airmen did we require and in what trades or skills? More than this, we had to try and work out the demand for front-line aircrew, and how we could balance demand with constantly changing strategic needs.

Recruiting was much more complicated than I imagined, for even after we had encouraged individuals to apply, we then had to work out how we selected them for what tasks. I can't say I could raise much enthusiasm for the job, especially having only just left a high-pressure role on the front line of the Cold War. I was, if I am honest, rather disappointed not to continue in the intelligence field but my late boss in that area felt I ought to have a less stressful job. My fifty-fifth birthday was a little under five years away – and compulsory retirement beckoned – probably while still in my office at Adastral House which was no longer on that prominent corner of Aldwych and Kingsway but in Theobalds Road, Bloomsbury.

I worked for a capable and energetic director-general at two-star rank and had two experienced deputy directors: there was an excellent inspector of recruiting who ran a field force of recruiting offices in some of the larger cities and towns. This organisation was in close touch with schools and colleges, and the employment world. Within the office I was again lucky with staff experienced in dealing with the advertising world, a strange new world for me. They organised campaigns which ranged from give-away leaflets showing our latest aircraft and equipment to posters on the sides of London's buses advertising for 'technocrats', a buzz word invented to attract those interested with the appropriate skills.

Perhaps the most time-consuming effort was put into aircrew recruiting and the aircrew selection board located at Biggin Hill. The cost of all this, especially the advertising budget which was farmed out by contract, was under constant scrutiny by our financiers, the Treasury and, at one time, by a parliamentary committee of enquiry. At one of these sittings to which I had been summoned to give evidence, a Welsh nationalist MP asked me why we didn't have our recruiting literature printed in the Welsh language. I tried to explain that as the RAF lived and operated in English it would be difficult to train anyone unable to read our recruiting literature. To my best knowledge, the RAF still operates in English to this day!

From my married quarters in Stanmore I commuted on the tube. This was convenient enough, but we knew friends who lived further into London, in Islington, where some prices were still low enough for us to join in the 'gentrification' that was then well underway. We were lucky to find an early Victorian terraced house near the canal, on which some modernisation had already been started. We also found a splendid lady architect who knew the planning regulations and the local planners. Thanks to her and a builder with whom she had often worked, we were able to combine a new roof with an extra storey – the old roof had been badly shaken in the bombing blitz and had a make-shift repair by covering the tiles with tar and tarpaulin. We also had a small south-facing yard and garden, with room for a small, lean-to greenhouse.

We were very happy there. The car could be parked in the street right outside though there was even the 38 bus that would take me from Islington Green to Holborn. However I soon found a walking route, through Clerkenwell and across towards Sadler's Wells, which often proved to be far more preferable to standing in a queue in the rain at the bus stop, and then struggling to stand on the bus when it finally arrived. We could even walk home at night from the Angel underground station, always in peace.

But while I was happy at home, I was not happy in my job and I'm afraid it showed. My boss knew it too and clearly I was quite unlikely to gain further promotion this way. Fortunately, I knew that a one-star post titled 'air commodore (intelligence)' was about to become vacant and it did not take too much effort to get myself moved just before my two-year spell was up. I was now back on the staff of the CAS, to whom I had direct access.

There were three of us one-star officers (one from each service) left in the constant re-organisation of the defence intelligence staff (DIS). They had created a 'central staff', not yet in purple uniforms, who reported to the chief of the defence staff, thence to the JIC itself. We were in fact single-service 'spies' in the central staff who could then brief their masters, who received all high-level service intelligence papers, on likely clashes ahead within the chiefs of staff.

One particular aspect of my job was visiting the many RAF representatives in the several civilian intelligence collecting agencies, as well as those in the intelligence collecting employ of a number of RAF units in the field. In all this the services kept their own liaison with their US opposite numbers. With all this centralisation I felt that in a number ways the single-service aspects were being forgotten, especially when under budgetary attacks.

A case in point was the pressure to get rid of the Eastern Sovereign Base Area in Cyprus (at Dhekelia) and so save money. A very senior soldier in the central organisation was quite unaware that it contained vital RAF aerials, a separate part of the OTHR system which was important to the US as well as to British interests. No doubt, this ignorance would have been spotted somewhere in the chain of command before the USAF would realise the danger of such a move and threaten 'to send in the marines'.

I don't think even our own top brass always realised the significance of work done often by small, dedicated dispersed staffs in small units. I made it my job to keep CAS briefed. This too, gave me the chance to travel overseas and to fly with the squadrons concerned and get visiting again.

The RAF had long collected photographic intelligence, first exploited for intelligence purposes in the First World War. We ran the school for photographic interpretation, which became something wider when we started collecting intelligence by infrared and radar scan. I was able to fly in the Nimrods of Coastal Command which, in their anti-submarine patrols collected an enormous amount of 'sonic' intelligence (the noise made by the cavitation of propellers) so naval intelligence could even tell one boat from another. Other RAF units collected signals intelligence of all sorts and I happened to be on one such visit to Cyprus when the 1973 'Arab/Israeli war' broke out. Some of Strike Command aircraft 'sampled' the atmosphere at high altitudes for traces of nuclear dust, for the high altitude winds carry such evidence of nuclear tests for a long time.

Space track was now beginning to overtake the land-based air defence radars, and the associated OTHR research was rather stopped in its tracks by the speed of developments in space. But the RAF had more than one finger in this, notably Fylingdales on those bitterly cold North Yorkshire moors. The Soviet Tupolev long-range maritime aircraft (Bears in NATO parlance) continued their own probes into our defences with a view to photographing anything new. These would be routinely intercepted by our Lightning supersonic interceptors from Leuchars. All in all, it was a most interesting time for me, particularly as I could follow Soviet air force developments from the time I had been able to see some of their prototypes in flight.

All good things come to an end sometime – in this case on my fifty-fifth birthday, though I did get one year's extension concerned with RAF co-operation with the US space track programme. This involved the RAF directly, and not the other two services. It was a long way from the parochial matter of 'equal careers for navigators' – but which had had its recruiting aspect, also.

In due course I received the inevitable letter from the minister for defence for the air force, one Brynmor John, who thanked me on behalf of Her Majesty "for my valuable services" and wished me well for the future. After a spell of 'gardening leave' in which we had built a new house, near Calshot to be next door to very old RAF friends, and carving a garden out of a green-field site, I applied for a job with help from the Officer's Association in the Foreign Office security department. I felt that with my experience in Washington (before the Burgess-Maclean affair burst onto an unsuspecting public) and in Moscow (soon after the Profumo/Vassall scandal and the Radcliffe commission report) I could claim qualifying experience. Fortunately, the interview panel – which included a retired chief constable of Bristol – thought so too, and I was delighted to be told that the job was mine.

CHAPTER 14

FINAL APPROACH

My new job was London-based, just as we were planning to move out of the city. It was far from ideal, but since I would be travelling a great deal, both around the UK and to Brussels and Paris, I could work from home for much of the time.

It was not highly paid by any means, and there was no such thing as an expense account and car which many of my ex-service colleagues seemed to enjoy. But I was working with congenial people, most of them ex-service, and the pace wasn't tiring. The salary (and later minis-cule pension) kept me in drink but little else. It didn't matter. We had our new house and garden, and all the fun, and hard work, of getting established, with the bonus of being able to crew in the Finnish motor-sailer of our great friend and neighbour. The job ended, as did my working life, when I turned sixty-five, and became an OAP.

Looking back on those last forty years, I cannot help but appreci-ate how extraordinarily lucky I have been: I might have been posted to France in early 1940, and been slaughtered as were so many Battle aircrew; I might easily have gone down with so many friends in Bomber Command. I was lucky also to have been around at the time of the selection of an RAF crew for Churchill's aircraft, with the right qualifications and a 'face' that evidently fitted.

The development of a new policy after the war of 'equal careers for navigators' undoubtedly opened up opportunities that might not have previously existed, and I found myself in a number of congenial appointments often, I have to admit, at the expense of 'family and fireside'. This is the cost of a service career but I was blessed with a wife who had put up with a gypsy life and my frequent absences, the latter often the result of my selfish desire to expand my flying experience and my love for foreign travel that still exists today.

In the course of my career I met and brushed shoulders with a wide range of important and historic figures – arguably the most important being The Owner himself, Winston Churchill.

I have often been asked: "What was the prime minister like?" Not an easy question to answer. Firstly, he was never one for small talk. If he sent for you in-flight, he could be direct, even a little fierce on occasions, and it was important to be on the ball at all times. You also needed to be consistent, for he had a prodigious memory for how you had answered a similar question last time. The questions were always factual ones about our height, speed, the weather etc. Only once did we have to postpone a flight – because of a bad route forecast for the last leg home. I had to be 'in attendance' with the captain to justify the decision to delay take-off. He never bullied – indeed he was scrupulously fair – but he would challenge you and it helped to have the facts at your fingertips.

Many biographies tell of his unreasonable working hours and his treatment of his closest staff, and I suppose this was true. We certainly got to know many of his habits, his likes, dislikes and eccentricities. We were familiar faces to him; he very much disliked the unfamiliar, but I doubt if he ever actually remembered our names, with the exception of the captain.

Once out of the UK we were on our own, and we had to be ready for anything. Actually, my duties as navigator were straightforward, even though the travel plan would get changed 'on the road'. Responsibility for the catering and domestic side of our operations was far more onerous. Fresh clean water, for example, was a necessity, and not always easy to come by when far from an allied base. The one who had the greatest amount of work to do, however, was Jack, our flight engineer, who needed to keep the machinery running smoothly (and that included the sanitary facilities).

We never lost sight of the fact that we were mere bit-part players on an otherwise enormous stage. Our task with The Owner and indeed all of our VIPs was to ensure their safe and timely air transportation: no more; no less.

I was privileged to have met His Majesty King George VI, and through him Her Majesty Queen Elizabeth in comparative informality when we were presented with our Victorian Orders. On the aircraft, there was no intimacy whatsoever. We were communicated with via his courtiers. Only when we went to the palace did his charm become more apparent, and Her Majesty was positively chatty.

While His Majesty visited Malta, we were accommodated in Monty's tented headquarters mess at Zuara, near Tripoli, and invited once to have tea with him in his famous caravan. In Moscow's Bolshoi Theatre we sat within feet of Stalin near the former royal box. Washington and Moscow brought me into the diplomatic world (the kiss of death for an RAF career I had been told, in 1943) and a variety of important people in their day.

We sometimes graded our passengers according to their treatment of us as a crew. Jan Smuts, for example, was always the gentleman; so too General Alexander. In contrast, de Gaulle was arrogant and dismissive. Some were amusing – the PM's great friend Duff Cooper and his troupe kept us very much entertained – and The Owner's son, Randolph always took full advantage of the delicacies that Ascalon had to offer.

My RAF career brought me into contact with a good many wartime personalities, and I have been able only to give a snapshot of some of these people in my story such as 'The Maestro', Kenneth Smith, Peter Cribb, Pat Daniels, 'Dinty' Moore, Bill Christie and Cyril Boothby. Others included: 'Crack 'em' Staton, David Green, David McKinley, Dickie Law, Stafford Coulson, Alan Frank, John Downey, Gus Walker, Sid Bufton, Dick Collard, 'Mouse' Fielden – the list is long.

If you asked me who was the most significant, then it would have to be Dickie Legg, a man of the highest professional and moral standards, and possessing huge integrity. It was Dickie who gave me my first break into the attaché world, and I never looked back. I admired him enormously.

Simple arithmetic shows that having joined the DSIR from school at my father's behest in 1936 and left the Foreign Office in 1983, I had served the crown for forty-seven years – under three monarchs,

Edward VIII, George VI and Elizabeth II; I was in the RAF for thirty-six of them. Considerable technological developments obviously took place over this period. Having been born and brought up within viewing distance of Croydon aerodrome on the edge of the North Downs at Sanderstead, I was not unnaturally air-minded – having got over the fright of seeing the airship, the R33, fly low over the house as it approached its temporary mooring mast on the old site of Plough Lane (an RFC aerodrome originally).

We lived not far from Kenley and my first view of the RAF was of the Bristol Bulldog single-seat fighters stationed there. Sir Alan Cobham's flying circus came to the vicinity twice before the war to my memory. The circus toured England with the objective of promoting air-mindedness. My pocket money didn't stretch to five shillings needed for a joy ride in his HP W20; and certainly not to the 7/6 required for a trip in the Spooner sisters' open-cockpit three-seat Spartan (they were both pilots with ground-engineer licences and great entrepreneurs).

Although the circus completed its objective in my case and contributed to my air-mindedness, I never did get to a Hendon Air Show and my first serious view of the RAF was at Castle Bromwich, in 1938, when it was open for an Empire Air Day and a Gladiator of 605 (County of Warwick AAF) gave a polished aerobatic performance. As previously recounted, it was flown by Flying Officer Denis Smallwood, the regular adjutant and training officer and (much) later C-in-C Strike Command. He was also a family friend, his parents lived in Moseley not far from where I was in 'digs' at the time, working in HM Customs and Excise in Birmingham. (Castle Bromwich was also the site of the Austin Shadow Factory at that time building Fairey Battles – subject of many memories.)

I would learn in due course that the RAF was very oriented towards 'a single-seat mentality' notwithstanding the few multi-crew bombers ex-First World War that were the core of an 'independent air striking force', or Bomber Command as it became. Trenchard's great idea developed in 1917/18 – but the additional crew were air gunners who were found from the armament tradesmen. Navigation – or pilotage – was conducted by the second pilot; it was only natural that pilots were the core of the flying air force. Serious navigation was being nurtured only in the general reconnaissance (GR) flying boat squadrons.

It is sometimes difficult to realise that those critical years leading up to the outbreak of the war in 1939 were only ten or so years after the outbreak of peace in 1918, when I was born. Little wonder, therefore, that the 1918 war mentality was so inbred in our senior officers. Much of my earliest training, as an observer, related to army co-operation. The syllabus included the 'three-letter reporting code' for the position of a marching column of troops, its head and its tail. I'm afraid the German Panzers were a bit too quick for such information – the message had to be encoded on the Syko machine, with the correctly dated card inserted!

The RAF with Trenchard's embryonic striking force and a few squadrons for the air defence of Great Britain, was fighting for its very independence, struggling for a limited amount of money then grudgingly allocated to defence between all three services. With the meagre air vote, Trenchard was determined to establish a highly trained core to his force, based on training at Cranwell for the GD pilots and at Halton for his skilled tradesmen. These two 'colleges' would be supported by a staff college at Andover. From this base, expansion could, and would, eventually come.

Far-sighted officers among the training staff realised that it would be difficult, and perhaps even impossible, to maintain flying training within UK airspace if hostilities were once again to break out. Thus the commonwealth air training plan was conceived and negotiated once a common syllabus and training standards had been agreed by the main players that comprised Canada (as the largest) followed by Australia, New Zealand, South Africa and Southern Rhodesia. They were to provide training in safety - their schools and airfields in excellent environments and in what seemed like unlimited airspace.

I was mobilised just prior to the very beginning of hostilities (the Phoney War, as this period came to be known) and was fed into the machine at a time when a limited amount of embryonic observer training was continuing in the UK and, for better or for worse, I missed out on the ITW stage. This meant that I reached the front line much sooner than many of my contemporaries in the VR.

The value of the high-grade core of navigation specialists, both pilots and observer/navigators, was later realised in the influence they had as instructors and in associated fields besides training, such as operational requirements, as well as in the world of aircraft and instruments production. I have in mind in particular those seconded to the British Air Commission in Washington DC, where these officers could explain the value of such things as offensive and defensive armament based on real operational experience or, in my case, the importance of astrodomes, an adequate navigator's position, and improved compass installations in various multi-crew aircraft.

RAF offensive thinking had been designed around daylight operations. The belief was that our sophisticated defensive armaments would see us through. When this failed, in spectacular and tragic fashion, we were obliged to rethink our strategy for the whole air offensive, at least in Europe. Night operations cruelly exposed our deficiencies in navigation and bomb aiming.

Our efforts in those early war years in which I took part were puny compared to what followed, but we were at least taking the fight to the enemy. Fortunately we were largely oblivious to our shortcomings, and the cost in lives. Had this not been the case, our morale might otherwise not have been as high as it was, considering that we were alone after the fall of France, the US had yet to enter the war, and the Germans had not embarked on their foolhardy invasion of Russia. With much improved training using experienced crews being 'rested', Bomber Command developed steadily into a potent weapon, however much one might argue about the targeting policy driven from on high. Pinpoint bombing was not possible on a large scale, in spite of the most significant developments in radar; area bombing and large-scale fire raids became the order of the day, and satisfying retaliation for the Luftwaffe raids on London and Coventry.

Complementing the RAF was the even more powerful weapon of what became the US Strategic Air Command. Post-war, both were to be armed with nuclear weapons. Aircraft were to be superseded by the surface-to-surface, or airborne GW to carry the deterrent weapons. The V2 rocket of 1945 had shown the way. The value of such weapons, however, still depends entirely on the political will to use them, and the enemy's perception of the threat.

I was privileged to serve in the USA immediately after the war and to learn more about our ally, whence back in the UK I returned to the field of navigation training and development. My career broadened out with intelligence duties in the Near East and various joint staff appointments. I saw the swing of influence from the single-seat world of the Battle of Britain fighters to the tactical requirements of NATO and to our dwindling overseas commitments. These in turn needed a transport force with adequate range to sustain them.

Navigation capabilities progressed through ground-based systems of greater and greater range which would in turn be superseded by self-contained technologies. First came inertial systems, quickly followed by sat nav, which might be described as spherical trigonometry using satellites instead of the stars. Ever-more sophisticated all-weather landing systems provide the terminal navigation. Things have come a long way since my Spec.N course in 1941!

My own career switched into the field of air intelligence and with embassy experience into foreign affairs. Having had a lucky start in Washington, I went to the opposite pole in Moscow, ending my service career on the defence intelligence staff in London. The struggle with other branches over the policy of 'equal career for navigators' – that is a career with equal prospects of promotion – had long been forgotten. Perhaps we will all have been put out of business in the years to come, as the whole offensive machine becomes more automated and controlled from the ground under a unified command alongside its political control. Maybe a cyber-war will revolutionise the ability to 'command and control'.

I often wonder what might have happened if my father had left me at school to at least reach the higher schools level and possibly a university education. I might have applied myself more effectively in whatever field I entered. The outbreak of the war would have affected me anyway. From my experience it was luck all the way through. Being in the right place, at the right time, with the right experience/qualifications is essential; looking back and wondering 'if only...' is a negative way of thinking.

I can only be eternally grateful to have survived.

APPENDIX I

First Tour of Operations, 58 Squadron					
DATE	PILOT/SECOND	TARGET	DURATION	OP	COMMENTS
1940					
29.7	S/L Bartlett P/O Ford	Düsseldorf (Reisholz oil refinery)	6.40	1	
1.8	S/L Bartlett Sgt Hughes	Düsseldorf (Reisholz oil refinery)	7.10	2	
2.9	S/L Bartlett Sgt Kerr	Genoa (docks)	10.20	3	Ditched in sea
8.9	Sgt Boothby P/O Robison	Ostend (docks and shipping)	5.45	4	
10.9	F/L Harding Sgt Hughes	Bremen (docks and warehouses)	6.40	5	
13.9	Sgt Boothby F/L Harding	Dunkirk (docks and shipping)	4.30	6	
18.9	P/O Brown Sgt Walters	Zeebrugge (docks and shipping)	4.20	7	
24.9	P/O Brown Sgt Walters	Berlin	2.50	–	DNCO. A/G sick
26.9	P/O Brown Sgt Walters	Le Havre (docks and shipping)	5.20	8	
29.9	P/O Brown Sgt Walters	Magdeberg (oil refinery)	8.00	9	
2.10	P/O Brown Sgt Walters	Stettin (bombed Hindenberg dam)	9.40	10	Abandoned
7.10	S/L Smith Sgt Stiles	Amsterdam (Fokker works)	5.05	11	
10.10	Sgt Christie Sgt Stiles	Leuna (oil refinery)	9.25	11	
14.10	Sgt Christie Sgt Stiles	Pollitz (Stettin – oil refinery)	9.15	12	

20.10	Sgt Christie Sgt Stiles	Pilsen (Skoda works)	11.10	13	10/10 Cloud
26.10	Sgt Christie Not listed in ORB	Stettin (Pollitz – oil refinery)	9.15	14	
14.11	Sgt Christie F/O Clementi	Berlin	10.05	15	Black Thursday
16.11	W/C Smith F/O Clementi	Hamburg (Blohm & Voss)	8.30	16	
26.11	Sgt Christie Sgt Johnston	Turin			DNCO Collision
11.12	Sgt Christie F/O Clementi	Mannheim (power station – blitz)	7.50	19	
16.12	Sgt Christie F/O Clementi	Mannheim (blitz)	7.40	20	
20.12	Sgt Christie F/O Clementi	Berlin (bombed Potsdam)	8.15	21	
1941					
6.2	Sgt Christie P/O Walker	Calais (docks and shipping)	4.45	22	
22.2	Sgt Fullerton P/O Carrapiett	Düsseldorf (blitz)	6.15	23	

Miscellaneous Operations

1943					
22.3	S/L Donaldson	St Nazaire	4.45	24	With 156 Sqn

APPENDIX TWO

The following officers were with the squadron on July 1, 1940 and served throughout the month:

NAME	DETAIL/FATE (WHERE KNOWN)
W/C John Sutton	Later station commander, Rabat (Sale). Survived the war.
S/L Michael Hallam	DFC. Later wing commander RAFO.
S/L John Bartlett	DFC. Killed in action 22.8.41.
F/L Frank Aikens	Later squadron leader DFC, AFC. Survived the war.
F/L Leopold Evershed	Ex-RFC. Survived the war.
F/O Paul Matthews	Short service commission officer (1936). Flight lieutenant (1940).
F/O Peter Cribb	Later air commodore CBE, DSO & Bar, DFC & Bar. Famous pathfinder.
F/O John Rail	Later flight lieutenant. Survived the war.
F/O Edward Francis	Later squadron leader. Survived the war.
F/O Mervyn Fleming	Later wing commander DSO, DFC. CO 419 Squadron RCAF.
F/O William Espley	Killed in action 3.10.40. Canadian.
P/O Thomas Robison	Killed in action 20.6.41 with 35 Squadron.
P/O Victor Pike	Killed in action 9.4.41 as flight lieutenant with 7 Squadron.
P/O Harold Welte	Later squadron leader. Medically unfit for service 1945.
P/O Richard Fennell	Later squadron leader. Survived the war.
P/O Arthur Wilding	Later DFC (with 138 Squadron) 1944.
P/O Thorfinn Gunn	Later wing commander DFC (with 161 Squadron), AFC, CdeG. Died 1996.
P/O Leslie Crooks	Later DSO, DFC. CO 426 Squadron, RCAF. Killed in action 18.8.43.

P/O Neville Clements	Later flight lieutenant. South African. Killed in action 5.12.44 with 24 Squadron.
P/O Richard Williams	Later flight lieutenant. Survived the war.
P/O James Thompson	Later squadron leader MBE. Survived the war.
P/O Danny Falconer	Killed in action 16.10.44.
P/O Peter Elliott	Later DFC with 35 Squadron. Killed in action 1.3.43.
P/O Brian O'Duffy	Later squadron leader AFC.

The following officers were posted to the squadron in July:

S/L John Tuck	DFC. Survived the war and medically discharged 1948.
P/O Eric Ford	Killed in action 18.9.40.
P/O Richard Phillips	Killed in action 9.10.40.
P/O John Mitchell	Retired as air commodore LVO, DFC, AFC.

The following airmen pilots were with the squadron on July 1, 1940 and served throughout the month:

Sgt J Archer	
Sgt Montague Terraneau	Later a DC4 pilot with Swiss Air.
F/S Dennis Moore	Later squadron leader DFC, DFM. Survived the war.
Sgt Cyril Boothby	Later flight lieutenant DFC, DFM. Killed in action 10.9.43
Sgt J Ashmore	
Sgt Herbert Cornish	Killed in crashed-landing 24.9.40.

The following airmen pilots were posted to the squadron in July:

Sgt Albert Crossland	Killed in action 18.9.40.
Sgt William Christie	Later flight lieutenant DSO, DFM. Killed in action 12.12.42.

Sgt R.A Gosling	Later warrant officer. Mentioned in Despatches.
Sgt Frederick Kerr	Shot down. POW.
Sgt Colin Hughes	Later squadron leader DSO, DFC. POW.

The authors would welcome any further information on the officers and men mentioned above, and their ultimate fates. (www.seanfeast.com).

THE VIP
PASSENGERS

Harold Alexander served with distinction in France during World War One, and between the wars, he served as a brigadier-general on the northwest frontier of India. At the start of World War Two, 'Alex' commanded the first division that was part of the British Expeditionary Force that landed in France. The first division was pushed back to Dunkirk – Alexander being the last officer to be evacuated. After trying to stem the onslaught of the Japanese in Burma, in August 1942, Churchill appointed Alexander C-in-C of the British forces in North Africa and he commanded the allied forces that landed in Sicily. He was promoted field marshal in 1944, and created a viscount in 1946. After his successful career in the military, he was appointed governor-general of Canada from 1946 to 1952. In 1952 he was made Earl Alexander of Tunis and he served in Winston Churchill's Conservative Cabinet as minister of defence from 1952 to 1954. He died in 1969.

Lord Beaverbrook was born William Maxwell Aitken, the son of a Presbyterian minister, and made his fortune from Canadian cement mills. After a move to Britain, he became the Conservative member for Ashton-under-Lyne. In 1918 David Lloyd George granted Aitken the title, Lord Beaverbrook and appointed him as minister of information. During the war Beaverbrook acquired a controlling interest in the *Daily Express*, turning it into the most widely read newspaper in the world. Beaverbrook also founded the *Sunday Express* (1921) and in 1929 purchased the *Evening Standard*. In the Second World War, Winston Churchill recruited Beaverbrook into his Cabinet where he served as minister for aircraft production (1940-41), minister of supply (1941-2), minister of war production (1942), and Lord Privy Seal (1943-45). Lord Beaverbrook died in 1964.

Alan Brooke joined the British Army and served in Ireland and India before going to France in 1914. He served on the Western Front and was mentioned six times in despatches. On the outbreak of the Second World War, Brooke went to France as a member of the British Expeditionary Force and played a leading role in the evacuation of British troops at Dunkirk. Brooke returned to Britain and in July 1940 became commander of the home forces. In this post Brooke had several major disagreements with Winston Churchill about military strategy. It therefore came as a surprise when Churchill appointed him chief of imperial general staff in December 1941. Promoted to field marshal in January 1944 he was created Baron Alan Brooke of Brookeborough in September 1945. Alan Brooke died in June 1963.

Sarah Churchill was the second daughter of Winston and Clementine Churchill. She was married three times, the first occasion to Victor Oliver, a comedian and musician. Sarah was herself an actress and dancer whose most famous role was arguably as Anne Ashmond, starring opposite Fred Astaire, in Royal Wedding. She died in 1982.

Archibald Clark Kerr entered the Foreign Service in 1906 and served as ambassador to China during the Japanese occupation of the late 1930s. From 1935 to 1938, he served as ambassador to the Kingdom of Iraq. Clark Kerr was moved to Moscow in February 1942 where he forged a remarkable relationship with Stalin. His work there and at the 'Big Three' conferences put him at the very centre of international politics. After the war he was appointed ambassador to the United States, and was created Baron Inverchapel in 1946. He died in July 1951.

John Colville joined the Foreign Office in 1937, and by 1939 he was appointed assistant private secretary to the prime minister, in which capacity he served Neville Chamberlain, Winston Churchill and Clement Attlee. The same six-year period also included an interim spell as an RAF fighter pilot. He later served as private secretary to Princess Elizabeth from 1947-49. Sir John Colville died in 1987.

Pierson Dixon was the principal private secretary to the foreign secretary between 1943 and 1948. He held the post of ambassador to

Czechoslovakia (1948–1950) and was invested as Knight Commander of the Order of St. Michael and St. George in 1950. He later held the offices of deputy under-secretary of state, Foreign Office (1950–1954) and permanent representative of the United Kingdom to the United Nations (1954–1960). He was involved during the Suez crisis in 1956. He also served as the ambassador to France between 1960 and 1964.

Duff Cooper joined the Foreign Office after Eton and Oxford and during the First World War fought on the Western Front with the Grenadier Guards. Cooper was elected to the House of Commons in 1924, and was appointed financial secretary to the War Office by Ramsay MacDonald in August 1931. Cooper was appointed as First Lord of the Admiralty in 1937 but resigned from office after the signing of the Munich Agreement. When Winston Churchill became prime minister in May 1940, he appointed Cooper as minister of information. He also served as chancellor of the Duchy of Lancaster (July 1941-November 1943). Cooper retired from the House of Commons in 1945 and became the ambassador in Paris. He was created Viscount Norwich in 1952 and died on January 1, 1954.

Anthony Eden was commissioned into the King's Royal Rifle Corps and served on the Western Front, winning the Military Cross at the Battle of the Somme in 1916. After the war Eden pursued a career in politics. When Stanley Baldwin became prime minister in 1935 he appointed Eden as his foreign secretary. Eden disagreed with Neville Chamberlain about the way to deal with fascism in Europe and in 1938 he resigned from office. When Winston Churchill took over from Chamberlain in 1940, Eden was reappointed as foreign secretary. He became prime minister in 1955 but was later obliged to resign over the Suez crisis. Created Earl Avon, he died in January 1977.

Charles de Gaulle was a veteran of the First World War. He was an early proponent of armoured warfare and advocate of military aviation, which he considered a means to break the stalemate of trench warfare. During World War Two he reached the temporary rank of brigadier-general, leading one of the few successful armoured counter-attacks in 1940, and then briefly served in the French government as France fell. He escaped to England and organised the Free French Forces with exiled French officers in Britain. By the time of the liberation of France in 1944 he was heading a government in exile. After the war he founded his own political party, the RPF. Although he retired from politics in the early 1950s after the RPF's failure to win power, the French Assembly voted him back to power as prime minister during the May 1958 crisis. de Gaulle led the writing of a new constitution founding the Fifth Republic, and was elected president of France. He remains the most influential leader in modern French history.

James Grigg achieved a first in the civil service examination of 1913 and served in the treasury. After the First World War, during which he served in the Royal Garrison Artillery, he returned to the treasury and in 1921 he became principal private secretary to the Chancellor of the Exchequer, serving several successive chancellors including Winston Churchill. In 1939 Grigg became permanent under-secretary of state for war. He proved an effective civil service head but it came as a great shock to many when in February 1942 Churchill dismissed Margesson and replaced him with Grigg. It was a response to considerable military setbacks such as the loss of Singapore. Grigg retained his post for the rest of the war. In the 1945 general election he lost his seat and left public life. He died in May 1964.

Alexander Hardinge served with the Grenadier Guards in the First World War, and won the Military Cross, but he received wounds that affected his health for the rest of his life. He became assistant private secretary to King George V in 1920 and held the post until the king's death in 1936. The new monarch, Edward VIII, made him his private secretary, but he was an early opponent of the king's relationship with Mrs Simpson. He played an important role in the abdication crisis by protecting the reputation of the monarchy and ensuring the smooth succession of George VI. Ill health and a difficult relationship with George VI led to his retirement in 1943, shortly after accompanying him on the visit to the troops in North Africa. He succeeded his father to the peerage in 1944 as 2nd Baron of Penshurst and died in May 1960.

Godfrey Huggins studied medicine in London before travelling to

Salisbury, Southern Rhodesia in 1911, initially to act as a locum but eventually deciding to stay. He served in the RAMC in the First World War in France, returning to Southern Rhodesia in time to deal with the influenza epidemic. He entered politics in 1924, becoming prime minister of Southern Rhodesia in 1933 when his reform party won that year's general election. Huggins won successive elections and was knighted in 1941 by King George VI. Huggins remained in office until 1956 and was elevated to the British peerage as Viscount Malvern prior to his retirement.

Hastings 'Pug' Ismay served with the 21st Cavalry Frontier Force in India and during the First World War fought in Somaliland. In 1926 Ismay joined the imperial defence committee and as major general became chief of staff to Winston Churchill in May 1940. Ismay retired from the British Army in 1946 as full general. He then went to India where he served under Lord Mountbatten as chief of staff. Lord Ismay, as he became, was the first secretary general of NATO (1952-57). Ismay died in 1965.

Dermot Kavanagh served in the 11th Hussars from 1909, and was the regiment's commanding officer between 1932-36. In 1939 he was promoted to colonel, and served in France in 1940. He was equerry to King George VI between 1937-1941, and crown equerry from 1941 to 1955. Sir Dermot Kavanagh died in 1958.

Robert Laycock was commissioned into the Royal Horse Guards in 1927. When the Second World War broke out a scientific bent caused Laycock to be appointed to the chemical warfare section of the BEF in France although he was back in England prior to Dunkirk. Appointed by Admiral of the Fleet Sir Roger Keyes to the commandos he took part in various raids against German and Italian airfields and fought heroically in Crete, being among the last to be evacuated along with his intelligence officer and friend, Evelyn Waugh. Laycock also led the 1941 raid to capture Rommel that failed with significant casualties. After taking part in the assault in Sicily, he succeeded Mountbatten as chief of combined operations, a position he held until 1947. He was later governor of Malta. Laycock died in March 1968.

Piers Legh was a military secretary during the First World War and was Mentioned in Despatches in 1919. He became equerry to The Prince of Wales until 1936 and then equerry and extra equerry to King George VI from 1937–46. In 1941, he became master of the royal household, a post he held until his retirement in 1953. Sir Piers Legh died in 1955.

George Marshall served in the First World War on the Western Front and directed the United States armed forces throughout World War Two. In 1944 Marshall was disappointed not to have been given command of the allied D-Day landings. However, Franklin D. Roosevelt argued that he could not afford to lose him as chief of staff. He was involved in the planning of the invasion and Winston Churchill later claimed that Marshall's achievements were monumental and described him as the "organiser of victory". Marshall was given the rank of a five-star general in December 1944. In 1953 he was awarded the Nobel Prize for Peace for his contribution to the recovery of Europe after the Second World War. George Marshall died in Washington in October 1959.

Fitzroy Maclean was Winston Churchill's special envoy to the Yugoslav leader Josip Tito in 1943–45. After Eton and King's College, Cambridge, Maclean was initially drawn to the academic life but the crisis in Europe in the early 1930s led him to the diplomatic service. He spent five years in France and Russia, before turning to politics and enlisting as a private in the Cameron Highlanders. Later commissioned, he joined the newly formed special air service, taking part in several spectacular raids. He parachuted into Yugoslavia with his mission in September 1943 and built up a personal rapport with Tito, which never faded. After the war he returned to the commons, and was created baronet in 1957. An admirer of Margaret Thatcher, he steered her through the intricacies of Yugoslav politics, advised her to put her political money on Gorbachev in 1985, and acted as special adviser to the Prince of Wales when he visited Tito in the 1970s.

Harold Macmillan was wounded three times in the First World War. He was elected a Conservative MP in 1924. In 1940 he was appointed a junior minister, and in 1942 became the resident minister at allied forces HQ in the Mediterranean, where he became a friend of General Eisenhower. He lost his seat in 1945 but returned soon after. In 1954 he became minister for defence, and in 1955 Anthony Eden appointed him foreign secretary and then Chancellor of the Exchequer. Following Eden's resignation over Suez, Macmillan became prime minister. In 1962 the government's general unpopularity led Macmillan to abruptly dismiss six Cabinet members, the so-called 'night of the long knives'. Macmillan fell ill in 1963 and resigned. He eventually returned to parliament in 1984 as a hereditary peer. He died in 1986.

Lord Moran, Churchill's personal physician, was born Charles McMoran Wilson. He served in the Royal Army Medical Corps during the First World War, winning the Military Cross. He was the Dean of St Mary's Hospital Medical School between 1920 and 1945, where he oversaw the rebuilding of the premises. He was a prominent scientist in his day, and was elected president of the Royal College of Physicians in April 1941 and was re-elected each year until 1950. He was knighted in 1942 and created Baron Moran in the New Year Honours of 1943.

Louis Mountbatten was the great grandson of Queen Victoria, and second cousin of George V. Mountbatten was educated at Osborne and Dartmouth Royal Naval College, serving in HMS *Lion* and HMS *Elizabeth* in the First World War. Mountbatten remained in the Royal Navy and on the outbreak of the Second World War was captain of the destroyer *Kelly*. He saw action during the Norwegian campaign and the ship was sunk off Crete on 23rd May 1940 with the loss of 130 men. Winston Churchill appointed Mountbatten head of Combined Operations Command in October 1941. He launched a series of commando raids including the disastrous Dieppe Raid in August 1942. The decision by Churchill to promote Mountbatten upset senior officers in the military establishment. In October 1943 Churchill appointed Mountbatten as head of the South East Asia Command (SEAC). Working closely with General William Slim, Mountbatten directed the liberation of Burma and Singapore. In 1947 Clement Attlee selected Mountbatten as viceroy of India and he oversaw the creation of the independent states of India and Pakistan. Mountbatten returned to service at sea and as Fourth Sea Lord was commander of the Mediterranean Fleet (1952-55). He was also First

Sea Lord (1955-59) and chief of defence staff (1959-65). Louis Mountbatten was murdered by an IRA bomb while sailing near his holiday home in County Sligo, Ireland, in August 1979.

Bernard Paget was commissioned into the Oxfordshire and Buckinghamshire light infantry in November 1907 and in the First World War was awarded the Military Cross in November 1915 and the Distinguished Service Order in January 1918. He was four times Mentioned in Despatches. By the start of World War Two, Paget was fighting in Norway, and on his return was promoted lieutenant general and made general officer commanding-in-chief South-Eastern Command in 1941. He was promoted general in July 1943, commanding 21st Army Group prior to Bernard Montgomery. In January 1944 he became C–in–C Middle East Command until October 1946, when he retired from the army. He died in 1961.

Manley Power joined the Royal Navy as a cadet in 1917. In the early part of his career, he served mainly in submarines, attaining his first command in 1934. In 1939 he was promoted to commander and appointed as staff officer (operations) to the C–in–C, Mediterranean, Vice-Admiral Sir Andrew Cunningham. In 1942, he was given command of HMS *Opportune*, escorting Arctic convoys, before returning as staff officer (operations) in the Mediterranean in September 1942, in preparation for the invasion of North Africa and then became staff officer (plans) for C–in–C, Mediterranean, assisting the planning of the invasion of Sicily. He was promoted captain in 1943, and deputy chief of staff (plans), and stayed in the Mediterranean until March 1944, planning the invasion of Italy and the Anzio landings. He was later appointed to command HMS *Saumarez* in the Eastern Fleet, and his flotilla destroyed the Japanese cruiser *Haguro* in May 1945. After the war a variety of senior appointments culminated in his promotion to admiral in 1960. He retired in 1961 and died in May 1981.

John Peck was a career Foreign Office official who after the war was instrumental in the establishment of the information research department to counter Soviet propaganda and disinformation during the Cold War. He was later ambassador to Ireland, 1970-1973.

Charles Portal transferred from the Royal Engineers to the Royal Flying Corps in 1915 and served with distinction in the First World

War. He remained in the recently created Royal Air Force, and at the start of World War Two was a member of the air council and head of Bomber Command (from April 1940), impressing Churchill with his performance. He was knighted in July 1940 and three months later was appointed chief of the air staff. As a member of the chiefs of staff committee, Portal had a significant influence on allied strategy and other important matters of military policy. Portal was created baron in August 1945 and the following year was raised to viscount. He died in April 1971.

Archibald Sinclair joined the Life Guards in 1910 and went on to serve in the First World War, for a time with Winston Churchill. The pair became close friends and later political allies. In 1912 Sinclair succeeded his grandfather to become the 4th Baronet of Ulster. In 1922, he was elected as Liberal MP for Caithness and Sutherland, and served until 1945. He became chief whip of the Liberals in 1930. He served in two national unity governments as secretary of state for Scotland (1931–32) and secretary of state for air (1940–45). He was created Viscount Thurso in 1952.

Jan Christian Smuts established himself as a guerrilla leader of exceptional talent during the Boer War. He was also one of the leading negotiators involved in the production of the Vereeniging Peace Treaty (1902). An opponent of extreme nationalism, Smuts argued that South Africa's future lay in co-operation with Britain. On the outbreak of the First World War, Smuts led South Africa's successful campaign in German East Africa. In 1917 David Lloyd George invited Smuts to join the Imperial War Cabinet in London. He soon obtained a high reputation and was an influential figure in devising allied war strategy. Smuts returned to South Africa after the war and soon afterwards became prime minister. Smuts lost power in 1924 but later returned to office as deputy prime minister (1933–39) and prime minister (1939–48). Smuts worked closely with Winston Churchill during the Second World War and was the only man to sign the peace treaties at the end of both wars. Smuts was also a leading figure in the drafting of the United Nations Covenant. Jan Christian Smuts died in 1950.

William Strang joined the diplomatic service after service in the

First World War and served at the British embassy in Belgrade from 1919 to 1922, at the Foreign Office from 1922 to 1930 and at the embassy in Moscow from 1930 to 1933. He returned to the Foreign Office in 1933. During the 1930s he was an adviser to the government at the major international meetings, and met Mussolini, Hitler and Stalin. He continued as an adviser during and after the Second World War and was present at the major conferences between the allied leaders. Strang again returned to the Foreign Office in 1947, retiring six years later. In 1954 he was made Baron Strang of Stonesfield. Lord Strang died at the age of eighty-five.

Arthur Tedder joined the Royal Flying Corps in 1916, and after carrying out bombing and reconnaissance missions he was given command of 70 Squadron. After the war he held various senior appointments, including air officer commanding Singapore. Tedder was appointed director-general of research and development in the Air Ministry in 1938. He held this post until he became air commander in the Middle East in 1940 and played an important role in the defeat of Erwin Rommel in the Desert War. After the successful conquest of Tunisia and Sicily he was appointed as deputy supreme allied commander under General Eisenhower. Tedder became chief of the air staff in 1946. After retiring from the RAF in 1950 Tedder, now the 1st Baron of Glenquin, was chairman of the British joint services commission in Washington. He died in June 1967.

Hesperus Andrias van Ryneveld began his military career serving in the Royal Flying Corps, where he distinguished himself as a fighter ace. After the war, van Ryneveld was called back to South Africa by Prime Minister Jan Smuts in order to set up a South African Air Force (SAAF). He flew back home, across Africa, in a Vickers Vimy – a pioneering feat for which he and his co-pilot Quintin Brand were both knighted. Colonel van Ryneveld established the SAAF in 1920, and directed it until 1933, when he was promoted to chief of the general staff, a position he held for sixteen years, including the whole of World War Two. He retired in 1949.

Henry 'Jumbo' Wilson served in South Africa in the Second Boer War, for which he was awarded the Queen's and King's South Africa medal each with two clasps. He fought throughout the First World

War being awarded the DSO in 1917 and was Mentioned in Despatches three times. At the start of the Second World War, Wilson fought with distinction against the Italians, achieving one of Churchill's first notable victories. He later fought against the Germans in Greece, before being appointed GOC Palestine and Trans Jordan and overseeing the successful Syria-Lebanon campaign. Wilson was Churchill's choice to succeed Auchinleck as commander of the Eighth Army in 1942, but Montgomery was appointed instead. Wilson was appointed C-in-C Middle East, organising an unsuccessful attempt to occupy the small Greek islands of Kos, Leros and Samos. He succeeded Eisenhower as the supreme allied commander in the Mediterranean, and was later promoted field marshal and sent to Washington to be chief of the British joint staff mission. He was created Baron Wilson, of Libya and of Stowlangtoft in the County of Suffolk.

BIBLIOGRAPHY/SOURCES

Much of this book is as original as possible, drawing on interviews, log-books, diaries, scrapbooks, letters, newspaper cuttings and the phenomenal memory that John still possesses.

Some squadron records were consulted, notably the Form 540 for 58 Squadron, July 1940 to February 1941.

The following books were also of use:

Ascalon, Jerrard Tickell, Hodder and Stoughton, 1964
Bomber Barons, Chaz Bowyer, Pen & Sword, 2001
Bomber Command War Losses, (Vols 1 and 2), Bill Chorley, Ian Allan, 1998
From Sky to Sea, Susan Van Hoek, Best Pub Co, 1993
From Dogfight to Diplomacy, Donald MacDonell, Pen & Sword, 2005
From Hull, Hell and Halifax, Chris Blanchett, Midland Publishing, 1998
High Endeavour, John Ivelaw Chapman, Pen & Sword, 1993
History of the US Air Force, David Anderton, Crescent Books, 1988
Master Bombers, Sean Feast, Grub Street, 2008
The RAF Source Book, Ken Delve, Airlife, 1994
The Whitley Boys, Larry Donnelly, Air Research Pub, 1998

Photography
All of the photographs come from John's private collection, including several contemporary images sent to him immediately after the events in which he took part. The photograph of John today is reproduced with thanks to *Aeroplane Monthly*.